English-Pashto
Pashto-English

Word to Word™
Bilingual Dictionary

Compiled by:
C. Sesma, M.A.

Translated by:
Sobia Kattak

Bilingual Dictionaries, Inc.

Pashto Word to Word™ Bilingual Dictionary
1st Edition © Copyright 2008

Published in the United States by:

Bilingual Dictionaries, Inc.
PO Box 1154
Murrieta, CA 92562
T: (951) 461-6893 • F: (951) 461-3092
www.BilingualDictionaries.com

ISBN13: 978-0-933146-34-1
ISBN: 0-933146-34-5

Preface

Bilingual Dictionaries, Inc. is committed to providing schools, libraries and educators with a great selection of bilingual materials for students. Along with bilingual dictionaries we also provide ESL materials, children's bilingual stories and children's bilingual picture dictionaries.

Sesma's Pashto Word to Word Bilingual Dictionary was created specifically with students in mind to be used for reference and testing. This dictionary contains approximately 17,500 entries targeting common words used in the English language.

List of Irregular Verbs

present - past - past participle

arise - arose - arisen
awake - awoke - awoken, awaked
be - was - been
bear - bore - borne
beat - beat - beaten
become - became - become
begin - began - begun
behold - beheld - beheld
bend - bent - bent
beseech - besought - besought
bet - bet - betted
bid - bade (bid) - bidden (bid)
bind - bound - bound
bite - bit - bitten
bleed - bled - bled
blow - blew - blown
break - broke - broken
breed - bred - bred
bring - brought - brought
build - built - built
burn - burnt - burnt *
burst - burst - burst
buy - bought - bought
cast - cast - cast
catch - caught - caught
choose - chose - chosen
cling - clung - clung
come - came - come
cost - cost - cost
creep - crept - crept
cut - cut - cut
deal - dealt - dealt

dig - dug - dug
do - did - done
draw - drew - drawn
dream - dreamt - dreamed
drink - drank - drunk
drive - drove - driven
dwell - dwelt - dwelt
eat - ate - eaten
fall - fell - fallen
feed - fed - fed
feel - felt - felt
fight - fought - fought
find - found - found
flee - fled - fled
fling - flung - flung
fly - flew - flown
forebear - forbore - forborne
forbid - forbade - forbidden
forecast - forecast - forecast
forget - forgot - forgotten
forgive - forgave - forgiven
forego - forewent - foregone
foresee - foresaw - foreseen
foretell - foretold - foretold
forget - forgot - forgotten
forsake - forsook - forsaken
freeze - froze - frozen
get - got - gotten
give - gave - given
go - went - gone
grind - ground - ground
grow - grew - grown
hang - hung * - hung *
have - had - had

hear - heard - heard	**ring -** rang - rung
hide - hid - hidden	**rise -** rose - risen
hit - hit - hit	**run -** ran - run
hold - held - held	**saw -** sawed - sawn
hurt - hurt - hurt	**say -** said - said
hit - hit - hit	**see -** saw - seen
hold - held - held	**seek -** sought - sought
keep - kept - kept	**sell -** sold - sold
kneel - knelt * - knelt *	**send -** sent - sent
know - knew - known	**set -** set - set
lay - laid - laid	**sew -** sewed - sewn
lead - led - led	**shake -** shook - shaken
lean - leant * - leant *	**shear -** sheared - shorn
leap - lept * - lept *	**shed -** shed - shed
learn - learnt * - learnt *	**shine -** shone - shone
leave - left - left	**shoot -** shot - shot
lend - lent - lent	**show -** showed - shown
let - let - let	**shrink -** shrank - shrunk
lie - lay - lain	**shut -** shut - shut
light - lit * - lit *	**sing -** sang - sung
lose - lost - lost	**sink -** sank - sunk
make - made - made	**sit -** sat - sat
mean - meant - meant	**slay -** slew - slain
meet - met - met	**sleep -** sleep - slept
mistake - mistook - mistaken	**slide -** slid - slid
must - had to - had to	**sling -** slung - slung
pay - paid - paid	**smell -** smelt * - smelt *
plead - pleaded - pled	**sow -** sowed - sown *
prove - proved - proven	**speak -** spoke - spoken
put - put - put	**speed -** sped * - sped *
quit - quit * - quit *	**spell -** spelt * - spelt *
read - read - read	**spend -** spent - spent
rid - rid - rid	**spill -** spilt * - spilt *
ride - rode - ridden	**spin -** spun - spun

spit - spat - spat
split - split - split
spread - spread - spread
spring - sprang - sprung
stand - stood - stood
steal - stole - stolen
stick - stuck - stuck
sting - stung - stung
stink - stank - stunk
stride - strode - stridden
strike - struck - struck (stricken)
strive - strove - striven
swear - swore - sworn
sweep - swept - swept
swell - swelled - swollen *
swim - swam - swum
take - took - taken
teach - taught - taught
tear - tore - torn

tell - told - told
think - thought - thought
throw - threw - thrown
thrust - thrust - thrust
tread - trod - trodden
wake - woke - woken
wear - wore - worn
weave - wove * - woven *
wed - wed * - wed *
weep - wept - wept
win - won - won
wind - wound - wound
wring - wrung - wrung
write - wrote - written

**Those tenses with an * also have
  regular forms.**

English-Pashto

Bilingual Dictionaries, Inc.

Abbreviations

a - article
n - noun
e - exclamation
pro - pronoun
adj - adjective
adv - adverb
v - verb
iv - irregular verb
pre - preposition
c - conjunction

A

abandon v پریښودل

abandonment n پریښودنه

abbey n لنګر

abbot n لنګر خانه

abbreviate v لنډول

abbreviation n لنډیز

abdicate v پریښودل

abdication n ګوښنه

abdomen n نس

abduct v تښتول

abduction n تښتونه

aberration n کږبدل

abhor v کرکه کول

abide by v عمل کول

ability n وړوالی

ablaze adj ځلاند

able adj وړ

abnormal adj بې قاعده

aboard adv .باندې

abolish v له منځه وړل

abort v نقصانول

abortion n بې وخته زیږبدنه

abound v ډېر

about pre په هکله

about adv شاو خوا

above pre پاس

abreast adv په کتار

abridge v لنډول

abroad adv د کوره د باندې

abrogate v لغوه کول

abruptly adv ناڅاپه

absence n غیرحاضری

absent adj غیر حاضر

absolute adj بشپړه

absolution n ازادي

absolve v بخښل

absorb v زغمل

absorbent adj جذبونکی

abstain v ډډه کول

abstinence n لاس اخیستنه

abstract adj لنډیز

absurd adj چټي

abundance n ډېرښت

abundant adj ډېر، زیات

abuse v ناړه ګټه کول

abuse n ښکنځا

abusive adj ناوړه

abysmal adj ژور

abyss n بې حده ژور ځند

academic adj داپلاتون فلسفي

academy n ښوونځی

accelerate v ګړندي کول

accent n لفظ

accept v منل

acceptable adj دمنلو وړ

acceptance n قبول شوب

access n لاس رسېدنه

accident n د تصادف حالت

accidental adj تصادفي

acclaim v چکچکب کول

acclimatize v عادي کول

accommodate v ځاي ور

accompany v ملګرتيا کول

accomplice n ملګري

accomplish v بشپړکول

accord n موافقه کول

according to pre سره سم

accordion n دساز بوه آله

account n کڼل, انګېرل

account for v تشريح کول

accountable adj شمبربدونکب

accountant n محاسب

accumulate v غونډول

accuracy n درستوالب

accurate adj درست

accusation n تور

accuse v تورلګول

accustom v اموخته کول

ace n خال

ache n درد

achieve v سرته رسول

achievement n سرته رسولنه

acid n تېزابي

acidity n تبره والب

acknowledge v معلومات لرل

acorn n د ځبري مبوه

acoustic adj صوتي

acquaint v بيا نول

acquaintance n پېژند ګلوب

acquire v لاس ته راورل

acquit v ازادول

acquittal n خلاصون

acrobat n جمناستک

act v عمل کول

action n کړنه

activate v فعالول

activation n په ګرندبتوب

active adj فعال

activity n کړنې

actor n اکټ کونکي

actress n اکټ کونکی

actual adj رښتبنب

actually adv په رښتبا سره

acute adj فعالول

adamant adj نه ماتبدونکب

adapt v توافق کول

adaptable adj توافق

adapter n برابرونکب

add v زباتول

addicted adj روردي	**adolescent** n خوان
addiction n روردبدنه	**adopt** v اقتباس كول
addictive adj عادي	**adoption** n نبونه
additional adj جمع	**adoptive** adj نبول شوى
address n اضافي	**adorable** adj عبادت
address v پته	**adoration** n نمانځنه
addressee n مرسل	**adore** v عبادت كول
adequate adj كافي	**adorn** v سبنگار
adhere v نښتل	**adrift** adv خوشي
adhesive adj سربښناک	**adulation** n ستاینه
adjacent adj گاونډي	**adult** n جوټه كونکى
adjective n صفت	**adulterate** v جوټه كول
adjoin v بو خاې كېدل	**adultery** n بد لمني
adjoining adj نزدي	**advance** v وراندې كول
adjourn v ځندول	**advance** n پر مختگ
adjust v براپرول	**advantage** n لوروالي
adjustable adj تنظبمولو	**Advent** n رسېدنه
adjustment n برابرونکي	**adventure** n پېښنه
administer v اداري	**adverb** n قید
admirable adj د شاباسي ور	**adversary** n دښمن
admirer n خوښونکي	**adverse** adj ضد
admissible adj د اجازې ور	**adversity** n توجه كول
admission n دننوتلو حق	**advertise** v خپرول
admit v اجازه وركول	**advice** n نصیحت
admittance n اجازه	**advisable** adj د تجوېز ور
admonish v نصیحت	**advise** v لارښودنه كول
admonition n مشوره	**adviser** n مشاور
adolescence n خواني	**advocate** v مدافع وكېل

aeroplane *n* الوتکه

aesthetic *adj* ښکلا پېژندنه

afar *adv* له وراپه

affable *adj* مهربان

affair *n* شغل ، مطلب

affect *v* اغبزه کول

affection *n* لمسونه

affectionate *adj* مبنه ناک

affiliate *v* پو ځای کول

affiliation *n* ترون

affinity *n* خپلوي

affirm *v* تصدیقول

affirmative *adj* مثبت (هو)

affix *v* گنډل

afflict *v* دردول

affliction *n* زور

affluence *n* شتمنې

affluent *adj* جارې

afford *v* زغمل

affordable *adj* د زغملو وړ

affront *v* مخامخ کبدل

affront *n* مخامخ

afloat *adv* په بحر کی

afraid *adj* ډار شوی

afresh *adv* نوی

after *pre* وروسته

afternoon *n* ماسپېنبېن

afterwards *adv* وروسته

again *adv* دوهم وار

against *pre* مقابل

age *n* عمر

agency *n* نمابندگي

agent *n* نمابنده

aggravate *v* ورانول

aggravation *n* کرکپچنوالې

aggression *n* تبرې

aggressive *adj* تبرې کونکې

aggressor *n* متجاوز

aghast *adj* هک پک

agile *adj* فعال

agitator *n* لسوونکي

agonize *v* کړبدل

agonizing *adj* کړبدنه

agony *n* کړاو

agree *v* موافق کبدل

agreeable *adj* مناسب

agreement *n* جوړه

agricultural *adj* زراعتي

agriculture *n* زراعت

ahead *pre* پر مختگ

aid *n* مرسته

aid *v* مرسته کول

aide *n* مرستندوي

ailing *adj* ناروغتبا

ailment *n* ناروغي

aim *v* نبنه کول

aimless adj بې کاره	**allegedly** adv د ادعا په توګه
air n هوا	**allegiance** n وفاداري
air v هوا ورکول	**allegory** n مجازي کبسه
aircraft n الوتکه	**allergic** adj تمثبلي
airline n هوايي کرښه	**allergy** n حساسيت
airliner n طياره	**alleviate** v سپکول
airmail n هوايي خط	**alley** n تنګه کوڅهٔ
airplane n الوتکه	**alliance** n بو والی
airport n هوايي ډګر	**allied** adj ارتباط
airspace n هوايي فضا	**alligator** n يو ډول تماس
airtight adj تنګه کوڅهٔ	**allocate** v نبنته
aisle n لار	**allot** v وبشل
ajar adj نبم کبنه	**allotment** n وبشنه
akin adj خپل هډ	**allow** v اجازه ورکول
alarm n د خطري زنګ	**allowance** n اجازه
alarming adj زنګبدنه	**alloy** n مخلوط فلزات
alcoholic adj شرابي	**allure** n راګبرول
alert n ناخاپي	**alluring** adj طمعدار کول
alert v تبار سب	**allusion** n اشاره
algebra n الجبر	**ally** n ملاتړ
alien n انتقال ورکول	**ally** v تړون کول
alight adv کوزبدل	**almanac** n کلبزه
align v په لبکه درول	**almighty** adj د مطلق واکدار
alike adj ورته	**almond** n د بادام ونه
alive adj ژوندي	**almost** adv نږدې
all adj ټول	**alms** n خبرات
allegation n ادعا	**alone** adj ځانته
allege v ادعا کول	**along** pre په اوږدو

alongside *pre* په څنګ کې	**ambivalent** *adj* غبر بقبني
aloof *adj* جلا	**ambush** *v* مورچه
aloud *adv* په جګ رغ	**amenable** *adj* مسول
alphabet *n* الفبا	**amend** *v* سمول
already *adv* پخوا	**amendment** *n* اصلاح
alright *adv* په صحيح توګه	**amenities** *n* خوروالی
also *adv* همداسې	**American** *adj* امربکايي
altar *n* د قربانی ځای	**amicable** *adj* د ملګرتبا ور
alter *v* اړول	**amid** *pre* په مېنځ کې
alteration *n* بدلون	**ammonia** *n* امونيا
altercation *n* جګړه	**ammunition** *n* حربي مهمات
alternate *v* په نوبت کول	**amnesia** *n* هېربجنتوب
alternate *adj* متناوب	**amnesty** *n* عمومي بخښنه
alternative *n* چاره	**among** *pre* په مېنځ کې
although *c* که څه هم	**amoral** *adj* غبر اخلاقي
altitude *n* جګوالې	**amorphous** *adj* بې ډوله
altogether *adj* ګرد سره	**amortize** *v* سپمول
aluminum *n* المونيم	**amount** *n* ختل
always *adv* تل	**amount to** *v* تول
amass *v* کوټه کول	**amphibious** *adj* دوه ژوندی
amateur *adj* شوقي	**ample** *adj* ارت
amaze *v* هک پک کول	**amplifier** *n* ارتوونکی
amazement *n* ارباني	**amplify** *v* ارتول
amazing *adj* حبرانوونکی	**amputate** *v* غوڅول
ambassador *n* سفبر	**amputation** *n* بلونه
ambiguous *adj* تت	**amuse** *v* لګبا کول
ambition *n* حرص	**amusement** *n* مشغولا
ambitious *adj* حربص	**amusing** *adj* پام غلطول

an *a* هو	**annex** *n* ترل
analogy *n* ورته والى	**annexation** *n* پيوند
analysis *n* تجزیه	**annihilate** *v* نابودول
analyze *v* تجزیه کول	**annihilation** *n* نابود
anarchist *n* د گډوډى طرفار	**anniversary** *n* کاليزه
anarchy *n* بې قانونى	**annotate** *v* تفسير ليكل
anatomy *n* اناتومي	**annotation** *n* تفسير
ancestor *n* نبکه	**announce** *v* اعلانول
ancestry *n* شجره	**announcement** *n* اعلان
anchor *n* لنگر	**announcer** *n* اعلانوونکى
ancient *adj* لرغونى	**annoy** *v* خورول
and *c* هم	**annoying** *adj* خوروونکى
anecdote *n* لنډه کېسه	**annual** *adj* کلنى
anemia *n* ربدپ	**annul** *v* نابودول
anemic *adj* ربدپ گل	**annulment** *n* فسخه کونه
anew *adv* بیا ، له سره	**anoint** *v* غوړول
angel *n* پرېښته	**anonymity** *n* ورته والپ
angelic *adj* پرېښته ډوله	**anonymous** *adj* ورک نومى
anger *v* غوسه کېدل	**another** *adj* یو بل
anger *n* غوسه	**answer** *v* خواب ورکول
angle *n* کوټ	**answer** *n* خواب
angry *adj* قارجن	**ant** *n* مېږى
anguish *n* کړاو	**antagonize** *v* د مخلفت
animal *n* څاروى	**antecedent** *n* مخکې کېدنه
animate *v* ژوند کول	**antecedents** *n* محکې کېدنې
animation *n* ژونديتوب	**antelope** *n* غرخه
animosity *n* دبنمني	**antenna** *n* بنکر
ankle *n* بننگرى	**anthem** *n* ترانه

antibiotic n انتي بيوتيک	**appeal** n عرض ،غوښتنه
anticipation n چمتوالى	**appealing** adj په زړه پورې
antipathy n کرکه	**appearance** n خرګندېدنه
antiquated adj زوړ	**appease** v راضي کول
antiquity n پخوانى زمانه	**appeasement** n آساآن
anvil n سندان	**appendicitis** n اپنډيسآيټ
anxiety n اندېښنه	**appendix** n مل
anxious adj اندېښمن	**appetite** n اشتها
any adj څينې	**appetizer** n اشتها ور
anybody pro هر څوک	**applaud** v چک کې وهل
anyhow pro په هر ډول	**applause** n شاباسى ويل
anyone pro هر يو	**apple** n مڼه
anything pro هر شى	**appliance** n اسباب
apart adv جلا	**applicable** adj د اجرا ور
apartment n استوګنځى	**applicant** n غوښتوونکى
apathy n بې دردي	**apply for** v عرض کول
ape n بيزو	**appoint** v ټاکل
apex n څوکه	**appointment** n ټاکلنه ، ګمارنه
apiece adv هر يوه ته	**appraisal** n ارزښت ټاکنه
apologize v مودبانه	**appraise** v بيه ټاکل
apology n بخښنه	**appreciate** v مننه کول
apostrophe n غبروندى	**appreciation** n نمانځنه
appall v وبرول	**apprehend** v نيول ،خپرېدل
appalling adj وبروونکى	**apprehensive** adj اندېښمن
apparel n ښکآره	**apprentice** n شاګرد
apparent adj جوت	**approach** v نږدې کول
apparently adv ظآهرآ	**approach** n رسونه
apparition n خرګندېدنه	**approachable** adj د رسونې ور

approbation n تصویب	**argue** v بحث کول
appropriate adj اختیارول	**argument** n ثبوت
approval n موافقه	**arid** adj وچه
approve v موافقه کول	**arise** iv پاڅیدل
approximate adj اټکلي	**aristocracy** n د اشرا فو ډله
apricot n زردالو	**aristocrat** n شریف
April n د اپریل میاشت	**arithmetic** n حساب
apron n پیش بند	**ark** n دنوح بیړۍ
aptitude n وړوالی	**arm** n مټ
aquatic adj دبنی	**arm** v په وسله سنبال
aqueduct n ناوه	**armaments** n جنگي سامان
Arabic adj عربي ژبه	**armchair** n ارامچي
arbiter n منځگړی	**armed** adj ترتبب والی
arbitrary adj په خپل سر	**armistice** n متارکه
arbitrate v روغه کول	**armpit** n تخرګ
arbitration n حاکمیت	**army** n لښکر
arc n لیندۍ	**aromatic** adj خوشبویه کول
archaic adj لرغونی	**around** pre نژدې
archbishop n ستر پادري	**arouse** v پارول، پاڅول
architect n معمار	**arrange** v برابرول
architecture n معماري	**arrangement** n تیاری
archive n عمومي اسناد	**array** n په لیکه درول
arctic adj شمالي قطب	**arrest** v گرفتارول
ardent adj سوځند	**arrest** n گرفتارونه
ardor n شهادت	**arrival** n رسیدنه
arduous adj مشکل	**arrive** v رسیدل
area n ساحه	**arrogance** n ځان ستاینه
arena n میدان، ډگر	**arrogant** adj په ځان غره

arsenal *n* وسله تون	**aspect** *n* اړخ
arsenic *n* ارسینیک	**asphalt** *n* قیر
arson *n* او ر اچونه	**asphyxiate** *v* خفه کول
art *n* هنر	**asphyxiation** *n* خفګان
artery *n* ارتباطي	**aspiration** *n* لویه هیله
arthritis *n* د بندو پاړسوب	**aspire** *v* لوړه ارزو لرل
article *n* مقاله	**aspirin** *n* اسپرین
articulate *v* ویاند	**assail** *v* یرغل کول
articulation *n* بند	**assailant** *n* یرغل ګر
artificial *adj* مصنوعي	**assassin** *n* قاتل
artillery *n* توپخانه	**assassinate** *v* وژل
artisan *n* کسب ګر	**assassination** *n* وژنه
artist *n* هنر مند	**assault** *n* حمله
artistic *adj* هنري	**assault** *v* حمله کول
as *c* په همدې ډول	**assemble** *v* یو کېدل
as *adv* په همدې ډول	**assembly** *n* ټولنه
ascend *v* ختل	**assent** *v* تصدیق
ascendancy *n* واک	**assert** *v* ښکاره کول
ascertain *v* یقیني کول	**assertion** *n* تائید
ascetic *adj* رهبز ګاري	**assess** *v* ټاکل, مالیه ټاکل
ash *n* کورنۍ نوم	**assessment** *n* ټاکنه
ashamed *adj* شرمېدلی	**asset** *n* دارايي
ashore *adv* غاړې ته	**assign** *v* ننه کول
aside *adv* پسیدا	**assignment** *n* ټاکنه
aside from *adv* د غاړې څخه	**assimilate** *v* یو شانته کېدل
ask *v* ورپسې ګرځېدل	**assimilation** *n* زغم
asleep *adj* بیده	**assist** *v* مرسته کول
asparagus *n* یو ډول سابه	**assistance** *n* مرسته

associate v يو ځای کېدل	atom n اتوم
association n ملګرتيا	atomic adj اتومي
assortment n طبقه بندي	atone v تلافي کول
assume v په غاړه اخيستل	atonement n سمون
assumption n انګېرنه	atrocious adj ډېر ظالم
assurance n ډاډينه	atrocity n بې رحمي
assure v ډاډ ور کول	atrophy v ډنګرېدل
asthma n نفس تنګي	attach v تړل
asthmatic adj د نفس تنګی	attached adj ضميمه
astonish v اريانول	attachment n ضميمه
astonishing adj اريانوونکی	attack n بريد
astound v اريانول	attack v بريد کول
astounding adj حېرانوونکې	attacker n بريد کوونکی
astray v بې لارې	attain v بری موندل
astrologer n نجوم پوه	attainable adj د لاس بريدو وړ
astrology n د نجوم علم	attainment n هڅه
astronomer n منجم	attempt v هڅه کول
astronomic adj پېژندنې	attempt n زيار
astute adj خيرک	attend v پاملرنه کول
asunder adv په جلا ډول	attendance n پاملرنه
asylum n مرستون	attendant n ملګری
at pre الحاد	attention n توجه
atheism n بې دنيي	attentive adj متوجه
atheist n انکار	attenuate v نري کېدل
athlete n اتل	attenuating adj نری شوی
athletic adj د پهلواني	attest v شهادت ورکول
atmosphere n اتموسفير	attic n بامبوتی
atmospheric adj اتموسفيري	attitude n کره وړه

attorney *n* څارنوال	automatic *adj* خپل کاري
attract *v* رابنـکل	automobile *n* موټر
attraction *n* رابنـکنه	autonomous *adj* خپل وا که
attractive *adj* په زړه پورې	autonomy *n* خپلواکي
attribute *v* ذاتي	autopsy *n* د مړيني معائينه
auction *n* ليلامول	autumn *n* مني
auction *v* ليلام	auxiliary *adj* معاون
auctioneer *n* ليلامکوونکی	avail *v* ګټه
audacious *adj* زړه ور	availability *n* شته وال
audacity *n* زړه ورتوب	avalanche *n* راشي
audible *adj* د اوربدو ور	avarice *n* حرص
audience *n* اوربدنه	avaricious *adj* حريص
auditorium *n* کنفرانس خونه	avenge *v* کسات اخيستل
augment *v* زياتول	avenue *n* ارت سړک
August *n* عالي	averse *adj* مخالف
aunt *n* توری	aversion *n* بېزاري
auspicious *adj* نيکمرغه	avert *v* مخ اړول
austere *adj* تند خويه	aviation *n* هوا نوردي
austerity *n* ترشوالی	aviator *n* هوا نورد
authentic *adj* واقعي	avid *adj* ليوال
authenticate *v* کره کول	avoid *v* مخه نيول
authenticity *n* اصليتوب	avoidable *adj* دمخنيوي ور
author *n* ليکوونکی	avoidance *n* مخنيوی
authoritarian *adj* اقتدار	avowed *adj* مکمل
authority *n* واک	await *v* انتظار وېستل
authorization *n* صلاحيت	awake *iv* وېښ
auto *n* په خپل سر	awake *adj* وېښنبدل
autograph *n* لاس ليک	awakening *n* وېښنتوب

award v تاوان وركول	**backbone** n شمزى
award n قضاوت	**background** n پخوانى
aware adj پوه	**backing** n ملاتړ
awareness n خبردارى	**backlash** n حساسيت
away adv لرې	**backlog** n ټولونه
awe n ډارول	**backpack** n طبراق
awesome adj هيبتناک	**backup** n همكاري
awful adj سهم ناک	**backward** adj شاته
awkward adj شواړه	**backwards** adv په شا
awning n څپرى	**backyard** n بڼ
ax n تبر	**bacteria** n بكتريا
axiom n منلى حقيقت	**bad** adj بد
axis n محور	**badge** n مټ ترونکى
axle n اكسل	**badly** adv نيمګړتوب
	baffle v ويجاړول
	bag n كڅوړه
	baggage n پنډه کى
B	**baggy** adj پرسيدلى
	bail n ضامن
	bail out v امنيت
babble v پرتپ ويل	**bait** n شومه
baby n تي خور ماشوم	**bake** v پخول
bachelor n ژنکى، كونډ	**baker** n نانوايي
back n شا	**bakery** n پخلنځى
back adv وروسته	**balance** v موازنه كول
back v ملاترل	**balance** n موازنه، تمادل
back down v پرېښنودل	**bald** adj ساده
back up v همكاري كول	**bale** n مصيبت

ballot n د رايپ کاغذ	**barber** n نايي
ballroom n دنڅا سالون	**bare** adj لوخ
balm n ويلنی	**barefoot** adj پنڅپ لوخپ
balmy adj نرم	**barely** adv په بربنده بنه
bamboo n بانکس	**barely** adv اوربشپ
ban n منع	**bargain** n جوړه
ban v منع کول	**bargain** v جوړه راتلل
banality n بپ خوندي	**barge** n سيند
banana n کيله	**bark** v غپا
band n وندنی، کړی	**bark** n دونپ پوستک
bandage n پټی	**barmaid** n هوټلی
bandage v پټی اپنپودل	**barman** n هوټلی
bandit n ياغي	**barn** n کودام
bang v ترک	**barracks** n بارکونه
banish v شپرل	**barrage** n مخنيونه
banishment n فرار	**barrel** n بيلر
bank n خنډه	**barren** adj شنډ
bankrupt v يووالی	**barricade** n خنډ
bankrupt adj مات شوی	**barrier** n سيمه
bankruptcy n تنګ لاسي	**barring** pre هيله لرل
banner n بيرغ	**bartender** n هوټل ساتونکی
banquet n ميلمستيا	**barter** v بدلول
baptism n تعميد غسل	**base** n سټه
bar n سيخ، ميله	**base** v ټيټول
bar v نبنلول	**baseball** n د بيسبال لوبه
barbarian n پردکی	**baseless** adj بپ اساسه
barbarism n بربريت	**basement** n زپر خانه
barbecue n وريت	**bashful** adj شپرميندونکی

basic *adj* اساسي	bean *n* باقلي
basics *n* لومړني	bear *n* اير
basin *n* تشت، کندول	bear *iv* محتکر، چالباز
basis *n* اساس	bearable *adj* د منني ور
bask *v* مرسته	beard *n* ږیره
basket *n* شکور	bearer *n* نیوونکی
bat *n* کوتک، سوټی لور	beast *n* څاروی
batch *n* خواله	beat *iv* وهل، ټکول
bath *n* غسل	beat *n* وار، ورخَبدنه
bathe *v* لمبل	beaten *adj* وهل شوی
bathrobe *n* دحمام چینه	beating *n* وهنه
bathroom *n* تشناب	beautiful *adj* ښکلی
bathtub *n* لامبل	beautify *v* ښایسته کول
baton *n* کوتک	beauty *n* ښکلا
battalion *n* لبوا	beaver *n* د اوبو سپی
batter *v* دربول	because *c* څکه
battery *n* دربونه	because of *pre* ددې په وجه
battle *n* جگړه	beckon *v* رابلل
battle *v* جگړه کول	become *iv* کبدل
battleship *n* جنگبالی	bed *n* کټ
bay *n* خلیج	bedding *n* د خوب سامان
bayonet *n* برچه	bedroom *n* د خوب خونه
bazaar *n* بازار	bedspread *n* پوښ
be *iv* اوسبدل	bee *n* مچی
beach *n* دسیند غاړه	beef *n* زور
beacon *n* دخطر نښنه	beehive *n* مچی خاله
beak *n* مبنوکه	beer *n* بیر
beam *n* تیر	beet *n* چوغندر

before *adv* پخوا	**bell** *n* زنګ، ترنګیار
before *pre* رومبی	**belly** *n* خیته
beforehand *adv* پخوا له پخوا	**belongings** *n* مربوط شیان
befriend *v* ملګرتیا	**beloved** *adj* کسران
beg *v* سوال کول	**below** *adv* لاندې
beggar *n* سوالګر	**below** *pre* لاندې تر
begin *iv* پیل کېدل	**belt** *n* ملاوستنی
beginner *n* پیل کوونکی	**bench** *n* اوږده چوکی
beginning *n* پیل	**beneath** *pre* لاندې تر
beguile *v* غولول	**benediction** *n* دخیر دعا
behalf (on) *adv* په خاطر	**benefactor** *n* خیر رسوونکی
behave *v* سلوک کول	**beneficial** *adj* ګټور
behavior *n* اجراء	**beneficiary** *n* ګټکوونکی
behavior *v* فعالیت	**benefit** *n* تخفه
behind *pre* شاته	**benefit** *v* تخفه ورکول
behold *iv* پام کول	**benevolence** *n* سخاوت
being *n* مجبوریت	**benevolent** *adj* مهربان
belated *adj* خندیدلی	**benign** *adj* خواخوري
belch *v* سابندول	**bequeath** *v* پریښودل
belch *n* سابندي	**bereaved** *adj* محرومواليب
belfry *n* د زنګ پرج	**bereavement** *n* خفګان
Belgian *adj* د بلجیمي	**beret** *n* بېره خولی
Belgium *n* بیلجیم	**berserk** *adv* لیونتوب
belief *n* عقیده	**beseech** *iv* زاري کول
believable *adj* دمنلو ور	**beset** *iv* ایسارول
believe *v* نظریه	**beside** *pre* برسېره پر
believer *n* منوونکي	**besides** *pre* بې له دې
belittle *v* وروکی کول	**besiege** *iv* ایسارول

best *adj* تر ټولو ښه	billionaire *n* ملبنر
bestial *adj* دڅاروي ډله	bin *n* کندو
bestiality *n* وحشي والي	bind *iv* تړل
bestiality *v* وحشي کول	binding *adj* ضرورت
bet *iv* شرط تړل	binoculars *n* دوربينونه
bet *n* شرط	biography *n* ژوند ليک
betray *v* خيانت کول	biological *adj* بيالوژيکي
betrayal *n* خيانت	biology *n* ژوند پوهنه
better *adj* ښه تر	bird *n* مسارغه
between *pre* تر منځ	birth *n* زيږيدنه
beverage *n* څښاک	birthday *n* د زيږيدنې ورځ
beware *v* پام ساتل	biscuit *n* بسکوټ
bewilder *v* وارخطايي	bishop *n* مسخي ملا
bewitch *v* کوډې کول	bison *n* د غره غوايي
beyond *adv* پورې خوا	bit *n* ګرمټ
bias *n* تعصب	bite *iv* ژوول، چيچل
bible *n* انجيل	bite *n* پرهار
biblical *adj* انجيلي	bitter *adj* تريخ
bicycle *n* بايسکل	bitterly *adv* عجيبه
bid *n* بيه	bitterness *n* غصه
bid *iv* بيه ټاکل	bizarre *adj* احساسا تي
big *adj* ستر	black *adj* تور
bigamy *n* ددوو ښځو لرنه	blackberry *n* سپنګور
bigotry *n* خرافات	blackboard *n* توره دره
bike *n* موټر سايکل	blackmail *v* بدنامول
bile *n* ژېر	blackness *n* تور والی
bill *n* مبنوکه، څوکه	blackout *n* پرکالتوب
billiards *n* د بيليارد لوبه	blacksmith *n* پښن

bladder *n*	مثانه
blade *n*	پانه
blame *n*	تور
blame *v*	تهمتي کول
blameless *adj*	ناملامته
bland *adj*	نرم
blank *adj*	تش
blanket *n*	کمپله
blaspheme *v*	لعنت ويل
blasphemy *n*	کفر
blast *n*	تند باد
blaze *v*	لمبه کېدل
bleach *v*	پاکول
bleach *n*	دپاکول اله
bleak *adj*	تت
bleed *iv*	وينې کول
bleeding *n*	خونړيزي
blemish *n*	ژوبلونه
blemish *v*	ژوبلول
blend *n*	ګډ
blend *v*	ګډول
blender *n*	ګډوونکی
bless *v*	برکت ورکول
blessed *adj*	خوشاله
blessing *n*	برکت
blind *v*	ړندول
blind *adj*	ړوند
blindfold *v*	سترګې ورتړل

blindness *n*	ړوند
blink *v*	ستر ګک وهل
bliss *n*	خوشالي
blissful *adj*	تل خوشاله
blister *n*	تناکه
blizzard *n*	دواوري توپان
bloat *v*	پړپدل
bloated *adj*	پړسوبوالي
block *n*	دره، چمبه
block *v*	چمبه وهل
blockade *v*	بنديز لګول
blockade *n*	بنديز لګونه
blockage *n*	لار بندول
blond *adj*	ژېر
blood *n*	وينه
bloodthirsty *adj*	خوني
bloody *adj*	خونړی
bloom *v*	ګل غوړېدنه
blossom *v*	غوړېدل
blot *n*	داغ
blot *v*	داغ ګر کېدل
blouse *n*	بلوز
blow *n*	غوټی
blow *iv*	غوړېدل
blow out *iv*	چاودېدل
blow up *iv*	وپچارول
blowout *n*	چاودېدنه
bludgeon *v*	په کوتک وهل

blue *adj* اسماني	bomb *v* بم چول
blueprint *n* پلان	bombing *n* قوت
bluff *v* لاپ وهل	bombshell *n* د بم گولی
blunder *n* خطا	bond *n* اسير، په بند کې
blunt *adj* پخ، بې پردي	bondage *n* غلامي
bluntness *n* عدالت	bone *n* بې هډوکو
blur *v* وريخ	bone marrow *n* د هډوکو منځ
blurred *adj* تتوالی	bonfire *n* ميرکن
blush *v* شرمېدل	bonus *n* بخشش
blush *n* شرم	book *n* کتاب
boar *n* نر خوگ	bookcase *n* د کتابونو بکس
board *n* دره، تخته	bookkeeper *n* دفتر دار
board *v* خوراک برابرول	bookkeeping *n* دفتر داري
boast *v* لاپ وهل	booklet *n* رساله
boat *n* وړه بېړۍ	bookstore *n* کتاب پلورنځی
bodily *adj* جسماني	boom *v* د بېړۍ لکره
body *n* جسم، صورت	boost *v* تېل وهل
bog *n* جبه	boost *n* تېله کونه
bog down *v* سپلاب . نبز . مد	boot *n* گته
boil *v* ايشېدل	booth *n* کوچنۍ کوټهٔ
boil down to *v* دلالت کول	booty *n* لوټ
boil over *v* حيرانوونکی	booze *n* الکولي څنباک
boiler *n* ايشولو لوښی	border *n* څنډه، ژۍ
boisterous *adj* زير	border on *v* نزدې کول
bold *adj* زرور، بې باک	borderline *adj* دسرحد کربنه
boldness *n* نر توب	bore *v* سورۍ کول
bolt *n* غشی، کلفک	bored *adj* بې خوندي
bomb *n* بم	boredom *n* ستومانۍ

B

boring *adj* ستومانوونکي	**bourgeois** *adj* دلوري طبقي
born *adj* ورل	**bow** *n* سرتیتونه
borough *n* ناحیه	**bow** *v* سر تیتول
borrow *v* پور ه ول	**bow out** *v* سپارل
bosom *n* غبر	**bowels** *n* نس
boss *n* مشر	**bowl** *n* کاسه، کنډی
boss around *v* اداره کول	**box** *n* بوکس
bossy *adj* حاکم	**boxing** *n* د سوکانو لوبه
botany *n* دبوټو علم	**boy** *n* هلک
botch *v* پینه کول	**boycott** *v* اریکي شلول
both *adj* دواړه	**boyhood** *n* هلکتوب
bother *v* ځورېدل	**bra** *n* برمه
bothersome *adj* ځوروونکي	**bracelet** *n* وښنی
bottle *n* بوتل	**bracket** *n* ستنه
bottle *v* جنګ	**brag** *v* باټي وهل
bottleneck *n* دجنګ حمله	**braid** *n* چوټي
bottom *n* بیخ	**brain** *n* ماغزه
bottomless *adj* بې پایه	**brainwash** *v* حالت
bough *n* څانګه	**brake** *n* ګڼ څنګل
boulder *n* پرنبه	**brake** *v* ورکول
boulevard *n* پراخه جاده	**branch** *n* څانګه
bounce *v* ټوپ وهل	**branch office** *n* فرعي دفتر
bounce *n* ټوپ وهنه	**branch out** *v* خارج څانګه
bound *adj* برید	**brand** *n* داغ، نښه
bound for *adj* هدایات ورکونه	**brand-new** *adj* نوی
boundary *n* سرحد	**brandy** *n* براندي
boundless *adj* بې سرحده	**brat** *n* ماشوم
bounty *n* خیرات	**brave** *adj* بنکلی

bravery n زړور

brawl n شخړه

breach n چاود، ماتونه

bread n ډوډۍ

breadth n پلنوالی

break n ماتونه، ماتېدنه

break iv ماتېدل

break away v یاغي کېدل

break away v سرکش

break free v تښتېدل

break off v بندول

break open v واز

break up v خپرول

breakable adj ماتېدونکی

breakdown n پرې وتنه

breakfast n ناری

breakthrough n ترقي کول

breast n سینه

breath n ورمه

breathe v تنفس کول

breathing n تنفس

breathtaking adj سا اخیستل

breed iv ډوله جوړول

breed n ډول

breeze n باد

brethren n رضایي ورونه

brevity n کموالی

brew v جوړول

bribe v فاسدول

bribe n ګازره

bribery n خیانت

brick n خری

bricklayer n د محکمي خری

bridal adj واده

bride n ناوې

bridge n پل

bridle n زیر وبنبتان

brief adj لنډ

brief v لړ

briefcase n سفرل بکس

briefing n غونډه

briefly adv د لر وخت لپاره

briefs n تفصیل

brigade n غونډ

bright adj ځلاند

brighten v روښانول

brightness n ځلا

brilliant adj روڼ

brim n څنډه

bring iv راوړل

bring back v بېرته ورل

bring down v د قیمت کوزېدل

bring up v روزل

brink n کرنګ

brisk adj چمتو

Britain n برطانوي

B

British *adj*	برتانوي
brittle *adj*	چغزی
broad *adj*	پلن
broadcast *v*	خپرول
broadcast *n*	خپور
broadcaster *n*	خپروونکي
broadcaster *v*	خبريال
broadly *adv*	په پراخه پيمانه
broadminded *adj*	زغمونکی
brochure *n*	رساله
broil *v*	وريتول
broiler *n*	دوريتول اله
broke *adj*	چاودلی
broken *adj*	زره ماتی
bronchitis *n*	برانشيت
bronze *n*	ژير
broom *n*	جارو
broth *n*	بنوروا
brothel *n*	فاحشه خانه
brother *n*	ورور
brotherhood *n*	ورورولي
brother-in-law *n*	اوبنی
brotherly *adj*	دوروری
brow *n*	تنډه
brown *adj*	نسواري
browse *v*	څيرېدل، لوستي
browser *n*	څربدونکی
bruise *n*	سربېرن زخم

bruise *v*	زخمي کول
brunch *n*	مېنبام
brush *n*	برس
brush *v*	رنګول
brush up *v*	تېزول
brusque *adj*	زبرد
brutal *adj*	وحشت
brutality *n*	بې معنا
brutalize *v*	حمله کول
brute *adj*	خالق
bubble *n*	پوکنی
bubble gum *n*	ژاوله
buck *n*	نر
bucket *n*	بوکه
buckle *n*	غوټه
buckle up *v*	تلوار کول
bud *n*	غوټی
buddy *n*	ملګری
budge *v*	بنوربدل
budget *n*	بوديجه
buffalo *n*	مېبنه
bug *n*	خسک
bug *v*	هسکول
build *iv*	ودانول
builder *n*	ورانوونکی
building *n*	ودانی
buildup *n*	قوي
bulb *n*	غوټه

bulge *n* پرسوب	**burglarize** *v* لوټل
bulk *n* لوېوالی	**burglary** *n* غلا
bulky *adj* لوي	**burial** *n* ښخونه
bull *n* غویی	**burly** *adj* قوي
bulldoze *v* درجه	**burn** *iv* سوځول
bullet *n* مردک	**burn** *n* سوځېدنه
bulletin *n* ورځپاڼه وره	**burrow** *n* سوری
bully *adj* خوروونکي	**burst** *iv* چاودل
bulwark *n* سنگر	**burst into** *v* په تېزی راتلل
bum *n* غالبوزه	**bury** *v* ښخول
bump *n* ټکر، ضربه	**bus** *n* بس
bumper *n* ډک گلاس	**bus** *v* دبس چلول
bumpy *adj* ژورب لروونکی	**bush** *n* بوټی
bun *n* کلوله	**busily** *adv* په فعاله توگه
bunch *n* وابنکی	**business** *n* مشغولیت
bundle *n* بنډل	**businessman** *n* تاجر
bundle *v* بنډل کول	**bust** *n* دوجود یوه برخه
bunk bed *n* دپوان	**bustling** *adj* مصروف
bunker *n* ناره وزمه ببری	**busy** *adj* لگیا
buoy *n* سپک جسم	**but** *c* خو
burden *n* بار	**butcher** *n* قصاب
burden *v* بارول	**butchery** *n* قصابي
burdensome *adj* دروند	**butler** *n* خانه سامان
bureau *n* دفتر	**butt** *n* ټاپه، لوي بیلر
bureaucracy *n* بیروکراسي	**butter** *n* کوچ
bureaucrat *n* بروکریټ	**butterfly** *n* پتنگ
burger *n* برگر	**button** *n* غوټه
burglar *n* لوټ ماري	**buttonhole** *n* غوړ یاشه

B
C

buy *iv* اخیستل

buy off *v* رشوت ورکول

buyer *n* اخیستوونکی

buzz *n* بنګبدل

buzz *v* بنګبدل

buzzard *n* پکه بابنه

buzzer *n* مجرد

by *pre* نردې

bye *e* خدای په امان

bypass *n* مخنیوی

bypass *v* مخنیوی کول

by-product *n* نتیجه

bystander *n* نندارچي

C

cab *n* ټکسي موټر

cabbage *n* کرم

cabin *n* وره خونه

cable *n* فلزي مزی

cafeteria *n* رستورانت

caffeine *n* کافین

cage *n* کپس

cake *n* کبک

calamity *n* مصیبت

calculate *v* شمبرل

calculation *n* سمبر

calculator *n* شمبر کوونکی

calendar *n* کلیزه

calf *n* خوسکی

caliber *n* ماهیت

call *n* غږ

call *v* غږ کول

call off *v* منسوخول

call out *v* مظاهره کول

calling *n* بلنه

calm *adj* وره خونه

calm *n* ارامي

calm down *v* تسلي ورکول

calorie *n* دتودوخی مقیاس

calumny *n* تهمت لګونه

camel *n* اوښ

camera *n* خونه

camouflage *v* کمپولاژ کول

camouflage *n* کمپولاژ

camp *v* موقتي اوسېدل

campaign *v* انتخابي مبازره

can *iv* توان

can *v* توان موندل

can *n* دبلی

cancel *v* فسخه کول

cancellation *n* فسخه کونه

candid *adj* بې ریا

candidacy n وراندیز	captivity n خوندي توب
candidate n کاندید	carat n قيراط
candle n شمع	caravan n کاروان
candlestick n د شمعي چوکه	carburetor n کار بېټر
candor n صميمي	carcass n لاپي
candy n خواږه	card n پتي، کارت
cane n ټانټه، گنی	cardboard n مقوا
cannibal n سړي خور	cardiac adj زړه ته منسوب
cannon n توپ خانه	cardiac arrest n زړه نیوونکی
canonize v سر لوړی کول	cardiology n دزړه ناروغي
cantaloupe n یو ډول ختکی	care n پاملرنه
canteen n کانتین	care v پاملرنه کول
canvas n تاپ	care about v عزت کول
canvas v عکس جوړول	care for v حفاظت کول
canyon n تنگه ژوره دره	career n مسلک
cap n خولی،سر پټونی	carefree adj خوشحاله
capability n توان	careful adj محتاط
capable adj ور	careless adj بې فکره
capacity n ظرفیت	carelessness n باحتیاطي
capital n مهم	carelessness n باحتیاطي
capital letter n اساسي مکتوب	caress v نازول
capitalism n سرمایه داري	caretaker n څارونکی
capitalize v سرمایه ورکول	cargo n مال
capsize v ویجاړول	caricature n ټوکیزې څبرې
capsule n کپسول	caring adj نیک
captain n رئس	carnage n زیاته ژوبله
captivate v مایل کول	carnal adj غوجن
captive n بندي	carnation n غوښن رنگ

C

carol *n* تعريف كول	catalog *n* اساسي لست
carpenter *n* ترکاڼ	catalog *v* اساسي لست
carpentry *n* ترکاڼي	cataract *n* لوي جروبی
carpet *n* غالی	catastrophe *n* غمجنه پيښه
carriage *n* بگی	catch *iv* نيول
carrot *n* گازره	catch up *v* نيول
carry *v* وړل	catching *adj* نيول شوی
carry on *v* جاري ساتل	catchword *n* چغه
cart *n* د غويو گاډی	category *n* ډول
cart *v* د غويو گاډی	cater to *v* په ناز لوبول
cartoon *n* توکيزۍ څبرې	caterpillar *n* ځيني حشرات
cartridge *n* کارتوس	cathedral *n* لويه کليسا
carve *v* تورل، کيندل	catholic *adj* جهاني
cascade *n* جروبی	Catholicism *n* کاتولبزم
case *n* صندوق، پوښ	cattle *n* څاروي
cash *n* نقدي پيسې	cauliflower *n* گوپي
cashier *n* خزانه دار	cause *n* سرک پخول
casino *n* تعمير	cause *v* سرک پخول
casket *n* تابوت	caution *n* اخطار
casserole *n* ارکاره	cautious *adj* محتاط
cassock *n* اورد کوټ	cavalry *n* رساله
cast *iv* تورل، شميرل	cave *n* سمځ
castaway *n* ايسته غورځول	cave in *v* ټوک ټوک کبدل
castle *n* حصار	cavern *n* غار
casual *adj* اتفاقي	cavity *n* سوری
casualty *n* پيښه	cease *v* درول
cat *n* پيشو	cease-fire *n* سوله
catacomb *n* د ښخولو ځای	ceiling *n* چت

celebrate v لمانځل	chagrin n پربشاني
celebration n لمانځنه	chain n خنځير
celebrity n نامتو سړی	chain v په خنځير تړل
celery n يو ډول سابه	chainsaw n د اړې خنځير
celestial adj اسماني	chair n څوکۍ
celibacy n لوند	chair v سرپ
cellar n زبر خانه	chairman n رئيس
cellphone n موبايل	chalet n بانډه
cement n سيمنټ	chalice n پياله
cemetery n هديره	chalk n تباشير
censorship n سمبال	chalkboard n د تباشير تخته
censure v تر ټنه	challenge v اعتراض کول
census n سر شمبرنه	challenge n اعتراض کول
centenary n سل کاله	challenging adj مشکل
center n مرکز	chamber n د خوب کوټه
center v متمرکز کول	champion n اتل
centimeter n سانتي متر	chance n تصادف، پيښه
central adj منځنی	chancellor n د پوهنتون رئس
centralize v مرکزي کول	chandelier n شمع دان
century n پيړۍ	change v بدلون
ceramic n کلالي	change n بدلونه
cereal n غله	chant n سندره
cerebral adj دماغي پرده	chaos n ګډوډي
ceremony n مراسم	chaotic adj ګډوډ
certain adj يقيني	chapel n ورہ کليسا
certainty n ډاډ	chaplain n پادري
certificate n تصديق نامه	chapter n څپرکی
certify v تصديقول	char v سکاره کول

C

character n کیفیت	check v نیول
characteristic adj خاصیت	check in v لاسلیک کول
charade n حرف جنگي	check up n ترکول
charcoal n د لرگو سکاره	checkbook n دکتنې کتاب
charge v بارول	cheek n بې پروایي
charge n بار، پیتی	cheeky adj بې باکه
charisma n جادو	cheer v خوشـالول
charismatic adj طلسـمي	cheer up v خوشـالول
charitable adj سخي	cheerful adj ورین تندی
charity n سخاوت	cheers n چک چکې کول
charm n جادو	cheese n پنیر
charming adj په زړه پورې	chef n د اشـپزانو مشر
chart n چارټ،نقشـه	chemical adj کیمیاوي
charter n منشـور	chemist n کیمیا پوه
chase n ښکار	chemistry n کیمیا
chase v ښکار کول	cherry n دګلاس مېوه
chase away v له کاره شړل	chess n سطرنج
chasm n تنگه دره	chest n سـینه، تیر
chaste adj پاک	chew v ژوول
chastise v وهل	chick n چرګوری
chastisement n سـمون	chicken n چرګه
chastity n پاکي	chicken pox n شرې
chat v ګپ شپ	chide v دغور تاوول
chauffeur n موټروان	chief n مشر
cheap adj ارزانه	chiefly adv په ابتدایي توګه
cheat v ټګي کول	child n کوچنی
cheater n ټګمار	childhood n کوچنیتوب
check n نیونه، تمبونه	childish adj سـاده والې

children n کوچنیان	chronicle n تاریخ
chill n ساړه، سا	chubby adj چاغ
chill v سړبدل	chuckle v مسکا کول
chill out v ارام کول	chunk n پنډه ټوټه
chilly adj یخ	church n کلیسا
chimney n دریخهٔ	chute n نل
chimpanzee n چیمپنزی	cider n د میو شیره
chin n زنه	cigar n سبار
chip n کوچنی ټوټه	cigarette n سیگریټ
chisel n ترښخ	cinder n نیم سوی سکاره
chocolate n چاکلیټ	cinema n سینما
choice n انتخاب	circle n دایره
choir n د سندر غاړو ډله	circle v دایره کول
choke v خفه کول	circuit n دوره
cholera n د کلورا ناروغي	circular adj دایروي
cholesterol n کلسترول	circulate v ګرڅیدل
choose iv انتخابول	circulation n متحدالمال
choosy adj انتخاب شوی	circumcise v سنت کول
chop v ماتول	circumcision n سنت کول
chop n ټوټه	circumstance n حالت
chopper n اورونکی	circus n سرکس
chore n وړه دنده	citizen n ښاري
chorus n کورس ډله	citizenship n تابعیت
christening n نوم	city n ښار
christian adj مسیحي	city hall n دښار سالون
Christianity n مسیحیت	civic adj مدني پوهنه
Christmas n مسیحیت	civil adj مدني
chronic adj مزمن	civilization n ښه سلوک

C

civilize v کلتور	**clear** adj روڼ، صاف
claim v حق غوښتل	**clear** v روڼول، صافول
claim n ادعا، تقاضا	**clearance** n تصفیه
clamor v په زوره غږ کول	**clear-cut** adj پاک صاف
clamp n نیوونکی	**clearly** adv په واقعي توګه
clan n قوم	**clearness** n پاکوالی
clandestine adj پټ	**cleft** n د تالونو کلي
clap v چک چکي کول	**clemency** n زړه سوی
clarification n تصدیقول	**clench** v ټینگ نیول
clarify v تصفیه کول	**clergy** n ملا
clarity n څرگند والی	**clergyman** n پادري
clash v ټکر کول	**clerical** adj د لیکلو کار
clash n ټکر	**clerk** n لیکوونکی
class n ټولګی، طبقه	**clever** adj څیرک
classify v تصنیف	**client** n مراجعه کوونکی
classmate n ټولگیوال	**clientele** n مشتریان
classmate n ټولگیوال	**cliff** n ګرنگ
classy adj درجه دار	**climate** n اقلیم
clause n فقره	**climatic** adj اقلیمي
claw n نوک	**climax** n لوړه درجه
claw v نوک، چمبه	**climb** v ختل
clay n خاوره	**climbing** n ختنه
clean adj پاک	**clinch** v کرول
clean v پاکول	**cling** iv په غبر نیول
cleaner n پاکوونکی	**clinic** n د ناروغانو کتنځی
cleanliness n مخنیوی کول	**clip** v غوڅول
cleanse v پاکول	**clipping** n پرې شوې ټوټه،
cleanser n پاک کوونکي	**clock** n چینه

C

clog v مخه نیول	coach n ښوونکی
cloister n صومعه	coaching n لارښووني
clone v کاپي ویستل	coagulate v ترل
cloning n غبرګوني	coagulation n ترل
close v ترل	coal n د ډبرو سکاره
close adj ترلی	coalition n یووالی
close to pre نږدې	coarse adj لاره
closed adj ترل شوی	coast n زیره
closely adv په ترلي توګه	coastal adj زیره
closet n الماری	coastline n زیره کرښه
closure n پای	coat n کرتی، بالاپوش
clot n پرنډ	coax v غوره مالي کول
cloth n رخت	cob n تیو
clothe v دجامو اخیستل	cobblestone n غرګی
clothes n کالي	cobweb n د غنې خاله
clothing n پوښاک	cocaine n کوکاین
cloud n وریځ	cock n چرګ
cloudless adj له وربخو پرته	cockpit n ژور ځای
cloudy adj یخ	cockroach n ګرندی
clown n مسخره	cocktail n یو ډول شراب
club v په لرګي وهل	cocky adj کبرجن
clue n نښه	cocoa n بې غوره چاکلیټ
clumsiness n وارخطاپي	coconut n کوپره
clumsy adj بې خونده	cod n یو ډول کب
cluster n غنچه	code n رمز، شفر
cluster v غونډېدل	codify v شفر جوړول
clutch n کلچ	coerce v ترې کول
coach v راسته کول	coercion n مکمکلېدنه

C

coexist v يو ځای اوسېدل	cologne n كلونيا
coffee n قهوه	colon n د شارحې نښه
coffin n تابوت	colonel n ډګروال
cohabit v ګډ ژوند کول	colonial adj استعماري
coherent adj نښتوونکی	colonization n هجرت
cohesion n نښه	colonize v مستعمره کول
coin n سکه	colony n مستعمره
coincide v برابرېدل	color n رنګ
coincidence n تصادف	color v رنګول
coincidental adj تصادفي	colorful adj رنګداره
cold adj ساړه	colossal adj ستر
coldness n يخ	colt n کوتی
colic n قولنج	column n ستن
collaborate v کار کېدل	coma n بې حالي
collaboration n ګروپي کار	comb n ږمنځ
collaborator n برخوال	comb v ږمنځول
collapse v ټوک ټوک کېدل	combat n مبارزه
collapse n ستونزه	combat v مبارزه کول
collar n غړوندی	combatant n عسکر
collarbone n د اوربې هډوکی	combination n ترکیب
collateral adj څنګ په څنګ	combine v يو کول
colleague n ملګری	combustible n اور اېستوونکي
collect v لنډ لمونځ	combustion n احتراق
collection n راټولېدنه	come iv راتلل
collector n راټولوونکی	come about v مخې ته تلل
college n پوهنځی	come across v په مخه ورتګ،
collide v نښتل	come apart v نړدې ورتلل
collision n واقعه	come back v بېرته راتلل

C

come down v بنکته راتلل	commit v ارتکاب کول
come forward v په وراندي تلل	commitment n وعده
come in v داخل ته راتلل	committed adj ربنتنی
come out v خارج ته تلل	committee n هئیت
come over v زیات تلل	common adj عمومي
come up v ستومانه کېدل	commotion n لمسون
comeback n بیا را ګرځېدنه	communicate v مخابره کول
comedian n مسخره	communication n مفاهمه
comedy n مزاحیه ډرامه	communion n ګډون
comfort n هوسا کول	communism n کمونیزم
comfortable adj ارام	communist adj کونست
comforter n هوسا کوونکی	community n ټولنه
comical adj عجیبه	commute v بدلون
coming n راتګ	compact adj لنډ
coming adj راتلونکی	compact v ټولول
comma n کامه	companion n ملګری
command v امر ورکول	companionship n ملګرتوب
commander n قوماندان	company n ملګرتیا
commandment n حکم	comparative adj د مقایسې ور
commemorate v په یادول	compare v مقایسه کول
commence v پیل کول	comparison n مقایسه
commend v سپارښت	compartment n خونه
commendation n منظوري	compass n قطب نما
comment v تبصره کول	compassion n خوا خوږي
comment n تبصره	compassionate adj نیک
commerce n سوداګري	compatibility n متناسبوالی
commercial adj تجارتي	compatible adj متناسب
commission n کمیسار	compatriot n هېوادوال

C

compel v مجبورول	**complimentary** adj تعارفي
compelling adj قويتوب	**comply** v موافق کېدل
compendium n قوي	**component** n جز
compensate v تاوان ورکول	**compose** v ترتيبول
compensation n مصارف	**composed** adj را ټول شوی
compete v سيالي کول	**composer** n ليکونکی
competence n ورتوب	**composition** n جوړښت
competent adj ور	**compost** n نباتي سره
competition n رقابت	**composure** n غلی
competitive adj ويښ	**compound** n يوځای
competitor n سيال	**compound** v يوځای کول
compile v تآليفول	**comprehend** v پوهېدل
complain v شکايت کول	**comprehensive** adj پراخ
complaint n شکايت	**compress** v خنډول
complement n بشپړ	**compression** n پنډوالی
complete adj پوره	**comprise** v شاملول
complete v پوره کول	**compromise** n روغه جوړه
completely adv په پوره توګه	**compromise** v روغه کول
completion n پای	**compulsion** n اړيستنه
complex adj مرکب	**compulsive** adj ښايسته
complexion n څېره	**compulsory** adj ضروري
complexity n ستونزه	**compute** v شمېرل
compliance n پر ځای کونه	**computer** n کمپيوټر
compliant adj شکايت	**comrade** n مل
complicate v پېچل	**conceal** v پټول
complication n مشکل	**concede** v منل
complicity n ګډون	**conceited** adj په ځان غره
compliment n مننه	**conceive** v بلاربېدل

concentrate v کول متمرکز	condo n غم شریکېدنه
concentration n توجه	condolences n غم
concept n مفکوره	condone v بخښنل دگنا
conception n بلاربوالی	conducive adj مرستندویه
concern n مسأله	conduct n اداره
concerning pre په باره کې	conduct v لاربنسوول
concert n کنسرت	conductor n عملي کوونکی
concession n تېربدنه	cone n مخروط
conciliate v پخلاکوال	confer v منظورول
conciliatory adj پخلاوالی	conference n مجلس
conciousness n خبرداري	confess v منل
concise adj لنډ	confession n مننه
conclusion n نتیجه، پای	confessor n اعتراف کوونکی
conclusive adj ډاډ	confidant n باوري
concoction n مخلوط، مرکب	confide v کول باور
concrete n خاص	confidence n وریا
concrete adj مشخص	confident adj په پته
concur v جوربدل	confidential adj اعتمادي
concussion n ټکر	confinement n بندي ساتل
condemn v ملامتول	confirm v کول ملاتړ
condemnation n ترټنه	confirmation n ملاتړ
condensation n خلاصه	confiscate v اخیستل
condense v ټینګول	confiscation n جدا کېدنه
condescend v شفقت کول	conflict n مخالفت
condiment n مرچ او مصاله	conflict v کول مخالفت
condition n شرط	conflicting adj نا خوښنه
conditional adj مشروط	conform v سمول
conditioner n وضع کوونکی	conformist adj روایتي

C

conformity n جوړه	**consecration** n لبوالتيا
confound v وارخطا کول	**consecutive** adj پرله پسې
confront v مخالفت کول	**consent** n رضايت
confrontation n مشکل	**consequence** n پايله
confuse v مغشوشول	**conservation** n ساتنه
confusing adj وارخطايي	**conservative** adj محافظه کار
confusion n مغشوش	**conserve** v ساتل
congenial adj خوا خوړی	**consider** v فکر کول
congested adj بوخاب والې	**considerable** adj دقدر ور
congestion n بوخاب توب	**considerate** adj پاملرونکي
congratulate v مبارکي ويل	**consideration** n پاملرنه
congratulations n مبارکي	**consignment** n لېږنه
congregate v يو ځای کېدل	**consist** v تشکيلېدل
congregation n ټو لنه	**consistency** n مقاومت
conjecture n ګمان	**consistent** adj د ډاډ ور، باوري
conjugal adj د واده	**consolation** n مرسته
conjugate v جوړه کول	**console** v دلاسه کول
conjunction n يووالی	**consolidate** v يو ځای کول
connect v مينبلول	**consonant** n موافق
connection n کړۍ	**conspicuous** adj څرګند
connive v تجاهل کول	**conspiracy** n دسيسه
connote v تجويز ورکول	**conspire** v چل کول
conquer v بری موندل	**constancy** n عزم
conqueror n فاتح	**constant** adj ثابت
conquest n بری	**constellation** n غوسکه
conscience n ضمير	**consternation** n وبره
conscious adj يوه	**constipate** v وبرېدل
conscript n پچه کښنبل	**constipated** adj وبرېدلی

constipation *n* قبضيت	content *v* راضي كول
constitute *v* مقررول	contentious *adj* مخالف
constitution *n* اساسي قانون	contents *n* مخالفت
constrain *v* ،درول	contest *n* جګړه كول
constraint *n* اجبار	contestant *n* مقابله كوونكى
construct *v* چل جوړول	context *n* قرينه
construction *n* جوړښت	continent *n* خان ژغورنه
constructive *adj* ګټور	continental *adj* ژغورونكى
consul *n* كونسل	contingency *n* استراري حالات
consulate *n* د كونسل دفتر	continuation *n* دوام
consult *v* سلا وركول	continue *v* جاري ساتل
consultation *n* بحث	continuity *n* تسلسل
consume *v* خرابول	continuous *adj* پرله پسې
consumer *n* مستهلك	contour *n* خاكه
consumption *n* مصارف	contract *v* لنډول
contact *v* تماس نيول	contract *n* قرار داد
contact *n* تماس	contraction *n* لرونه
contagious *adj* ساري	contradict *v* مخالف كول
contain *v* درلودل	contradiction *n* ضد
container *n* لوښى	contrary *adj* برعكس
contaminate *v* فاسدول	contrast *n* تفاوت
contamination *n* فساد	contribute *v* مرسته كول
contemplate *v* چورت وهل	contributor *n* مرستندوي
contemporary *adj* معاصر	contrition *n* پښېماني
contempt *n* كركه	control *n* كنترول
contend *v* مجادله كول	control *v* كنترولول
contender *n* مجادله كوونكى	controversial *adj* رسوايي
content *adj* راضي	controversy *n* رسوا

C

C

convalescent *adj* رسوا شوی	coolness *n* یخ
convene *v* غونډبدل	cooperate *v* مرسته کول
convenience *n* غونډ	cooperation *n* مرسته
convenient *adj* هوسا	cooperative *adj* کوپراتیف
convention *n* جرګه	coordinate *v* منظم کول
conversation *n* مرکه	coordination *n* منظم
converse *v* مرکه کول	coordinator *n* همکار
conversely *adv* په برابره توګه	cop *n* جګړه
conversion *n* تغیر	cope *v* جګړه کول
convert *v* اړول	copier *n* کاپي کوونکی
convert *n* په بل دین شوی	copper *n* مسي
convey *v* وړل، لېږل	copy *v* کافي اخیستل
convict *v* تهمتي کول	copy *n* کافي
conviction *n* ګرمتیا، ملامتیا	copyright *n* دچاپولو حق
convince *v* رضا کول	cord *n* پړی، رسی
convincing *adj* رضاکونه	cordial *adj* رښتنی
convoluted *adj* کږی والج	cordless *adj* ګرځندنه با تار
convoy *n* بدرګه	cordon *n* ننبان
convulse *v* لړزول	cordon off *v* جدا کول
convulsion *n* ټکان	core *n* مرکز
cook *v* پخول	cork *n* کارک
cook *n* اشپز	corn *n* غله
cookie *n* کلچه	corner *n* ګوټ،کنج
cooking *n* پخول	cornerstone *n* د کنج تیږه
cool *adj* یخنی، ساړه	cornet *n* تروم
cool *v* یخول	corollary *n* وړل، لېږل
cool down *v* د یخ لاندې	coronary *adj* کنجکي
cooling *adj* یخوالی	corporal *adj* مادي

corporal n فرقه مشر	counsel v مشوره کول
corporation n اتحادیه	counsel n سلا، مشوره
corpse n مړی	counselor n مشاور
corpulent adj ګردی	count v شمېرل
corpuscle n ذره	count n مخه ور
correct v سیخول	countdown n شمارل
correct adj سیخ	countenance n بڼه
correction n سیخالی	counter n شمېرونکی
correspond v مکاتبه کول	counter v کږبدل، چپبدل
correspondent n خبریال	counteract v مخالفت کول
corresponding adj سم	counterfeit v جعلي
corridor n دهلبز	counterfeit adj جعلي
corroborate v کره کول	counterpart n جوړه
corrupt v فاسد	countess n ماینه
corrupt adj فاسد	countless adj بې شمېره
corruption n سینګار شیان	country n هېواد، سیمه
cosmetic n سینګار شیان	countryman n هېوادوال
cosmic adj نړیوال	countryside n کلیوالي
cost iv ارزښت	county n ولایت
cost n ارزښت	coup n اولسوالۍ
costly adj قیمتي	couple n جوړه، تړیا
costume n جامې	coupon n کوپون
cottage n جونګړه	courage n مېړانه
cotton n مالوچ	courageous adj زړه ور
couch n کوچ	courier n قاصد
cough n ټوخی	course n کورس
cough v ټوخبدل	court n انګړ، دربار
council n ټولنه	court v دمینب څرګندول

C

courteous adj مودب	**cramped** adj محدود
courtesy n ادب	**crane** n کرین
courthouse n محکمه	**crank** n پرزه یوه دموټر
courtship n مینتوب	**cranky** adj تند مزاجه
courtyard n غولی	**crap** n کریپ
cousin n دتره څوي	**crappy** adj کریپي
cove n لغم	**crash** n تصادم
covenant n ترون	**crash** v ماتبدل
cover n پوښ، تپت	**crass** adj بې تهذیبه
cover v پوښبـول، پټول	**crater** n ارشیند
cover up v پوښ ورکول	**crave** v غوښبتل
coverage n احاطه	**craving** n مینه
covert adj پټ	**crawl** v تلل په خاپورو
coverup n دوسیه	**crayon** n پاستـل
covet v غوښبتل	**craziness** n بې عقلي
cow n غوا	**crazy** adj لیونی
coward n بې زره	**creak** v غچبدل
cowardice n وبره	**creak** n غچبدنه
cowardly adv کمزوری	**cream** n پیروی
cowboy n غوبه	**creamy** adj نرم
cozy adj مستریح	**crease** n کات کول
crab n چنکاښ	**crease** v کات کول
crack n چاودنه	**create** v خلق کول
cradle n زانگو	**creation** n پیدایښت
craft n هنر، ارټ	**creative** adj اخترع کوونکی
craftsman n هنر مند	**creativity** n لومړی والی
cram v ژر ژر خوړل	**creator** n خالق
cramp n بربښ	**creature** n مخلوق ژوندی

credibility n دباورمنتوب	**crook** n کروپ
credible adj باوري	**crooked** adj کوږ،
credit n اعتبار	**crop** n کروپ
creditor n پور کوونکی	**cross** n چليپا
creed n عقيده	**cross** adj چليپا شوی
creek n وياله	**cross** v چليپا رابنسکل
creep v خکبدل	**crossfire** n بالمقابل ډزي
creepy adj وبروونکی	**crossing** n د تقاطع ځای
cremate v دمړي سوځول	**crossroads** n غوڅونه
crest n څوکه	**crosswalk** n دباره کتل
crevice n درز	**crossword** n بالمقابل الفاظ
crib n اخور	**crouch** v تيتيدل
cricket n يو ډول لوبه	**crow** n دچرگ اذان
crime n جرم	**crow** v اذان کول
criminal adj مجرم	**crowbar** n اړم
cripple v گوډ ول	**crowd** n ډله
crisis n بحران	**crowd** v ټولنه
crisp adj گونجي گونجي	**crowded** adj ټولبدل
crispy adj سخت	**crown** n تاج
criss-cross v شبکه	**crown** v تاج يبنسودل
criterion n معيار	**crowning** n د ټولو څخه لوړ
critical adj بحراني، انتقادي	**crucial** adj قاطع
criticism n انتقاد	**crucifix** n عيسوي سمبول
criticize v انتقاد کول	**crucify** v په دار څرول
critique n انتقادي نظر	**crude** adj بې خونده
crockery n خاورين لوښی	**cruel** adj بې رحمه
crocodile n تمساح	**cruelty** n ښاورتوب
crony n انډيوال	**crumb** n کوچنی ټوټه

C

C

crumble *v* ټوټه ټوټه کول	cup *n* پياله
crunchy *adj* کرسن	cupboard *n* الماری
crusade *n* صليبي جګړه	curable *adj* دعلاج وړ
crush *v* میده کول	curator *n* ولي
crushing *adj* میده شوی	curb *v* مخ نیول
crust *n* قشر، پوټکی	curb *n* مخنیوی
crusty *adj* سخت	curdle *v* تومنه کول
crutch *n* د ګوډ لکړه	cure *v* علاج کول
cry *n* ژړا	cure *n* علاج
cry *v* ژړل	curiosity *n* اور وژنه
crying *n* ژړېدونکی	curious *adj* لټوونکی
crystal *n* کرسټل	curl *v* ول ول کول
cube *n* مکعب	curl *n* ول کونه
cubic *adj* مکعب غوندې	curly *adj* ول شوی
cubicle *n* خونه	currency *n* مروجب پیسب
cucumber *n* پادرنګ	current *adj* بهاندب اوبه
cuddle *v* په غیږ کې نیول	currently *adv* اوس
cuff *n* کپ، ولچک	curse *v* لعنت ویل
cuisine *n* پخلنځی	curtail *v* لنډول
culpability *n* مسئوولیت	curtain *n* پرده
culprit *n* مجرم	curve *n* کوروالی
cult *n* لمانځنه	curve *v* کوروالی
cultivate *v* کرل	cushion *n* بالښت
cultivation *n* کرنه	cushion *v* بالښت
cultural *adj* کرل شوی	cuss *v* ښنبرا کول
culture *n* دستور	custard *n* یو ډول خواړه
cumbersome *adj* دروند	custodian *n* ساتوونکی
cunning *adj* ښیرک	custody *n* خوندي توب

custom n دود	**dairy farm** n د لبنباتو فارم
customary adj عادي	**daisy** n داودي ګل
customer n بی پار	**dam** n بند
customs n دستور	**damage** n زیان
cut n پری کونه	**damage** v ویجاړول
cut iv پری کېدل	**damaging** adj وران شوی
cut back v کمول	**damn** v لعنت ویل
cut off v اریکه قطع کول	**damnation** n لعنت
cut out v خرابېدل	**damp** adj لوند والی
cute adj چالاک	**dampen** v لندېدل، لوندېدل
cutlery n غوښوونکي اله	**dance** n نڅا
cutter n غوښوونکی	**dance** v نڅېدل
cycle n بایسکل	**dancing** n نڅا
cyclone n بور بوره کی	**dandruff** n د سرپخه
cylinder n سلېنډر	**danger** n وبره
cynic adj بد بین	**dangerous** adj وبروونکی
cynicism n بد بینی	**dangle** v ځړېدل
cypress n د سبر ونه	**dare** v جرآت کول
cyst n مثانه	**dare** n جرآت
	daring adj جسارت
	dark adj تورتم
	darken v تیاره کول
	darkness n تیاره

D

dad n نرمر	**darling** adj په زړه پورې
dagger n خنجر	**darn** v پینه کول
daily adv ورځنی	**dart** n نوکداره ګولی
	dash v زورور ګوزار
	dashing adj ویښ

D

data n معلومات

date n نېټه

date v نېټه ټاکل

daughter n لور

daughter-in-law n خينه

daunt v ډارول

daunting adj ډاربدنه

dawn n دسباوون رنا

day n ورځ

daydream v خيال پلو

daze v گنگسول

dazed adj گډ وډ

dazzle v مبهوت

dazzling adj بربنښبدونکی

dead adj مړ

dead end n مرګونې پاې

deaden v له منځه وړل

deadlock adj ځنډ

deadly adj مهلک

deaf adj کوڼ

deaf adj کوڼ

deafen v کوڼ کول

deafening adj کوڼ والی

deafness n کوڼوالی

deal iv اندازه

deal n وېره

dealer n تجار

dealings n معامله کول

dean n کليسا مشر

dear adj ښاغلی

dearly adv په زياته پيمانه

death n مړينه

death toll n د تلفاتو شمېر

death trap n د مرګ لومه

deathbed n د مرګ کټ

debase v سپکول

debatable adj د بحث وړ

debate v مناظره

debate n مناقشه

debit n قرضداري

debrief v قرض ورکول

debris n هبرول

debt n پور

debtor n پوروړی

debunk v هوا ايستل

debut n لومړی کوشش

decade n لس کاله

decadence n زوال

decapitate v سر غوڅول

decay v ورستېدل

decay n خرابوالی

deceased adj مړينه

deceit n تبر ايستنه

deceitful adj بې ايمانه

deceive v خطا ايستل

December n دسمبر مياشت

decency *n* درنښت	deduct *v* جلا کول
decent *adj* شریف	deductible *adj* جلا شوی
deception *n* تېروتنه	deduction *n* جلا
deceptive *adj* بې اعتماده	deed *n* عمل
decide *v* فیصله کول	deem *v* اټکلول
deciding *adj* فیصله کن	deep *adj* ژور
decimal *adj* عشاري	deepen *v* ژوربدل
decipher *v* د رمز ترجمه	deer *n* هوسۍ
decision *n* فیصله	deface *v* بڼه ور خرابول
decisive *adj* مهم	defame *v* د چا نوم بدلول
deck *n* د بېړۍ عرشه	defeat *v* ماتې ور کول
declaration *n* اعلان	defeat *n* ماتې
declare *v* اعلانول	defect *n* نیمګرتیا
declension *n* لوبدنه	defect *v* عیب
decline *v* پرېوتل	defection *n* ناکامي
decline *n* پرېوتنه	defective *adj* نا مکمل
decompose *v* تحلیل کول	defend *v* دفاع کول
décor *n* سینگار	defendant *n* متهم
decorate *v* سینگارول	defender *n* دفاع کوونکی
decorum *n* بنه خوی	defense *n* دفاع
decrease *v* کمول	defenseless *adj* کمزوری
decrease *n* کمونه	defer *v* ځندول
decree *n* حکم	defiance *n* جنگ ته رابلل
decree *v* حکم کول	defiant *adj* سپک خولی
decrepit *adj* زوړ	deficiency *n* کموالی
dedicate *v* وقف کول	deficient *adj* کمبود
dedication *n* شوق	deficit *n* کسر
deduce *v* نتیجه کښنل	defile *v* تنگي

D

define *v* تعریف کول	delegation *n* خوشالونکی
definite *adj* قطعي	delete *v* ضررناک
definition *n* تعریف	deliberate *v* سنجول
definitive *adj* څرگند	deliberate *adj* سنجول شوی
deflate *v* تشول	delicacy *n* نزاکت
deform *v* مسخ کول	delicate *adj* نازک
deformity *n* اړونه	delicious *adj* خوندور
defraud *v* تبرایستل	delight *n* ښادي
defray *v* تادیه کول	delight *v* ښادي کول
defrost *v* گرم	delightful *adj* پوره خوشالي
deft *adj* ماهر	delinquency *n* شرارت
defuse *v* خاموش	delinquent *adj* بدعمله
defy *v* جگړې ته لمسول	deliver *v* تسلیمول
degenerate *v* کم اصل کېدل	delivery *n* ازادونه
degenerate *adj* کم اصل	delude *v* گمراه
degeneration *n* د نسل کمېدنه	deluge *n* داوبو سیل
degradation *n* تپتول	delusion *n* تصور
degrade *v* ښکنبمانبدل	deluxe *adj* تجمل
degrading *adj* شرمناک	demand *v* غوښتل
degree *n* درجه	demand *n* غوښتنه
dehydrate *v* اوبو کموالی	demanding *adj* غوښتل شوی
deign *v* تنزیل کول	demean *v* کښته کول
deity *n* الوهیت	demeaning *adj* اخلاقي
dejected *adj* خفه	demeanor *n* اخلاق
delay *v* ځنډول	demented *adj* لیونی
delay *n* ځنډیدنه	demise *n* انتقال
delegate *v* هئیت	democracy *n* دخلکو حکومت
delegate *n* د هئیت غړي	demolish *v* ویجاړول

demolition *n* خرابتيا	deplete *v* كمول
demon *n* شيطان	deplorable *adj* د خواشينى ور
demonstrate *v* څرگندول	deplore *v* غم كول
demonstrative *adj* مدلل	deploy *v* اوردول
demoralize *v* بى زره كول	deployment *n* سپرل
demote *v* تنزيل وركول	deport *v* شړل
den *n* غار	deportation *n* نقليه وسايل
denial *n* انكار	depose *v* معزولول
denigrate *v* كبنته كښل	deposit *n* كافي ذخيره
Denmak *n* ډنمارک	depot *n* ډيپو، تحويلخانه
denote *v* دلالت	deprave *adj* خرابول
denounce *v* تورول	depravity *n* فساد
dense *adj* خند، كپ	depreciation *n* تنزيل
density *n* پند والى	depress *v* لرول
dent *v* غاښ جوړول	depressing *adj* خفه
dent *n* غاښ	depression *n* ټيټوالى
dental *adj* غاښيز	deprivation *n* محرومول
dentist *n* دغاښونو ډاكتر	deprive *v* محرومول
dentures *n* د طبعت بدلول	deprived *adj* بى كښې
deny *v* انكار كول	depth *n* كنده
depart *v* مړ كېدل	derail *v* غمجن
department *n* دايره	derailment *n* غمجنتيا
departure *n* روانېدنه	deranged *adj* ساده
depend *v* متكي كېدل	derelict *adj* پرې اېښي
dependable *adj* د اتكا ور	deride *v* ملنډ وهل
dependence *n* اتكا	derivative *adj* مشتق
dependent *adj* تر لاس لاندې	derogatory *adj* كبنته كبدل
depict *v* انځورول	descend *v* ښكته كبدل

D

D

descendant *n* زوزات	despotic *adj* ظالمانه
descent *n* لوېدنه،ګوزېدنه	destination *n* د وتلو ځای
describe *v* روښانول	destiny *n* قسمت
description *n* سپرنه	destitute *adj* ډېر غریب
descriptive *adj* تشریحي	destroy *v* ویجاړول
desecrate *v* ملوث کول	destroyer *n* ویجاړوونکی
desegregate *v* بو کول	destruction *n* ویجاړتوب
desert *n* د شګو بیدیا	destructive *adj* مخرب
desert *v* پرېښوول، تښتېدل	detach *v* جلا کول
deserted *adj* بېباپب	detachable *adj* د جلا کېدو وړ
deserter *n* خاېن	detail *n* تفصیل
deserve *v* وړ کېدل	detail *v* تفصیل ورکول
deserving *adj* استحقاق موندل	detain *v* بندي کول
design *n* پلان ، طرحه	detect *v* موندل
designate *v* ټاکل	detective *n* منصبدار
designate *adj* غوره شوی	detector *n* کشفول
desire *n* غوښتنه	detention *n* توقیف
desire *v* غوښتل	deter *v* وېرول
desist *v* درېدل	detergent *n* ویجاړ
desk *n* مېز، منبر	deteriorate *v* ویجاړول
desolate *adj* ویجاړ	deterioration *n* ویجاړ
desolation *n* ویجاړتیا	determination *n* پرېکړه
despair *n* مایوسي	determine *v* پرېکړه کول
desperate *adj* مایوسه	deterrence *n* مخنیوی
despicable *adj* دسپکتیا وړ	detest *v* نفرت کول
despite *c* سره له دې	detestable *adj* بد ښېنې راتلل
despondent *adj* غمجن	detonate *v* چول
despotic *n* ظلم	detonation *n* چاودنه

D

detour n لار موقتي	**dial** n ساعت مبخ
detriment n زيان	**dial** v خرگندول
detrimental adj ضررناک	**dial tone** n اواز داپر د
devaluation n کول بدي خوا	**dialect** n لهجه
devalue v کول ارزانه	**dialogue** n اترې خبرې
devastate v ويجاړول	**diameter** n پرپر
devastating adj لرزوونکی	**diamond** n الماس
devastation n انحراف	**diaper** n ټوکر دکتان
develop v وروکول انکشاف	**diarrhea** n اسهال
development n اکشاف	**diary** n يادابنتونه ورځ
deviation n روانبدنه	**dice** n پاو چکه
device n اله	**dictate** v ويل املا
devil n شيطان	**dictator** n مستبد
devious adj سرگردانه	**dictatorial** adj ظالمانه
devise v کول تدبير	**dictionary** n قاموس
devoid adj خالي	**die** v کبدل مړ
devote v وقفول	**die out** v ختمبدل
devotion n وقف	**diet** n خواړه
devour v کول ضايع	**differ** v بېلبدل
devout adj پاک	**difference** n فرق
dew n پرخه	**different** adj توپېر
diabetes n ناروغي دشکري	**difficult** adj گران
diabetic adj شکري	**difficulty** n گراني
diabolical adj پساتې	**diffuse** v شيندل
diagnose v کول تشخيص	**dig** iv کيندل
diagnosis n موندنه	**digest** v مجموعه
diagonal adj وبېنته	**digestion** n جمع
diagram n انځور	**digestive** adj شوی جمع

D

dignify v واکمن	**disability** n کمزورېتوب
dignitary n دعزت مقام	**disabled** adj کمزورې کول
dignity n درنښت	**disadvantage** n تاوان
digress v یوې خوا ته کېدل	**disagree** v ناموافق
dilapidated adj ویجاړ شوی	**disagreeable** adj بدخوبه
dilemma n دمشکل انتخاب	**disagreement** n مخالفت
diligent adj خواري کښ	**disappear** v اه نظره پټېدل
dilute v اوبلنول	**disappearance** n غایب
dim adj قت	**disappoint** v مایوس کول
dim v قت کول	**disappointing** adj مایوس کدپنه
dime n دلسو سنټو سکه	**disappointment** n مایوستوب
dimension n اندازه	**disapproval** n خپکان
diminish v لرول	**disapprove** v بد ګڼل
diner n ډوډۍ خورونکی	**disarm** v بې وسلې کول
dinner n د مابښام ډوډۍ	**disarmament** n بې وسلې والی
diphthong n هیجا	**disaster** n ناوړه
diploma n دیپلوم	**disastrous** adj ډاروونکې
diplomacy n دیپلوماسي	**disbelief** n بد ګمانې
diplomat n سیاستمدار	**discard** v اېسته غورخول
diplomatic adj سیاسي	**discern** v لېدل
dire adj ډېر وبروونکی	**discharge** v تشول
direct adj نیغ	**discharge** n تش , رخصت
direct v لارښوونه کول،	**disciple** n شاګرد
direction n لارښونه،	**discipline** n دسپلېن سمون
director n مدېر	**disclaim** v انکار کول
directory n د یاداشت کتابچه	**disclose** v خرګندول
dirt n خاوره	**discomfort** n نا ارامه
dirty adj چاتلې	**disconnect** v جلا کول

D

discontent *adj* نا راضه	disguise *n* شکل بدلونه
discontinue *v* پرې کول	disgust *n* کرکه
discord *n* بل والې	disgusting *adj* تربړ کونکې
discordant *adj* غبر موافق	dish *n* خوراک
discount *n* لروونه	dishearten *v* بې زره کول
discount *v* لروول	dishonest *adj* منافق
discourage *v* بنه نه کېل	dishonesty *n* منافقت
discouragement *n* مخالفت	dishonor *n* سپکوالې
discouraging *adj* اختلاف	dishonorable *adj* شرم ناک
discourtesy *n* بې ادبي	disinfect *v* د عفونې ضدکول
discover *v* موندل	disinherit *v* عاق کول
discovery *n* موندنه	disintegrate *v* تت و پرک کول
discredit *v* بې اعتباري	disintegration *n* لوبدنه
discreet *adj* محتاط	disinterested *adj* بې طرفه
discrepancy *n* توپیر	disk *n* تبی
discretion *n* واک	dislike *v* نفرت کول
discriminate *v* توپیر کول	dislike *n* نفرت
discrimination *n* خیانت	dislocate *v* بې ځایه کول
discuss *v* مباحثه کول	dislodge *v* ابستل
discussion *n* مرکه	disloyal *adj* بې وفا
disdain *n* سپک کېل	disloyalty *n* بې وفایي
disease *n* داروغې	dismal *adj* سور
disentangle *v* نه کډول	dismantle *v* لغرول
disfigure *v* بې بنې کول	dismay *n* بې زره توب
disgrace *n* سپک والې	dismay *v* وبرول
disgrace *v* سپکه ول	dismiss *v* موقفول
disgraceful *adj* شرم ناک	dismount *v* پلی کېدل
disguise *v* بنه بدلول	disobedience *n* نا فرماني

D

disobedient adj نامنونکې	**disruption** n ماتېدل
disobey v غاړه غرونکې	**dissatisfied** adj ناراض
disorder n ګډوډي	**disseminate** v پاشل
disorganized adj ګډوډپدبنه	**dissent** v مخالفت کول
disown v انکار کول	**dissident** adj مخالفت کونه
disparity n توپیر	**dissimilar** adj ناوته
dispatch v لېرل	**dissipate** v جلا کول
dispel v ابستل	**dissolute** adj بد اخلاقه
dispensation n وبستنه	**dissolution** n تباهي
dispense v وبشل	**dissolve** v ویلي کول
dispersal n تبت وپرک کونه	**dissonant** adj ناروغتیا
disperse v تبت وپرک کول	**dissuade** v ګرزول
displace v بې ځایه کول	**distance** n فاصله
display n نمایش	**distant** adj لېرې
display v څرګندول	**distaste** n بې خونده
displease v خپه کول	**distasteful** adj بېزاره
displeasing adj مضر	**distill** v څخبدل
displeasure n خپګان	**distinct** adj څرګند
disposable adj سمونه	**distinction** n څرګندوالي
disposal n واک	**distinctive** adj تاکلی
dispose v سمول	**distinguish** v توپیر ورکول
disprove v غلط ثابتول	**distort** v اړول
dispute n جګړه	**distortion** n اړونه
dispute v جګړه کول	**distract** v ګرزول
disrepair n نه تر میمیدونکی	**distraction** n پارول
disrespect n بې احترامۍ	**distraught** adj لېونۍ
disrespectful adj بې ادبۍ	**distress** n غم
disrupt v ماتول	**distress** v غمګین کبدل

distressing *adj* خپه کېدنه

distribute *v* وېشل

distribution *n* خپرول

district *n* سيمه

distrust *n* بې اعتباري

distrust *v* بې اعتباري کول

distrustful *adj* شک

disturb *v* گډوډ کول

disturbance *n* لاس و پښه کول

disturbing *adj* لاس و پښه کونه

disunity *n* بې اتفاقي

disuse *n* بې پروایي کول

ditch *n* لښتی

diver *n* شو پشو کېدل

diverse *adj* خو

diversify *v* توپیرورکول

diversion *n* کږیدنه

diversity *n* توپیر

divert *v* اړول

divide *v* تقسیمول

dividend *n* برخه

divine *adj* مقدس

diving *n* اسماني

divinity *n* الوهيت

divisible *adj* د وشپلو ور

division *n* وېش

divorce *n* طلاق

divorce *v* طلاقول

divorcee *n* طلاق

divulge *v* څرگندول

dizziness *n* پرکالتوب

dizzy *adj* خوبولي

do *iv* اجرا کول

docile *adj* د تابع کېدو ور

docility *n* دابلېدو ور

dock *n* شلخي

dock *v* پرکول

doctor *n* طبیب

doctrine *n* عقیده

document *n* سند

documentary *n* مستند

dodge *v* بوې خواته کېدل

dog *n* سپی

dogmatic *adj* داخپلي

doll *n* نانزکه

dollar *n* ډالر

dolphin *n* نهنگ

dome *n* گنبزه

domestic *adj* کورنۍ

domesticate *v* اهلي کول

dominate *v* حاکميت لرل

domination *n* واک

domineering *adj* مشري کونکی

dominion *n* قلمرو

donate *v* بسپنه ورکول

donation *n* اینبل

D

donkey *n* خر	**downstairs** *adv* ښکته تر
donor *n* بښنه وړکونکی	**down-to-earth** *adj* قابل عمل
doom *n* حکم	**downtown** *n* کوزه برخه
doomed *adj* په تقدیر کی	**downtrodden** *adj* زره ماتی
door *n* ور	**downturn** *n* غوټه وړکول
doorbell *n* د ور زنگ	**dowry** *n* جهیز
doorstep *n* د وره زینه	**doze** *n* پر مخکی ورنه
doorway *n* مدخل	**doze** *v* پر مخکی ورل
dope *n* بی عقله	**dozen** *n* درجن
dope *v* بی عقله کول	**draft** *n* حواله ، مسوده
dormitory *n* لیلیه	**draft** *v* حواله کول
dossier *n* دوسیه	**draftsman** *n* نخشه کښ
dot *n* ټکی	**drag** *v* کښول
double *adj* غبرگ	**dragon** *n* ښامار
double *v* غبرگول	**drain** *v* وچول
double-check *v* چاڼ ورکول	**drainage** *n* وچونه
double-cross *v* خیانت کول	**dramatic** *adj* ډراماتیک
doubt *n* شک	**drastic** *adj* غبنتلی
doubt *v* شکمن کیدل	**draw** *n* کش
doubtful *adl* شکمن	**draw** *iv* کښول ،راښکل
dough *n* خمیره	**drawback** *n* مخ نیوی
dove *n* کوتره	**drawer** *n* حواله کونکی
down *adv* لاندی خوا	**drawing** *n* نقاشی
downcast *adj* غمجن	**dread** *v* ډارول
downfall *n* لویدنه	**dreaded** *adj* ډارونه
downhill *adv* ښکته خوا	**dreadful** *adj* ډارونکی
downpour *n* ګن باران	**dream** *iv* خوب لیدل
downsize *v* سپما کول	**dream** *n* خوب لیده

D

dress n كالي	**drowsy** adj نيم ويده
dress v كالي اغوستل	**drug** n دارو
dresser n د سپنګار ميز	**drug** v دارو وركول
dressing n پټی	**drugstore** n دوا خانه
dried adj وچ	**drum** n ډول
drift v ګردله	**drunk** adj نشه
drifter n ابله ګرد	**drunkenness** n نشه توب
drill v سورې كول	**dry** v وچول
drill n افريقايي بيزو	**dry** adj وچ
drink iv څكل	**dryclean** v پاک
drink n مشروب	**dryer** n وچوونك
drinkable adj پاک	**dual** adj دوه ګون
drinker n څښونكى	**dubious** adj شكی
drip v څڅول	**duck** n هلی
drip n څڅبدل	**duck** v غوټه كول ، ټيټول
drive n ابستل ، شړل	**duct** n نل
drive iv چلول	**due** adj ور
drive at v هدف ته رسبدل	**dues** n دنده
drive away v پورې وهل	**dull** adj لټ
driver n موټروان	**duly** adv په مناسب توګه
driveway n د چلولو لاره	**dumb** adj پوټ خولي
drizzle n نرۍ باران	**dummy** n سر مشق
drop n څاڅكی ، تنزبل	**dummy** adj نقلي
drop v څخول	**dump** v بار چپه كول
drop off v پربشاني ورل	**dump** n بارچپه
drop out v خارجول	**dung** n خوشايي
drought n وچكالي	**dungeon** n زندان
drown v ډوببدل	**dupe** v ژر غولبدونكب

duplicate v دوه ګون

duplication n دوه ګونې

durable adj کلک

duration n موده

during pre په ترځ کې

dusk n تباره

dust n خاوره

dusty adj ګردجن

Dutch adj ګرد

duty n دنده

dwarf n ټپټیکې

dwell iv مېشته کېدل

dwelling n کور

dwindle v مراوب کېدل

dye v رنګ

dye n رنګول

dying adj رنګونه

dynamic adj فعال

dynamite n چاودونکې مواد

dynasty n کورنۍ

E

each adj هر

each other adj یو د بل سره

eager adj لېوال

eagerness n لېوالتیا

eagle n عقاب

ear n غور، مننه

earache n د غوږ درد

eardrum n لقب با جاپداد

early adv وختي

earmark v علامه

earn v ګټل

earnestly adv په کلکه

earnings n بچت

earphones n ګوشکي

earring n غوروالی

earth n مځکه

earthquake n زلزله

earwax n غوږ خیرک

ease v بې غمه کول

ease n سهولت

easily adv په اسانۍ

east n ختیځ

eastbound adj ختیځه پوله

eastern adj شرقي

eastward adv مخ په لمر خاته

easy adj اسان	**effigy** n خبره
eat iv خورل	**effort** n هڅه
eat away v خورل	**effusive** adj ناکنتوباث
eavesdrop v غوږ نیول	**egg** n هګۍ
ebb v جزرورکول	**egg white** n د هګۍ سپین
eccentric adj ګوښه ګیر	**egoism** n ځانمني
echo n غږ	**egoist** n په ځان مین
eclipse n خسوف	**eight** adj اته
ecology n ژوند پوهنه	**eighteen** adj اتلسم
economical adj اقتصادي	**eighth** adj اتم
economize v سپما کول	**eighty** adj اتیا
economy n سپما	**either** adj یا
ecstasy n نشه	**either** adv بله دا چې
ecstatic adj خوندور	**eject** v شرل
edge n څنډه	**elapse** v تېربدل
edgy adj عصبي	**elastic** adj د بدلیدو ور
edible adj د خوراک	**elated** adj ڼاربدلی
edifice n ماڼۍ	**elbow** n څنګل
edit v نشر ته چمتو کول	**elder** n مشر
edition n عمومي ګنه	**elderly** adj پوخ سړی
educate v روزل	**elect** v غوره
educational adj تعلبمي	**election** n انتخاب
eerie adj ډار شوب	**electric** adj برقي
effect n اغېزه	**electrician** n د برښنا ماهر
effective adj اغېزناک	**electricity** n برق
effectiveness n اغېزناکي	**electronic** adj برښناپب
efficiency n مستعد	**elegance** n بنه ذوق
efficient adj موثر	**elegant** adj خور ژبب

E

element n عنصر
elementary adj ساده
elephant n پیل
elevate v جگول
elevation n جگونه
elevator n د غلې گودام
eleven adj یولس
eleventh adj یولسم
eligible adj مستحق
eliminate v لیرې کول
elm n نارون
eloquence n فصاحت
else adv بل
elsewhere adv په بل ځاي کې
elude v ځان بچول
elusive adj غلوونکی
emaciated adj نري
emanate v خپرېدل
emancipate v ازادول
embalm v مومباپې کول
embark v لگیا کېدل
embarrass v بې واره کول
embassy n سفارت
embellish v سینگارول
embers n اپرې
embezzle v غلا کول
embitter v قارول
emblem n نښان

embody v مجسم کول
emboss v برجسته کول
embrace v غیږ کېدل
embrace n ښه هرکلی
embroider v گل دوزې کول
embroidery n گل دوزې
embroil v په جنگ اچول
embryo n جنین
emerald n زمروت
emerge v ظاهر کېدل
emergency n اضطراري حالت
emigrant n مهاجر
emigrate v مهاجرت کول
emission n خوشې
emit v اچول
emotion n احساس
emotional adj احساساتي
emperor n امپراتور
emphasis n زور
emphasize v زور اچول
empire n امپراتورۍ
employ v کارول
employee n کارگر
employer n کار فرما
employment n کار
empress n د امپراتور ښځه
emptiness n تشوالی
empty adj تش

empty v تشول	**engagement** n نبونه، کوزده
enable v وركول	**engine** n انجن
enchant v زره ورل	**engineer** n انجبنر
enchanting adj زره ورونكي	**England** n انګلستان
encircle v را چاپيربدل	**English** adj انګربزي
enclave n اتحاديه	**engrave** v كبندل
enclose v بندول	**engraving** n كبندونكي
enclosure n چاپيربال	**engrossed** adj مقبوضه
encompass v را چاپيرول	**engulf** v څوبول
encounter v مقابله كول	**enhance** v غوټه كول
encounter n مقابله	**enjoy** v خوند اخبستل
encourage v تشوبقول	**enjoyable** adj خوندور
encyclopedia n دابرت المعارف	**enjoyment** n مزب
end n پاپ	**enlarge** v ارتول
end v پاپ ته رسول	**enlargement** n ارتونه
end up v په پاي كپ	**enlighten** v روښانول
endeavor v هڅه كول	**enormous** adj ستر
endeavor n كوشش	**enough** adv بس
ending n پاپ	**enrage** v قارول
endless adj بب پاپه	**enrich** v دولت مند كول
endorsement n لاس لبك	**enroll** v شامول
endure v زغمل	**enrollment** n استخدام
enemy n غلبم	**ensure** v ډاډه كول
energetic adj تكړه	**entail** v په غبر كپ نبول
energy n قوت	**entangle** v نبول
enforce v اړكول	**enter** v ننوتل
engage v لګبا كول	**enterprise** n دستګاه
engaged adj لګبا	**entertain** v مبلمه كول

entertaining *adj* مبلمه کونکی	epilepsy *n* عصبي ناروغي
entertainment *n* سات تيري	episode *n* پيښه
enthrall *v* غلامول	epistle *n* لیک
enthralling *adj* غلامونکی	epitaph *n* دبر لیک
enthuse *v* پارول	epitomize *v* لنډول
enthusiasm *n* شوق او ذوق	epoch *n* دوره
entice *v* اغوا کول	equal *adj* برابر
enticement *n* غولونه	equality *n* مساوي
enticing *adj* لمسونکي	equate *v* مساوي کول
entire *adj* ټوله	equation *n* موازنه
entirely *adv* په بشپړه توګه	equator *n* د استوا کرښه
entrance *n* سرېزه	equilibrium *n* توازن
entreat *v* غوښتل	equip *v* سمبالول
entree *n* دننوتو لار	equipment *n* سامان
entrenched *adj* ټاکل شوې	equivalent *adj* معادل
entrepreneur *n* تشبث کونکي	era *n* دور
entrust *v* ور سپارل	eradicate *v* ولې ابستل
entry *n* گډون کونه	erase *v* پاکول
enumerate *v* شمېرل	eraser *n* پاکونکی
envelop *v* تاوول	erect *v* نبغول
envelope *n* کثوره	erect *adj* نبغ
envious *adj* کستمن	err *v* خطا کېدل
environment *n* چاپېربال	errand *n* رسالت
envisage *v* تصورکول	erroneous *adj* غلطه
envoy *n* استاځي	error *n* غلطي
envy *n* حسد	erupt *v* راخوتيول
envy *v* حسدکول	eruption *n* راخوتيدنه
epidemic *n* ساري	escalate *v* بنست اپښنودل

escapade n تښتنته	eve n ماښام
escape v تښتېدل	even adj سم
escort n بدرګه	even if c وي سم چېرې که
esophagus n مرۍ	even more c وي نور چېرې که
especially adv خصوصاً	evening n ماښام
espionage n جاسوسي	event n پېښه
essay n کوښښ کول	eventuality n امکان
essence n جوهر	eventually adv کې پای په
essential adj ضروري	ever adv تل
establish v تپنګول	everlasting adj ابدي
estate n رتبه	every adj هر
esteem v کول قدر	everybody pro څوک هر
estimate v اټکلول	everyday adj ورځ هره
estimation n اټکلونه	everyone pro څوک هر
estranged adj جلاکېدنه	everything pro شي هر
eternity n بقا	evict v لنډول لاس
ethical adj سم	evidence n نښه
ethics n اخلاقي	evil n شیطان
etiquette n دود	evil adj خراب
euphoria n خوشالي	evoke v پارول
Europe n اروپا	evolution n تکامل تدریجي
European adj اروپايي	exact adj اړکول
evacuate v تشول	exaggerate v لوبول
evade v تښتېدل	exalt v لورول
evaluate v ټاکل ارزښت	examination n امتحان
evaporate v کېدل براس	examine v امتحانول
evasion n تښتنته	example n مثال
evasive adj غولونکي	exasperate v غمول

excavate v کنبدل	**exercise** v تمرین کول
exceed v تېرېدل	**exert** v واردول، اچول
excel v زباتوالپ	**exertion** n برېد، هڅه
excellence n غوره والپ	**exhaust** v تشول
excellent adj غوره	**exhausting** adj تشونه
except pre بې له	**exhaustion** n ستومانتیا
exception n استثنا	**exhibit** v ښودل
exceptional adj استثنايي	**exhibition** n نندارتون
excerpt n اخبستنه	**exhilarating** adj څرگندونه
excess n پرېمانپ	**exhort** v اړکول
excessive adj ډېر زيات	**exile** v شړل
exchange v بدلون	**exile** n شړنه
excite v پارول	**exist** v ژوندکول
excitement n هېجان	**existence** n ژوندکول
exciting adj پارونکپ	**exit** n وتنه
exclaim v چغپ کول	**exodus** n مهاجرت
exclude v ایستل	**exonerate** v پاکول
excruciating adj دردناک	**exorbitant** adj ډېر زيات
excursion n تفريحي گرڅېدنه	**exorcist** n کوډگر
excuse v بښنل	**exotic** adj ناشنا
excuse n معذرت	**expand** v غورول
execute v سرته رسول	**expansion** n توسعه
executive n اجرائیه	**expectancy** n امېد
exemplary adj د مثال	**expectation** n هېله
exemplify v مثال ورکول	**expediency** n غوره توب
exempt adj معاف	**expedient** adj وړ
exemption n بښنل	**expedition** n چمتو والپ
exercise n تمرین	**expel** v شړل

E

expenditure *n* خرڅ	**exquisite** *adj* ژور
expense *n* لګښت	**extend** *v* غزول
expensive *adj* ګران	**extension** *n* غزونه
experience *n* تجربه	**extent** *n* مبچ
experiment *n* تجربه	**extenuating** *adj* د اندازي ور
expert *adj* ماهر	**exterior** *adj* خارجي
expiate *v* مجراکول	**exterminate** *v* وبجارول
expiation *n* مجرا	**external** *adj* خارجي
expiration *n* پوره کېدنه	**extinct** *adj* ابرې شوب
expire *v* تېرېدل	**extinguish** *v* وژل
explain *v* بيانول	**extort** *v* شکول
explicit *adj* ښکاره	**extortion** *n* شوکه
explode *v* چول	**extra** *adv* سربېره
exploit *v* چمتوکول	**extract** *v* ابستل
exploit *n* استثمار	**extradite** *v* محکمه بدلول
explore *v* لټول	**extraneous** *adj* پردې
explorer *n* سپړونکې	**extravagance** *n* بې څابه
explosion *n* چاودنه	**extravagant** *adj* بې ګټې
explosive *adj* چاودېدونکې	**extreme** *adj* اخبري
export *v* د باندې لېږنه	**extremist** *adj* اطرفب سړې
expose *v* برېندول	**extremities** *n* بد مرغې
exposed *adj* لوڅ	**extricate** *v* خلاصول
express *adj* څرګند،روښان	**extroverted** *adj* مدلل
express *v* څرګندول،وېل	**exude** *v* زېم اچول
expression *n* څرګندونه	**exult** *v* وباړل
expressly *adv* په څرګند ډول	**eye** *n* سترګه
expropriate *v* اخبستل	**eyebrow** *n* وروځب
expulsion *n* شړنه	**eyeglasses** *n* چشمب

eyelash n بانه

eyelid n پزراله

eyesight n نظر

eyewitness n د سترګو لیدنه

E

F

F

fable n کیسه

fabric n جوړښت

fabricate v جوړول

fabulous adj اړبانوونکی

face n مخ

face up to v مخ ور ګرخول

facet n ارخ ، با مخ

facilitate v اسانول

facing pre کف

fact n رښتیا

factor n کرونب

factory n فابریکه

factual adj رښتینب

faculty n فاکولته

fad n تلوسه

fade v رژېدل

faded adj خړ

fail v ناکامېدل

failure n ناکامي

faint v پرکاله کېدل

faint n پرکالتوب

faint adj پرکال

fair n بازار

fair adj ښکلب،مناسب

fairness n ښکلا

fairy n ښاپیرۍ

faith n ایمان،وفا

faithful adj وفادار

fake v جعل کاري کول

fake adj غولونه

fall n لوېده ،بربادي

fall iv لوېدل،غورځېدل

fall back v وروسته تګ

fall behind v وروسته پاتب

fall down v ښکته غورځېدل

fall through v ناکام کېدل

fallacy n درغلب

fallhood n د بحث لاندي

fallout n بحث کونه

falsify v غلط ختل

falter v زړه کېدل

fame n شهرت

familiar adj پېژندوي

family n کورنب

famine n سوکړه

famous adj مشهور

fan n ببوزي، پکي	**father-in-law** n خسر
fanatic adj متعصب	**fatherly** adj پتبم
fancy adj خبالي	**fathom out** v پوره پوهول
fang n داړه	**fatigue** n ستړپا
fantastic adj اربانوونکب	**fatten** v خربول
fantasy n خبال پلو	**fatty** adj غوږبن
far adv لبرب	**faucet** n شبردان
faraway adj خوبولب	**fault** n سهوه
farce n لوبه	**faulty** adj عببب
fare n په سفر تلل	**favor** n مبنه
farewell n خداى پامانب	**favorable** adj منلب
farm n فارم	**favorite** adj په زړه پورب
farmer n بزګر	**fear** n ډار
farming n کرنه	**fearful** adj ډارونکب
farmyard n د فارم انګړ	**feasible** adj ممکن
farther adv وراندب	**feast** n مذهبب
fascinate v جلبول	**feat** n عمل
fashion n دود	**feather** n بڼکه
fashionable adj چولب	**feature** n شکل
fast adj دروند	**February** n فبرورب
fasten v کلکول	**fed up** adj غمجن
fat n وازګه	**federal** adj اتحادبه
fat adj چاغ	**fee** n اجوره
fatal adj مهلک	**feeble** adj کمزورب
fate n قسمت	**feed** iv مړول
fateful adj وبرجن	**feedback** n نصبحت
father n پلار	**feel** iv احساسول
fatherhood n پلارولب	**feeling** n احساس

feelings *n* تماس	**feud** *n* بدي
feet *n* پښې	**fever** *n* تبه
feign *v* بهانه کول	**feverish** *adj* تبجن
fellow *n* ملګری	**few** *adj* څو
fellowship *n* ملګرو ډله	**fewer** *adj* لږ
felon *n* مجرم	**fiber** *n* تار
felony *n* جرم	**fickle** *adj* زړه نا زړه
female *n* ښځینه، مونث	**fiction** *n* خیالي
feminine *adj* ښځینه	**fictitious** *adj* نا څله
fence *n* کټاره	**fiddle** *n* وایلون
fencing *n* مدافعه	**fidelity** *n* وفا
fend *v* بچول	**field** *n* میدان
fend off *v* مخنیوی کول	**fierce** *adj* شدید
fender *n* سپر	**fiery** *adj* تاوجن
ferment *v* خمبره	**fifteen** *adj* پنځلس
ferment *n* پاربدل	**fifth** *adj* پنځم
ferocious *adj* توندخوی	**fifty** *adj* پنځوس
ferocity *n* بې رحمي	**fifty-fifty** *adv* په برابر توګه
ferry *n* پوري وتل	**fig** *n* اینځر
fertile *adj* برکتب	**fight** *iv* جګړه کول
fertility *n* حاصل خیزه	**fight** *n* جګړه
fertilize *v* ښبرازه کول	**fighter** *n* جنګي
fervent *adj* تود	**figure** *n* شکل
fester *v* ورستیدل	**figure out** *v* باور کول
festive *adj* د جشن	**file** *v* لیکه کول، کتارول
festivity *n* جشن	**file** *n* لیکه، کتار
fetid *adj* بد بویه	**fill** *v* ډکول
fetus *n* جنین	**filling** *n* پربمانه

film n فلم	**fireman** n د اطفایي غړی
filter n فلتر	**fireplace** n نغری
filter v چنول	**firewood** n د سونگ لرګی
filth n چټلي	**fireworks** n اتشبازي
filthy adj مردار	**firm** adj کلک
fin n د کب وزر	**firm** n شرکت
final adj د پای	**firmness** n کلکوالی
finalize v ملاتړ کول	**first** adj لومړی
finance v مالیه	**fish** n کب
financial adj مالي	**fisherman** n کب نیوونکی
find iv موندل	**fishy** adj غبر رسمي
find out v پلټنه کول	**fist** n سوک
fine n ناغه	**fit** n حمله
fine v بنه	**fit** v برابرول
fine adv په بنه توګه	**fitness** n وړوالی
fine adj بنه	**fitting** adj وړ
fine print n بنه پرنټ کول	**five** adj پنځه
finger n ګوته	**fix** v سمول
fingernail n نوک	**fjord** n تنګي
fingerprint n د ګوتې نبنه	**flag** n جنډه
fingertip n دګوتې سر	**flagpole** n د بیرغ لکړه
finish v سر ته رسول	**flamboyant** adj ځلند
Finland n فنلند	**flame** n لمبه
Finnish adj ختمول	**flammable** adj اور اخیستونکی
fire v اور ،لبوالتبا	**flank** n اړخ
fire n اور	**flare** n بربښ
firecracker n پټاخي	**flare-up** v ځلیدل
firefighter n اور	**flash** n پرک

flashlight *n* چراغ دستي	**floor** *n* فرش
flashy *adj* لباسي	**flop** *n* نا كامبدل
flat *n* پور	**floss** *n* اومه ربينم
flat *adj* سم	**flour** *n* اوره
flatten *v* پلنوالى	**flourish** *v* سبنگارول
flatter *v* چاپلوسي	**flow** *v* بهبدل
flattery *n* غوره مالي	**flow** *n* بهبدني
flaunt *v* نخري كول	**flower** *n* ګلُ
flavor *n* خوند مزه	**flowerpot** *n* گل داني
flaw *n* عبب	**flu** *n* انفلو انز
flawless *adj* بې عببي	**fluctuate** *v* تغبر خورل
flea *n* ورره	**fluently** *adv* په رواني
flee *iv* تبنتبدل	**fluid** *n* سباله ماده
fleece *n* ورګ	**flunk** *v* ناكامه كبدل
fleeting *adj* تبربدنه	**flute** *n* ببكر
flesh *n* غوښه	**flutter** *v* رپبدل
flex *v* كربدل	**fly** *iv* الوتل
flexible *adj* كمبدونكي	**fly** *n* د ببرغ ازاده برخه
flicker *v* وروستي رپ	**foam** *n* ځک
flier *n* الوتونكي	**focus** *n* مركز
flimsy *adj* نازك	**focus on** *v* متمركز كبدل
flip *v* ډكه كول	**foe** *n* غلبم
flirt *v* ناز كول	**fog** *n* بدل
flock *n* ډله	**foggy** *adj* تت
flog *v* په متروكه وهل	**foil** *v* ماته وركول
flood *v* سبلاب	**fold** *v* كتول
flooding *n* سبلاب	**folder** *n* دوسبه
floodlight *n* لوي څراغ	**folks** *n* خلک

folksy adj ساده	**foreigner** n خارجي سړی
follow v منل	**foreman** n مشر
follower n شاګرد	**foresee** iv پیش بینی کول
folly n حماقت	**foreshadow** v د مخه خبرول
fond adj مبنه ناک ،لبوال	**foresight** n پیش بینی
fondle v ناز ورکول	**forest** n ځنګل
fondness n مبنه	**foretaste** n مخکې څکل
food n خواړه	**foretell** v پیش ګویي کېدل
foodstuff n غذايي مواد	**forever** adv د تل دپاره
fool v بې عقل کول	**foreword** n سر لیک
fool adj ساده	**forfeit** v جریمه کول
foolproof adj اسانه	**forge** v نغړی
foot n پینه	**forgery** n جعل کاري
football n فوټ بال	**forget** v هېرول
footnote n لمن لیک	**forgivable** adj د پوهیدو وړ
footprint n پل	**forgive** v بخښل
footstep n ګام	**forgiveness** n معافي
footwear n څپلۍ	**fork** n بناخی
for pre دپاره	**form** n شکل
forbid iv منع کول	**formal** adj رسمي
force n قوه	**formality** n تشریفات
force v مجبوره کول	**formalize** v لمانځل
forceful adj قوي	**formally** adv په رسمي ډول
forcibly adv په شدت	**format** n جوړښت
forecast iv پیش بینی کول	**formation** n رغونه
foreground n پیش نظر	**former** adj لرغونی
forehead n تندی	**formerly** adv پخوا
foreign adj خارجي ،پردی	**formidable** adj ډارونکی

F

formula *n* طريقه	**frailty** *n* کمزوري
forsake *iv* خوشي کول	**frame** *n* مزاج، خوي
fort *n* کلا	**frame** *v* په جوکار
forthcoming *adj* راتلونکی	**framework** *n* اډونه
forthright *adj* سم	**France** *n* فرانسه
fortify *v* قوي کول	**franchise** *n* قانوني حق
fortitude *n* زغم	**frank** *adj* روک
fortress *n* نظامي کلا	**frankly** *adv* په روکه
fortunate *adj* نبکمرغه	**frankness** *n* سپينه وينا
fortune *n* بخت	**fraternal** *adj* د وروري
forty *adj* څلويښت	**fraternity** *n* وروركلوي
forward *adv* مخ ته	**fraud** *n* ټګي
foster *v* روزل، وده کول	**fraudulent** *adj* ټګ
foul *adj* ناوړه	**freckled** *adj* خالداره
foundation *n* بنسټ، اساس	**free** *v* ازادول
founder *n* موسس	**free** *adj* ازاد، خپلواک
fountain *n* فواره	**freedom** *n* ازادي
four *adj* څلور	**freeway** *n* ارت ښکلی واټ
fourteen *adj* څوارلس	**freeze** *iv* کنګل کول
fourth *adj* څلورم	**freezer** *n* بخچال
fox *n* ګبدره	**freezing** *adj* بخ لرونګی
foxy *adj* مکار	**freight** *n* کرايه
fraction *n* کسر	**French** *adj* فرانسوي
fracture *n* ماتوالي	**frenetic** *adj* ساده
fragile *adj* نازک	**frenzied** *adj* لېونی
fragment *n* ټوټه	**frenzy** *n* هېجان
fragrance *n* خوش بوی	**frequency** *n* فريکونسي
fragrant *adj* معطر	**frequent** *adj* عادي

fresh *adj* تازه	fruit *n* میوه
freshen *v* تازه کول	fruitful *adj* مفبد
freshness *n* تازه والی	fruity *adj* میوه داره
friction *n* مښبود، مښبونه	frustrate *v* بې اثره کول
Friday *n* جمعه	frustration *n* ماته
fried *adj* د کب بچبان	fry *v* سور کول
friend *n* ملګری	fuel *n* دسونګ مواد
friendship *n* ياري	fugitive *n* فراري
fries *n* پخونکی	fulfill *v* سر ته رسول
fright *n* ناخاپي	fulfillment *n* اجرا
frighten *v* وبرول	full *adj* ډک
frightening *adj* وبرونه	fully *adv* کاملا
frigid *adj* بخ	fume *n* لوګی
fringe *n* حاشبه، چرمه	fumigate *v* تبخبر کول
frivolous *adj* سپک	fun *n* ساتبري
frog *n* چونګښه	function *n* دنده
from *pre* له	fund *n* وجه
front *n* مخ، دمخه	fund *v* ذخبره کول
front *adj* مخامخ کبدنه	fundamental *adj* اساسي
frontage *n* حربم	funds *n* پبسی
frontier *n* سرحد	funeral *n* جنازه
frost *n* پرخه	fungus *n* فنجي
frostbite *n* یخبدنه	funny *adj* مسخره
frostbitten *adj* یخوالی	fur *n* پت لرونکي
frosty *adj* بخ شوپ	furious *adj* قار
frown *v* تندي تربو کول	furiously *adv* په قار
frugal *adj* اقتصادي	furnace *n* داش
frugality *n* امساک	furnish *v* مجهز کول

F

furnishings n لوازم

furniture n چوکی، میز

furor n لهوالتپا

furrow n لبکه

furry adj پت لرونکی

further adv په زیاته اندازه

furthermore adv علاوه پر دي

fury n قهر

fuse n فیوز

fusion n سره کډیدنه

fuss n پاریدنه

fussy adj وسواسي

futile adj عبث

futility n عبثوالي

future n راتلونکی وخت

fuzzy adj پت لرونکی

G

gadget n سامان

gag n چپول

gag v چپول، دروغ

gage v ضمانت کول

gain v گټه کول

gain n گټه

gal n کهکشان

galaxy n د اسمان لار

gale n سیلي

gall bladder n مثانه

gallant adj زړه ور

gallery n دالان

gallon n گبلبن

gallop v په ټرات تلل

gallows n دار

galvanize v بنورول

gamble v جواري کول

game n لوبه

gang n ټولپ

gangrene n خس مار

gap n چاک. درز

garage n گاراج

garbage n خځلي

garden n باغ

gardener n باغوان

gargle v	غرغره کول
garland n	امبل
garlic n	ووږه
garment n	کالي
garnish v	سبنګارول
garnish n	سبنګار
garrison n	چاونۍ
garrulous adj	کرتن
garter n	دجراپوگاليس.
gas n	ګبس
gash n	پرهار
gasoline n	پترول
gasp v	تيګاوهل
gastric adj	دمعدي
gate n	لوپ ور
gather v	ټولول
gathering n	ټولونه
gauge v	اندازه کول
gauze n	نازکه جالۍ
gaze v	ځبر کېدل
gear n	کالي
geese n	قاز
gem n	غمی
gender n	جنس
gene n	د شجرې
general n	عمومي
generalize v	عمومي کول
generate v	توليدول

generation n	نسل
generator n	توليدونکی
generic adj	جنسي
generosity n	سخاوت
genetic adj	ارثي
genial adj	خوشال
genius n	نابغه
genocide n	د خلکو ازمبنت
genteel adj	نرم
gentle adj	پوست
gentleman n	نباغلی
gentleness n	نرموالي
genuflect v	ګونډه کېدل
genuine adj	واقعي
geography n	جغرافبه
geology n	ځمکه پژندنه
geometry n	هندسه
germ n	تخم
German adj	جرمن
Germany n	المان
germinate v	راشبن کېدل
gestation n	انکشاف
get iv	کېل
get along v	ترقي کول
get away v	روانېدل
get back v	ببرته راګرځېدل
get by v	حاصلول
get down v	کوزېدل

get in v منتخب کېدل	**glance** n کتنه
get off v کوزېدل	**gland** n پرکی
get out v لري کېدل	**glare** n ځلېدل
get over v روغېدل	**glass** n شېشه
get together v خاصه غونډه	**glasses** n چشمه
get up v رسېدل	**gleam** n ځلول
ghastly adj وېرونکی	**gleam** v ځلېدل
ghost n روح	**glide** v ښوېدل
giant n دېب	**glimmer** n رڼا کېدل
gift n سوغات	**glimpse** n لنډ نظر
gifted adj ځېرک	**glimpse** v سرسري کتل
gigantic adj ستر	**glitter** v ځلېدل
gimmick n وسېله	**globe** n توپ
ginger n شونډي	**globule** n کردۍ ذره
gingerly adv په پام سره	**gloom** n تباره
giraffe n زرافه	**gloomy** adj تت
girl n جینۍ	**glorify** v غټول
girlfriend n انډېواله	**glorious** adj لوړ
give iv ورکول	**glory** n برم
give away v سستول	**gloss** n لمن لېک
give back v بېرته ورکول	**glossy** adj روڼ
give in v منل	**glove** n لاس ماغو
give out v تقسېمول	**glow** v ځلا
give up v پرېښنودل	**glucose** n گلوکوز
glad adj خوشاله	**glue** n سرېښ
gladiator n پهلواني	**glue** v سرېښنول
glamorous adj زړه ورونکي	**glut** n مړېدل
glance v کتل	**glutton** n خېتو

gnaw v شکول	goof n غلطي
go iv تلل	goose n بته
go ahead v مخکې تلل	gorge n مړی
go away v په مخه تلل	gorgeous adj برم ناک
go down v تبرول	gorilla n ببزو
go in v کار پیل کول	gory adj له وېنو ډک
go on v جاري ساتل	gospel n تار
go out v بندبدل	gossip v اوازه کول
go over v معاینه کول	gossip n اوازه
go through v لبدل	gout n کوټ
go under v غرکبدل	govern v حکومت کول
go up v جګبدل	government n حکومت
goad v چوکه کول	governor n والي
goal n ګول، مقصد	gown n ګون
goalkeeper n ګول ساتونکې	grab v نبول
goat n بزه	grace n ناز
gobble v نغرل	graceful adj رحبم
God n خښتن تعالی	gracious adj مهربانه
goddess n الوهبت	grade n درجه
godless adj بې له خدایه	gradual adj تدربجي
gold n سره	graduate v فارغ التحصبل
golden adj دسرو	graduation n فراغت
good adj بنه	graft v پېوندکول
good-looking adj بنه بنکاربدنه	graft n پېوند
goodness n بنه والي	grain n غله
goods n سامان	gram n ګرام
goodwill n بنه نبت	grammar n صرف او نحوه
goof v غلطي کول	grand adj مهم

grandchild n لمسی

granddad n آبا

grandfather n نیکه

grandmother n نبا

grandparents n نبا او نیکه

grandson n لمسی

grandstand n بیگار

granite n کرونده

granny n نیا

grant v ورکول

grant n منل

grape n تور انگور

grapefruit n چکوتره

grapevine n بی اساسه

grasp n درک

grasp v نبول

grass n واښه

grassroots adj کاریگر

grateful adj خوښ

gratify v خوشالول

gratifying adj خوشالبدنه

gratitude n مننه

gratuity n انعام

grave adj کنبدنه

grave n د قبر کنبستل

gravel n کربر

gravely adv جغل کبدنه

gravestone n د قبر شنابښته

graveyard n هدیره

gravitate v جذب کېدل

gravity n درننښت

gravy n د غوښی لعاب

gray adj خړ

grayish adj ابرن

graze v څرل

graze n سپک تماس

grease v غوړول

grease n غوړي

greasy adj غوړ

great adj ستر

greatness n غټ والي

Greece n یونان

greed n حرص

greedy adj حرصتوب

Greek adj یونان

green adj شین

green bean n شنه پلی

greenhouse n شنه مانی

Greenland n سپزه زار

greet v سلام اچول

greetings n سلام

gregarious adj راټولبدونکی

grenade n لاسی بم

greyhound n تازی سپی

grief n غم

grievance n دغم علت

grieve v خپه کول	growth n غنیدنه
grill n دکباب سیخ	grudge n ضد
grim adj پروسوالی	grudgingly adv په بې مبلې
grimace n پروستوب	gruelling adj سر تربدنه
grime n چتیلتوب	gruesome adj ډارونکې
grind iv اوره کول	grumble v غوربدل
gripe n ټپنګ	grumpy adj توند مزاجه
grisly adj ډارونکې	guarantee v ضمانت کول
groan v وبر کول	guarantee n ضمانت
groan n زګبروپ	guarantor n ملاتړ
groceries n غذایي مواد	guard n ساتونکې
groom n زومر	guardian n محافظه
groove n کبله	guerrilla n سر تبرپ
gross adj زبر ، شډل	guess v ګمان کول
grossly adv په زبروالي	guess n ګمان
grotesque adj بې ډوله	guest n مبلمه
grotto n غار	guidance n مشرتوب
grouch v کبله کول	guide v لارښودل
grouchy adj غوربدونکې	guide n لارښود
ground n مخکه	guidebook n د لارښودنه کتاب
ground floor n د تعمیر فرش	guidelines n قاعده
groundless adj بې اساسه	guild n تحادبه
groundwork n بنسټ	guile n ټګې
group n ډله	guilt n ګناه
grow iv وده کول	guilty adj ګناهګار
grow up v بالغ کبدل	guise n کره وره
growl v غررنه	guitar n ګبتار
grown-up n ځوان	gulf n خلبج

gull n سمندري موغه

gullible adj ساده والي

gulp v غورپول

gulp n غورپ

gum n خچنې، اوركـ

gun n توپک

gun down v د وسلو تربیه

gunfire n ډزې

gunman n وسله وال

gunpowder n باروت

gunshot n په توپک وېشـتنه

gust n سبلۍ

gusto n ذوق

gusty adj طوفاني

gut n کلمه

guts n د ملاتبر

gutter n لښتۍ

guy n سړی

guzzle v نغررل

gypsy n جټ

H

habit n جامه

habitable adj د اوسـېدو وړ

habitual adj عادي

hack v زور اس

haggle v لړل

hail n ږلۍ

hail v ږلۍ اورېدل

hair n وېښته

hairbrush n د وېښتو برش

haircut n ذ وېښتو تپاري

hairdo n د وېښتو ډول

hairdresser n نايی

hairy adj وېښتن

half n نېم

half adj نېم

hall n سالون

hallucinate v خوب لېدل

hallway n دالان

halt v درول

halve v نېمول

hamburger n کوفته

hamlet n کوچنی کلی

hammer n څټک

hand n لاس

hand down v انتقالول

hand in v ورکول	harass v خوړول
hand out v پلاس تقسیمول	harassment n کبنرونوخ
hand over v چا ته ورکول	harbor n بندر
handbag n لاسي بکسه	hard adj کلک
handbook n لاسي کتاب	harden v کلکول
handcuff v ولچک کول	hardly adv په کلکه توګه
handcuffs n د لاس زولانه	hardness n کلکولي
handful n لپه	hardship n ستونځه
handgun n تماچه	hardware n د اوسپنې اوزار
handicap n عیب	hardwood n کلک لرګي
handkerchief n دسمال	hardy adj زړه ور
handle v لاس کې نیول	hare n سوی
handle n لاستي	harm v تاوان ورکول
handout n خبرنامه	harm n تاوان
handrail n برغل	harmful adj ضررناک
handshake n لاس کې ټینګول	harmless adj بې ضرره
handsome adj ښکلی	harmonize v سمول
handwritting n لاس لیک	harmony n سموالي
handy adj نژدې	harp n د موسقی اله
hang iv خرول	harrowing adj غاښور کونه
hang around v شرمبدونکی	harsh adj خبر
hang on v انتظار کول	harshly adv په خبر والي
hanger n کړۍ	harshness n خبروالي
hangup n کشاله	harvest n درمن
happen v واقعي کبدل	harvest v درمندول
happening n واقع کبدل	hashish n میدول
happiness n خوشالي	hassle v خوړول
happy adj خوشال	hassle n ناکاره

haste *n* چټکتیا	**headphones** *n* غوشکب
hasten *v* چټکول	**headquarters** *n* مرکز
hastily *adv* په بیړه	**headway** *n* پرمختک
hasty *adj* بیړناک	**heal** *v* رغول
hat *n* خولۍ	**healer** *n* درمل
hatchet *n* تبر	**health** *n* صحت
hate *v* کرکه	**healthy** *adj* صحت مند
hateful *adj* منغور	**heap** *n* کوټه
hatred *n* تنفر	**heap** *v* کوټه کول
haughty *adj* کبرجن	**hear** *iv* اوربدل
haul *v* کشول	**hearing** *n* اوربدنه
haunt *v* راشه درشه کول	**hearsay** *n* اوازه
have *iv* لرل	**hearse** *n* تابوت
have to *v* بابد	**heart** *n* زړه
haven *n* گودر	**heartbeat** *n* زړه غورځیدنه
havoc *n* ورانونه	**heartburn** *n* زړه سوی
hawk *n* بار	**hearten** *v* زړه ورکول
hay *n* پروړه	**heartfelt** *adj* د زړه له کومې
haystack *n* د پروړې کوټه	**hearth** *n* دیوالي بخارۍ
hazard *n* خطر	**hearty** *adj* صمیمي
hazardous *adj* خطرناک	**heat** *v* گرمول
haze *n* غبار	**heat** *n* گرمي
hazy *adj* تت	**heater** *n* منقل
head *n* سر	**heathen** *n* کافر
head for *v* تر لري سر	**heathing** *n* گرم
headache *n* سر دردۍ	**heatstroke** *n* دگرمی اسباب
heading *n* سر لېک	**heatwave** *n* د گرمی وخت
head-on *adv* مخامخ	**heaven** *n* هسک

H

heavenly *adj* اسماني	herald *n* جاچپ
heaviness *n* درونډوالپ	herb *n* کوچنپ بوټپ
heavy *adj* درونډ	here *adv* دلته
heckle *v* ږمنخول	hereafter *adv* ده له وروسته
hectic *adj* تبجن	hereby *adv* پدپ ډول
heed *v* پام کول	hereditary *adj* میراثپ
heel *n* پونده	heresy *n* کفر
height *n* قد	heretic *adj* کفرپ
heighten *v* لوروالپ	heritage *n* میراث
heinous *adj* ناروا	hermetic *adj* جادوپپ
heir *n* میراث خور	hermit *n* زاهد
helicopter *n* هلپ کوپتر	hero *n* اتل
hell *n* دوزخ	heroic *adj* د اتلتوب
hello *e* ږغ کول	heroin *n* اتله
helm *n* سټپرنګ	heroism *n* اتلتوب
helmet *n* داوسپنپ خولپ	hers *pro* ددپپ
help *v* مرسته کول	herself *pro* دا پخپله
help *n* مرسته	hesitate *v* زره نا زره کېدل
helper *n* مرسته کونکپ	hesitation *n* تردد
helpful *adj* کومکپ	heyday *n* خوشالپ
helpless *adj* بپ وسپ	hiccup *n* سلګپ
hem *n* ژپ	hidden *adj* پټ
hemisphere *n* مورکه	hide *iv* پټول
hemorrhage *n* وینپ کبدنه	hideaway *n* پټ
hen *n* چرګه	hideous *adj* وبروونکپ
hence *adv* څکه چه	high *adj* اوچت
henchman *n* مزدور	highlight *n* ځرګندول
herald *v* زبرپ کول	highly *adv* بپ پابه

H

Highness n ستروالي	**hit back** v انتقام
highway n لویه لار	**hitch** n رچول
hijack v نیول	**hitch up** v په دېکه پاسول
hijack n نیونه	**hitchhike** n ټکان
hijacker n نیونکی	**hitherto** adv تردې وخته
hike v تلل	**hive** n څاله
hike n تګ	**hoard** v پاسره
hilarious adj خوښ	**hoarse** adj زبر
hill n غونډی	**hoax** n ټوکی
hillside n غونډی لمن	**hobby** n ذوقي کار
hilltop n د غونډی سر	**hog** n خوګ، ناولي
hilt n لاستی	**hoist** v اوچتول
hinder v درول	**hoist** n اوچتول
hindrance n ممانعت	**hold** iv نیول
hindsight n بیا کتنه	**hold back** v درول
hinge v چپراسول	**hold on to** v نیول
hinge n چپراس	**hold out** v قایم ساتل
hint n اشاره	**hold up** v سم ودربدل
hint v اشاره کول	**holdup** n څنډونه
hip n کوناټی	**hole** n سوري
hire v اجاره کول	**holiday** n رخصتی
his adj دده	**holiness** n تقدس
Hispanic adj هسپانوی	**Holland** n هالېند
hiss v پوکی	**hollow** adj ګوګ
historian n تاریخ پوه	**holocaust** n په اور وژنه
history n تاریخ	**holy** adj پاک
hit n وهل ، توافق	**homage** n درناوی
hit iv وهل	**home** n کور

homeland *n* هېواد	horrible *adj* ډاروونکې
homeless *adj* بې کوره	horrify *v* ډارول
homely *adj* کورنۍ	horror *n* ډار
homemade *adj* دوطن	horse *n* اس
homesick *adj* وطن پسې خفه	hose *n* اوردې جرابې
hometown *n* دزبردنه	hospital *n* هپستال
homework *n* کورنۍ کار	hospitality *n* مېلمه پالنه
homicide *n* قاتل	hospitalize *v* خدمت کول
homily *n* وېنا	host *n* کوربه
honest *adj* رښتبا	hostage *n* برغمل
honesty *n* په رښتبا	hostess *n* کوربنه
honey *n* شات	hostile *adj* دښمن
honk *v* د هارن اواز	hostility *n* دښمنۍ
honor *n* شهرت	hot *adj* گرم
hoodlum *n* لوچک	hotel *n* مېلمستون
hoof *n* سوه	hound *n* تازې
hook *n* چنګ، کرۍ	hour *n* ساعت
hooligan *n* باغي	hourly *adv* هر ساعت
hop *v* توپ	house *n* کور
hope *n* امبد	household *n* خپلخانه
hopeful *adj* هېله مند	housekeeper *n* د کور خاوند
hopefully *adv* په هېله توب	housewife *n* د کاله مبرمن
hopeless *adj* نا امبد	housework *n* د کور کار
horizon *n* اسمان	hover *v* وزروهل
horizontal *adj* افقي	how *adv* څه ډول
hormone *n* هارمون	however *c* په هر حال
horn *n* ښکر	howl *v* انګلل
horrendous *adj* بې خونده	howl *n* انګولا

H

huddle v پر له اچول	**hurl** v اچول
hug v په غبږ نيول	**hurricane** n توپان
hug n په غبږ نيول	**hurriedly** adv په تلوار
huge adj خورا ستر	**hurry** v تلوار کول
hum v زمزمه کول	**hurt** iv وړول
human adj بشر	**hurt** adj ژوبلوالی
humanities n موجودات	**hurtful** adj رنبتنی
humankind n بشر	**husband** n ميړه
humble adj کمينه	**hush** n کراربدنه
humbly adv په تواضع	**hush up** v غلی
humid adj لوند	**husky** adj شډل
humidity n لندبل	**hustle** n دلی کول
humiliate v ټيټول	**hut** n کوډله
humility n ټيټ والی	**hydrogen** n هايدروجن
humor n خوش طبعي	**hyena** n کوړ
humorous adj ټوکي	**hymn** n مذهبي سندرې
hump n بوک (کوهان)	**hyphen** n داتصال ننبه
hunch n غونډول	**hypnosis** n مصنوعي
hunchback n شاکوپې	**hypocrisy** n دوه مخي
hunched adj غونډوالی	**hypocrite** adj ريا کاره
hundred adj سل	**hypothesis** n فرضيه
hundredth adj سلم	**hysteria** n بېسدي
hunger n لوږه	**hysterical** adj بېسدتيا
hungry adj وږی	
hunt v لټول	
hunter n ښکاري	
hunting n ښکار	
hurdle n شپول	

I

I *pro* زه

ice *n* يخ

ice cream *n* شيريخ

ice cube *n* د يخ ټوټه

ice skate *v* د واورو لوبه

iceberg *n* د يخ يوه ټوټه

icebox *n* د يخي بكس

icon *n* تمثال

icy *adj* ډېر سور

idea *n* مفكوره

ideal *adj* خيالي

identical *adj* كټ مټ

identify *v* تشخيصول

identity *n* هويت

ideology *n* دمفكورو علم

idiom *n* اصطلاح

idiot *n* احمق

idiotic *adj* په احمقانه ډول

idle *adj* بې اساسه

idol *n* مجسمه

idolatry *n* بت پرستي

if *c* كه چېرې

ignite *v* سبځل

ignorance *n* ناپوهي

ignorant *adj* ناپوه

ill *adj* ناروغي

illegal *adj* غير قانوني

illegible *adj* د نه لوستلو وړ

illegitimate *adj* نامشروع

illicit *adj* نا روا

illiterate *adj* نالوستى

illness *n* ناروغي

illogical *adj* بې دليله

illuminate *v* خلا

illusion *n* وهم / خيال

illustrate *v* تمثيل كول

illustration *n* تصوير

illustrious *adj* خلا

image *n* تصوير

imagination *n* خيال

imagine *v* تصور كول

imbalance *n* بې تناسبي

imitate *v* پيښپ كول

imitation *n* پيښپ

immaculate *adj* سپيڅلى

immature *adj* نامكمل

immediately *adv* سم د لاسه

immense *adj* ستر

immensity *n* ستروالى

immerse *v* غوټه كول

immersion *n* غووټه

immigrate *v* مهاجرت كول

immigration *n* هجرت

imminent *adj* تهدیدووکي	**implement** *v* دکار وسیله
immobile *adj* بې حرکته	**implicate** *v* دلالت کول
immobilize *v* ولاړ	**implication** *n* بنوونه
immoral *adj* نه مړ کېدنه	**implicit** *adj* بنودل شوی
immorality *n* تل ژوندی	**implore** *v* خواهش
immortal *adj* نه فنا کېدونکی	**imply** *v* استنباط
immortality *n* تل یادونکي	**impolite** *adj* بې ادبه
immune *adj* مصئون	**import** *v* واردول
immunity *n* مصئونیت	**importance** *n* اهمیت
immunize *v* خوندي کول	**importation** *n* واردونه
immutable *adj* اوښتونې	**imposing** *adj* اثرناک
impact *n* تماس	**imposition** *n* بارونه
impact *v* خته کول	**impossibility** *n* ناشونی کار
impair *v* لړول	**impossible** *adj* نه کېدونکی
impartial *adj* بې تعصبه	**impotent** *adj* سست
impatience *n* بې صبري	**impound** *v* اخیستل
impatient *adj* بې صبره	**impoverished** *adj* مات شوی
impeccable *adj* بې عیبه	**impractical** *adj* ناشونی
impediment *n* محنیوک	**imprecise** *adj* ناسم
impending *adj* پیښېدونکی	**impress** *v* بېگارول
imperfection *n* نیمگړتیا	**impressive** *adj* اثرناک
imperial *adj* ټول واکمني	**imprison** *v* بندي کول
imperialism *n* امپریالېزم	**improbable** *adj* لبري
impersonal *adj* بې طرفه	**impromptu** *adv* ناڅاپه
impertinence *n* سپین سترګي	**improper** *adj* ناوړه
impertinent *adj* بې ربطه	**improve** *v* سمول
impetuous *adj* تند	**improvement** *n* سمون
implant *v* اینبول	**improvise** *v* بې تیاری ویل

impulse *n* پورۍ وهنه	incline *v* ترتیبول
impulsive *adj* پورۍ وهونکی	include *v* درلود ل
impunity *n* له جوا خلاصون	inclusive *adv* پوره
impure *adj* کډوډ	incoherent *adj* نا لایقه
in *pre* په کې	income *n* ګټه
in depth *adv* په واسطه	incoming *adj* عادي
inability *n* نالایقي	incompetence *n* حماقت
inaccurate *adj* غلط	incompetent *adj* بې مهارته
inadequate *adj* لږ	incomplete *adj* طرفدار
inadmissible *adj* دنه منلو	inconvenient *adj* مشکل
inappropriate *adj* نا وړه	incorporate *v* واحد د یو بدن
inasmuch as *c* له دې کبله	incorrect *adj* غلط
inaugurate *v* پرانیستل	incorrigible *adj* جلبونکي
inauguration *n* پرانستنه	increase *v* لوریدل
incapable *adj* ناوړه	increase *n* لوریدنه
incapacitate *v* ناوړه کول	increasing *adj* لور شوی
incarcerate *v* بندي کول	incredible *adj* غبر یقیني
incense *n* پارول	increment *n* لور
incentive *n* هڅونه	incriminate *v* دلالت کول
inception *n* پیل	incur *v* وروسته کول
incessant *adj* جاري	incurable *adj* وروستی
inch *n* انچ	indecency *n* یرغل
incident *n* واقع کېدنه	indecision *n* بې تکل توب
incidentally *adv* ناڅاپه	indecisive *adj* بې پایه
incision *n* غوڅ	indeed *adv* واقعي
incite *v* لمسول	indefinite *adj* تت
incitement *n* هڅونه	indemnify *v* پوښ
inclination *n* غوړه توب	indemnity *n* مخنیوی

independence n خپلواكي	**inevitable** adj منل شوى
independent adj ازاد	**inexcusable** adj شدل
index n رهنما	**inexpensive** adj ارزان
indicate v څرګندول	**inexperienced** adj بې ګناه
indication n سلا	**inexplicable** adj قوي
indict v ملامتول	**infallible** adj پوره
indifference n بې پروايي	**infamous** adj رسوا
indifferent adj بې حسه	**infancy** n کوچنيتوب
indigent adj غريب	**infant** n کوچنى
indigestion n بد هضمي	**infantry** n عسکر
indirect adj شا وخوا	**infect** v فاسدول
indiscreet adj بې پامه	**infection** n ناروغي
indiscretion n بې پروايي	**infectious** adj ساري
indispensable adj مهم توکی	**infer** v نتيجه کښنل
indisposed adj نا خوښنه	**inferior** adj وروکى
indisputable adj منلى	**infertile** adj عسکري تربيت
indivisible adj نه بېلېدونکى	**infested** adj ککړ
indoctrinate v پروګرام	**infidelity** n خيانت
indoor adv دننه	**infiltrate** v ورننوتل
induce v تشديقول	**infiltration** n تماس
indulge v ډېر خواړ ورکول	**infinite** adj بې شمېره
indulgent adj سخي	**infirmary** n روغتون
industrious adj مصروف	**inflammation** n سوربخن
industry n تجارت	**inflate** v ټبل وهل
ineffective adj بې ګټې	**inflation** n لوړبدل
inefficient adj لګاوو	**inflexible** adj سخت
inept adj نا مبده	**inflict** v درست
inequality n بدلون	**influence** n توان

influential *adj* توانا	initially *adv* په اصلي بنه
influenza *n* انفلوانزا	initials *n* لومړي
influx *n* رسېدنه	initiate *v* پیل
inform *v* معلومات	initiative *n* تجویز
informal *adj* غیر رسمي	inject *v* ورپیژندل
informality *n* بلدتیا	injection *n* پیچکاري
informant *n* سیمه	injure *v* خورول
information *n* معلومات	injurious *adj* ژوبلوونکی
informer *n* ځان ایستل	injury *n* ژوبله
infraction *n* تجاوز	injustice *n* تېری
infrequent *adj* ناموندونکی	ink *n* رنگ
infuriate *v* پارول	inkling *n* اشاره
infusion *n* ترکیب	inland *adv* دننه
ingenuity *n* نظر	inland *adj* دننی
ingest *v* تېرول	in-laws *n* خپلوان
ingot *n* غیری	inmate *n* ملگری
ingrained *adj* ثابت	inn *n* هوټل
ingratiate *v* چاپلوس	innate *adj* ذاتي
ingratitude *n* بغیر له فراغته	inner *adj* دننه
ingredient *n* برخه	innocence *n* بې گناهي
inhabit *v* لگیا کول	innocent *adj* بې گناه
inhabitant *n* استوگن	innovation *n* ابتکار
inhale *v* تیکا وهل	innuendo *n* اشارتآ رسول
inherit *v* لاس ته راورل	innumerable *adj* خورا ډېر
inheritance *n* میراث	input *n* لاسته راورنه
inhibit *v* کمول	inquest *n* خبرنه
inhuman *adj* سخت زړی	inquire *v* پوښتنه کول
initial *adj* اصلي	inquiry *n* پلټنه

inquisition *n* تحقیقات

insane *adj* لیونی

insanity *n* لیونتوب

insatiable *adj* قانع کېدونکی

inscription *n* ثبت

insect *n* حشره

insecurity *n* ناخوندیتوب

insensitive *adj* بې حسه

inseparable *adj* نه جلا کېدنکی

insert *v* وراچول

insertion *n* ځایونه

inside *adj* داخلي

inside *pre* دننه

insignificant *adj* بې ارزښته

insincere *adj* ټګي

insincerity *n* ټګ

insinuate *v* اشاره کول

insinuation *n* اساره

insipid *adj* بې خونده

insist *v* اصرار

insistence *n* تجزیه کول

insolent *adj* بدغوني

insomnia *n* بې خوبي

inspect *v* څېرل

inspection *n* کتنه

inspector *n* پلټونکی

inspiration *n* پارونه

inspire *v* زړه رکونه

instability *n* ناکراري

install *v* مقررول

installation *n* درونه

installment *n* کښت

instance *n* نمونه

instance *n* مرحله

instantly *adv* په بېره سره

instead *adv* په بدل

instigate *v* تحریکول

instil *v* څخول

instinct *n* شعور

institute *v* بنسټ

institution *n* بنسټ اېښودنه

instruct *v* خبرول

instructor *n* ښوونکی

insufficient *adj* نیمګړی

insulate *v* جلا کول

insulation *n* جلاوالی

insult *v* ښکنځل

insult *n* ښکنځا

insurance *n* بیمه

insure *v* ذمه وهل

insurgency *n* یاغي توب

insurrection *n* ارو دور

intact *adj* روغ رمټ

intake *n* اوبه خور

integrate *v* یو لاس کول

integration *n* بشپړونه

integrity *n* بشپړتیا	intersect *v* پرېکول
intelligent *adj* څیرک	intertwine *v* غبرګول
intend *v* تکل کول	interval *n* ټال
intend *adj* توجه کول	intervene *v* تر منځ راتلل
intensify *v* ډېرول	intervention *n* مداخله
intensity *n* سختي	interview *n* خبري اترې
intensive *adj* ډېروونکی	intestine *n* کولمه
intention *n* تصمیم	intimacy *n* ګرانښت
intercede *v* ګواښ کول	intimate *adj* خُرګندول
intercept *v* پرېکول	intimidate *v* ډارول
intercession *n* ښواښ	intolerable *adj* سخت زغ ری
interchange *v* مبادله کول	intolerance *n* تعصب
interchange *n* بدلزل	intoxicated *adj* زره ور
interest *n* ګټة	intravenous *adj* لیکه توب
interested *adj* فیصله شوی	intrepid *adj* بې پروا
interesting *adj* په زړه پورې	intricate *adj* پیچلی
interfere *v* مداخله کول	intrigue *n* چل
interference *n* مداخله	intriguing *adj* زره رابښکوونی
interior *adj* دننی	intrinsic *adj* ذاتی
interlude *n* خند	introduce *v* ور پېژندل
intermediary *n* منځنی	introduction *n* سریخه
intern *v* داخلي	intrude *v* ورننه ایستل
interpret *v* ترجمه کول	intruder *n* څوروونکی
interpretation *n* ژباړه	intrusion *n* وتنه
interpreter *n* ژباړونکی	intuition *n* شعور
interrogate *v* پوښتنه کول	inundate *v* تر لاندې کېدل
interrupt *v* غوڅول	invade *v* یرغل کول
interruption *n* غوڅونه	invader *n* یرکوونکی

invalid *n* ناروغه	**ironic** *adj* پیغور
invalidate *v* بی اثره کول	**irony** *n* طعنه
invaluable *adj* بې قیمته	**irrational** *adj* بی خایه
invasion *n* چپاو	**irrefutable** *adj* منلی
invent *v* اخترع کول	**irregular** *adj* بې قاعدي
invention *n* اخترع	**irrelevant** *adj* بې ربطه
inventory *n* وجودي	**irreparable** *adj* نه جوړبدنکی
invest *v* رسمآ مقررل	**irresistible** *adj* بې اعتنايي
investigate *v* پلټل	**irreversible** *adj* مقامي
investigation *n* پلټنه	**irrevocable** *adj* نه رګرزبدنکی
investment *n* پانګه اچونه	**irrigate** *v* اوبول
investor *n* پانګه اچوونکي	**irrigation** *n* پنه
invisible *adj* لیدل کېدونکی	**irritate** *v* لمسول
invitation *n* بلنه	**irritating** *adj* د بدن یوه غړي
invite *v* میلمه کول	**Islamic** *adj* اسلامي
invoice *n* بېجک	**island** *n* ټاپو
invoke *v* دعا کول	**isolate** *v* جلا کول
involve *v* ګېرول	**isolation** *n* جلا
involved *v* اړه لرل	**issue** *n* موضوع
involvement *n* برخوال	**Italian** *adj* اېټالوي
inward *adj* وننه لوری	**italics** *adj* اېټالوي ژبه
inwards *adv* زړه او ځیګر	**Italy** *n* اېټالیا
iodine *n* خوا بدی شوی	**itch** *v* خارښت کول
irate *adj* په غصه	**itchiness** *n* عکس المل
Ireland *n* ایرلیند	**item** *n* ماده
Irish *adj* ایرلیندي	**itemize** *v* شمېرل
iron *n* اوسپنه	**itinerary** *n* تګلاره
iron *v* پوست یا خوبه	

J

jackal *n* سور لنډيان

jacket *n* کرتۍ

jackpot *n* سور لنډيان

jail *n* بندي خانه

jailer *n* د بنديخان امر

jam *n* مربا،درول

janitor *n* ور ساتونکی

January *n* جنوري

Japan *n* جاپان

Japanese *adj* جاپاني

jar *n* کوزری

jasmine *n* ياسمين

jaw *n* زامه

jealous *adj* کستمن

jealousy *n* زخه

jeans *n* پتلون

jerk *v* ټکان ورکول

jerk *n* ټکان

jersey *n* جرسي

Jew *n* جهود

jewel *n* غمی

Jewish *adj* اسراييلي

job *n* دنده

jobless *adj* بې کار

join *v* نښلول

joint *n* بند

jointly *adv* يو ځای

joke *n* ټوکه

joke *v* ټوکې کول

jokingly *adv* په ټوکو

jolly *adj* خوشاله

jolt *v* ټکان خورل

jolt *n* ټکان

journal *n* ورځپانه، مجله

journalist *n* خبريال

journey *n* سفر

jovial *adj* خوشاله

joy *n* خوسالي

joyful *adj* هک پک کوونکی

joyfully *adv* په خوښی

jubilant *adj* خوښ

Judaism *n* د يهودو دين

judge *n* قاضي

judgment *n* قضاوت

judicious *adj* د تميز خاوند

jug *n* صراحي

juggler *n* جادوګر

juice *n* شيره

juicy *adj* بنبراز

July *n* جولاي

jump *v* تو پ وهل

jump *n* ټوپ

jumpy *adj* غصبي

jungle *n* ځنګل	kid *n* ماشوم، مرغومی
junior *adj* کشر	kidnap *v* تښتول
junk *n* فضوله شیان	kidnapper *n* تیوونکی
jury *n* مشر	kidnapping *n* تښتونه
just *adj* عادلانه	kidney *n* پډوډی
justice *n* عدالت	kidney bean *n* لوبیا
justly *adv* په عادلا نه توګه	kill *v* وژل
juvenile *n* زپی	killer *n* وژونکی
juvenile *adj* کوچنیوالی	killing *n* وژنه
	kilogram *n* کیلو ګرام
	kilometer *n* کیلو متر
	kilowatt *n* کیلو واټ

K

	kind *adj* نیک
	kindle *v* بلول
	kindly *adv* خواخوري
kangaroo *n* کانګرو	kindness *n* نیکي
karate *n* کراټي	king *n* پاچا
keep *iv* ساتل	kingdom *n* پاچايي
keep on *v* جاري ساتل	kinship *n* خپلوي
keg *n* کوچنی بیرل	kiosk *n* کوچنی خونه
kennel *n* کوډله	kiss *v* مچول
kettle *n* چای جوش	kiss *n* مچه
key *n* کلي، لارښود	kitchen *n* پلنځی
key ring *n* کلي بند	kite *n* پتنګ
keyboard *n* کلیدره	kitten *n* پیشنګوری
kick *v* په پښه وهل	knee *n* زنګون
kickback *n* د شا لغته	kneecap *n* د زنګون سترګه
kickoff *n* هوابی لغته	kneel *iv* ګونډه کېدل

knife *n* چاقو	**lagoon** *n* کوچنی جهیل
knit *v* اوبدل	**lake** *n* ناور
knob *n* کوبه	**lamb** *n* وری
knock *n* وهل	**lame** *adj* نیمگری، معیوب
knock *v* تک تک وهل	**lament** *v* ویر کول
knot *n* لانجه	**lament** *n* ویر
know *iv* پیژندل	**lamp** *n* څراغ
know-how *n* مهارت	**lamppost** *n* د کوڅي څراغ
knowingly *adv* قصداً	**lampshade** *n* د څراغ پوښ
knowledge *n* پوهه	**land** *n* ځمکه
	land *v* ځاې
	landfill *n* د ځمکې جوړول
	landlady *n* مالکه
	landlocked *adj* په وچه ایسار
L	**landlord** *n* مالک
	landscape *n* طبعي منظره
	lane *n* نری لار
lab *n* ننبه	**language** *n* ژبه
label *n* پیژند پاڼه	**languish** *v* ناتوانه کېدل
labor *n* کار گران	**lantern** *n* ډیوه
laborer *n* کار کوونکي	**lapse** *n* ښویېدنه، غلطي
labyrinth *n* کور وور ځاې	**lapse** *v* ښویېدل
lack *v* ارتیا لرل	**larceny** *n* غلا
lack *n* ارتیا	**lard** *n* د وازکب غوړي
lad *n* ځلمی	**large** *adj* ستر
ladder *n* زینه	**larynx** *n* سره غاړه
laden *adj* تر بار لاندې	**laser** *n* شاع
lady *n* مبرمن	**lash** *n* متروکه
ladylike *adj* ښځنی	

K
L

lash *v* په متروکه وهل	lavish *v* ډبرول
lash out *v* مزمت کول	law *n* قانون
last *v* قالب کول	law-abiding *adj* قانون منونکی
last *adj* اخر	lawful *adj* قانوني،حقوقي
last name *n* وروستی نوم	lawmaker *n* سیاستوال
last night *adv* تېره شپه	lawn *n* چمن
lasting *adj* دوامداره	lawsuit *n* دعوه
lastly *adv* په پای کې	lawyer *n* قانون پوه
latch *n* قفل	lax *adj* سست
late *adv* ډیل	laxative *adj* جلاب
lately *adv* اوسنی	lay *n* غزل
later *adv* ارخیز	lay *iv* دروغ ویل،
later *adj* وروسته	layer *n* پوړ
lateral *adj* افقي	lay-out *n* نقشه
latest *adj* نوی	laziness *n* بې کاري
lather *n* ځگ	lazy *adj* لټ
latitude *n* ازادي	lead *n* د سربو څخه جوړ
latter *adj* وروستی	leaded *adj* بنودل شوی
laugh *v* خندل	leader *n* لاربنوونکی
laugh *n* خندا	leadership *n* مشر توب
laughable *adj* د خندا وړ	leading *adj* رهنمايي
laughing stock *n* مسخرچي	leaf *n* پاڼه
laughter *n* بنادي	leaflet *n* کومکي پاڼه
launch *n* دغرمې ډوډۍ	league *n* د واټن واحد
launch *v* پیل کول	leak *v* چاودېدل
laundry *n* د مینځلو کالي	leak *n* چاود
lavatory *n* تشناب	leakage *n* څخوبی
lavish *adj* زښت ډېر	lean *adj* ډنګر ، ضعیف

L

lean iv خنگ لګول	**legion** n يو غنډ عسكر
lean back v شاته تيتيدل	**legislate** v قانون جوړول
lean on v ارام دپاره	**legislature** n مقننه قوه
leaning n خرګدوالی	**legitimate** adj مشروع
leap iv ټوپ وهل	**lemon** n ليمو
leap n ټوپ	**lemonade** n د ليمو شربت
leap year n كبيته كال	**lend** iv پور وركول
learn iv زده كول	**length** n اوږد والی
learned adj عالم	**lengthen** v اوږدول
learner n زده كوونكی	**lengthy** adj اوږد
learning n زده كړه	**leniency** n نرمي
lease v په اجاره وركول	**lenient** adj نرم
lease n اجاره	**lense** n د كمري لېنز
leash n رسی	**Lent** n پور وركول
least adj ډېر كوچنی	**lentil** n پلی
leather n څرمن	**leper** n جذامي سړی
leave iv اجازه	**leprosy** n جذام
leave out v پرېښودل	**less** adj لږ
lecture n لكچر	**lessee** n اجاره كوونكی
leech n ژوره	**lessen** v لږول
leftovers n پاتې شونی	**lesser** adj ټيټ
leg n لينگی	**lesson** n لوست
legacy n ميراث	**let** iv مانع
legal adj شرعي	**let down** v لاندې كول
legality n قانونيت	**let go** v بې قابو كېدل
legalize v رسمي كول	**let in** v اجازه وركول
legend n نكل	**let out** v تبزې سره وتل
legible adj څرګند	**lethal** adj وژونكی

letter *n* لیک، خط	**lifeguard** *n* ساتل ژوند
lettuce *n* کاهو	**lifeless** *adj* مړ
leukemia *n* یو نوع مرض دی	**lifestyle** *n* رنگ ژوند د
level *v* برابرول	**lifetime** *adj* وخت ژوند د
level *n* درجه، مرتبه	**lift** *v* جگول
lever *n* ارم	**lift off** *v* ختل افقي
levy *v* غصبول	**lift-off** *n* ختنه افقي
lewd *adj* شهوت پرسته	**ligament** *n* پله
liability *n* وعده	**light** *iv* روښانول
liable *adj* گرم	**light** *adj* روښانه
liaison *n* یو ځای کېدنه	**light** *n* روښان
liar *adj* دروغجن	**lighter** *n* لایټر
libel *n* سپکاوی	**lighthouse** *n* روښانه کور
liberate *v* ازدول	**lighting** *n* روښانتیا
liberation *n* نجات	**lightly** *adv* ګلانده
liberty *n* ازادي	**lightning** *n* برېښنا
librarian *n* کتابدار	**likable** *adj* پوري زړه په
library *n* کتابتون	**like** *pre* غوندي
lice *n* سپږي	**like** *v* خوښول
license *n* اجازه لیک	**likelihood** *n* امکان
lick *v* څټل	**likely** *adv* مناسب
lid *n* پوښ	**likeness** *n* والی ورته
lie *iv* واقع کېدل	**likewise** *adv* څول همدا
lie *v* پربوتل	**liking** *n* میل
lie *n* دروغ	**limb** *n* اندام
lieu *n* ځای پر	**lime** *n* چونه
lieutenant *n* وکیل نایب	**limestone** *n* ډبره داهاکو
life *n* ژوند	**limit** *n* حد، برید

L

limit v محدودول	**literature** n ادبيات
limitation n محدوديت	**litigate** v اسره كول
limp v تلل ګوډ ګوډ	**litigation** n دعوه
limp n تلل ګوډ ګوډ	**litter** n تزکره
line n رسۍ	**little** adj کوچنی
linen n سان	**little bit** n لږ
linger v ځنډول	**little by little** adv کم ارزښته
lingerie n زبر جامې	**liturgy** n د لمانځه اداب
lingering adj دربدونکی	**live** adj ژوندی، تکړه
lining n استر	**live** v ژوند کول
link v اړيکه	**live off** v توقع کول
link n رابطه	**live up** v د ژوند معنا
lion n زمرى	**livelihood** n د ژوندانه شيان
lioness n د افريقا پيشو	**lively** adj تکړه
lip n شونډه	**liver** n ينه
liquid n مايع	**livestock** n څاروي
liquidate v پور ادا کول	**livid** adj پولادي
liquidation n پرېکړون	**living room** n اوسېدو کوټه
liquor n مشروب	**lizard** n کربوری
list v لست کې نيول	**load** v پيټی ورل
list n لست	**load** n پيټی
listen v اورېدل	**loaded** adj تر بار لاندې
listener n اورېدونکي	**loaf** n بشپړه ووډۍ
litany n دعا	**loan** v قرض کول
liter n لېټر	**loan** n قرض
literal adj ټکي په ټکي	**loathe** v کرکه کول
literally adv په صحيح ډول	**loathing** n نفرت
literate adj ادبي	**lobby** v د انتظار کوټه

L

local *adj* محلي، خای	long-term *adj* اوږده موده
localize *v* خای کول	look *n* لیدنه، کتنه
locate *v* په نښه کول	look *v* لیدل، کتل
location *n* خای	look after *v* تعقبول
lock *v* کوثی کول	look at *v* زره رانښکوونکی
lock *n* کوثی	look down *v* سپکتل
lock up *v* وروکپ دوکان	look for *v* احترام کول
lock up *n* جیل	look forward *v* هبله لرل
locksmith *n* قلف ساز	look into *v* تماشه کول
locust *n* ملخ	look out *v* پلټنه کول
lodge *v* کوچنی کور	look out *v* لټول
lofty *adj* لوړ	look out *v* لټول
log *n* کرکه، ستپه	looking glass *n* هنداره
log *v* دونو وهل	looks *n* لیدل
log in *v* شروع کول	loom *n* بنکاربدل
log off *v* ختمول	loom *v* تنسته
logic *n* منطق	loophole *n* مورچل
logical *adj* منطقي	loose *v* ایله
loin *n* ملا	loose *adj* نا تړلی
loiter *v* تالبدل	loosen *v* غرندول
loneliness *n* یوازې	loot *v* لوټول
lonely *adv* غمجن	loot *n* لوټ
loner *n* زاهد	lord *n* بادار
lonesome *adj* زړه تنګوونکی	lordship *n* خاني
long *adj* اوږد	lose *iv* یجاړول
long for *v* د اوږدې مودې	loser *n* بایلوونکی
longing *n* تلوسه	loss *n* ویجاړتوب
longitude *n* اوږدوالی	lot *adv* قرعه

lotion n محلول

lots adj ډېر

lottery n پچه

loud adj لوړ

loudly adv تېز والي

loudspeaker n لسپکر

lounge n ستړيا کښنل

louse n سپېره

lousy adj سپېرن

lovable adj د مينې وړ

love v مينه کول

love n مينه

lovely adj ښکلی

lover n ممين

loving adj په مينه

lower adj تريو

lowkey adj حياناک

lowly adj خاکسار

loyal adj وفاداري

loyalty n وفادري

lubricate v غورول

lubrication n غورونه

lucid adj څلاند

luck n بخت

lucky adj بختور

lucrative adj گټور

ludicrous adj د خندا وړ

luggage n پنډه

lukewarm adj تومن

lull n غلی

lumber n زور سامان

luminous adj څلاند

lump n کوټه، ډېری

lump together v بدشکله

lunacy n ليونتوب

lunatic adj ليونی

lunch n د غرمې ډوډی

lung n سرى

lure v لمسول

lurid adj پيکه

lurk v پټ کښنباستل

lush adj سمسور

lust v شهو ت لرل

lust n غوښتنه

lustful adj شهواني

luxurious adj عياش

luxury n تجمل

lynch v مر کول

lynx n صحرايي پيشو

lyrics n کلمې

M

machine n ماشـین

machine gun n ماشـین دار

mad adj سـاده

madam n میرمن

madden v لیونی کول

madly adv لیونتوب

madman n لیونی سری

madness n لیونتوب

magazine n مغازه

magic n جادو

magical adj جادويي

magician n جادوگر

magistrate n قاضي

magnet n مقناطیس

magnetic adj مقناطیسـي

magnetism n د جاذبې قوه

magnificent adj پرتمین

magnify v لویول

magnitude n پراخوالی

maid n پیغله

maiden n پیغلتوب

mail n بریښنالیک

mailman n ډاکي

maim v کلک زخمي کول

main adj لومړنی

mainland n اصلي خاوره

mainly adv اساسا

maintain v ساتل

maintenance n ساتنه

majestic adj برم لرونکی

majesty n جلال

major n لوي

major adj ستر

major in v زیات تعداد

major in n لوړ نمره

make n ډول

make iv جوړول

make up v سـبنګارول

make up for v ارایش جوړول

maker n جوړوونکی

makeup n جوړښت

malaria n ملاریا

male n نر

malevolent adj بد خوا

malfunction v ماتېدل

malfunction n مات

malice n دښـمني

malign v بد نیتي

malignancy n مضر

malignant adj خطر ناک

mall n د چکر ځای

malnutrition n ناوړه تغذیه

malpractice v نا وړه اداره

mammal *n* تي لرونگي	manure *n* سره ورکول
mammoth *n* ماموت پيل	manuscript *n* نسخه
man *n* سرى	many *adj* ډېر
manage *v* اداره کول	map *n* نقشه
manageable *adj* وړ دادراي	marble *n* مرمر
management *n* اداره تنظیم	march *v* مارش کول
manager *n* کوونکی اداره	March *n* سرحد
mandate *n* قومانده	mare *n* اسپه
mandatory *adj* قيموميت	margin *n* بريد
maneuver *n* مانو وره	marginal *adj* ژی
manger *n* اخور	marine *adj* سمندري
mangle *v* غوخول	marital *adj* واده
manhandle *v* پورې وهل	mark *n* نشانه
manhunt *n* مجرم	mark *v* نښه کول
maniac *adj* لبونی	mark down *v* قيمت ټيټول
manifest *v* څرګندول	marker *n* مارکر
mankind *n* انسان	market *n* مارکيټ
manliness *n* نارينتوب	marmalade *n* مربا
manly *adj* مېرنی	marriage *n* واده
manner *n* دود	married *adj* مېروبنه
mannerism *n* خاص رويش	marry *v* واده کول
manners *n* ماهده	Mars *n* مريخ
manpower *n* انسانی قوت	marshal *n* مارشل
mansion *n* مانۍ	martyr *n* خان شهيدول
manslaughter *n* بې اردې وژنه	martyrdom *n* شهادت
manual *n* لاسي کتاب	marvel *n* معجزه
manual *adj* لاسي	marvelous *adj* عجيبه
manufacture *v* جورول	Marxist *adj* سوسياليست

M

Marxist adj ماركبست

mash v د څاروو خواړه

mask n د څاروو خواړه

masochism n ماسکوژم

mason n ختګر

masquerade v اوښتي بنه

mass n کتله، ډله

massacre n ټولیزه وژنه

massage n مساژ

massage v مساژ کول

masseur n مساژ کوونکی

massive adj لوي

mast n ستنه

master n خاوند

master v لاس موندل

mastermind n اداره کوونکی

mastermind v اداره کوونکی

masterpiece n شاهکار

mastery n مهارت

mat n تت

match n اور لګیت، ګوګړ

match v وده ول

mate n جوړه

material n مواد، جنس

materialism n د مادي فلسفه

maternal adj مورنۍ

maternity n مورنۍ خوي

math n ریاضي

matrimony n واده

matter n مواد، ماده

mattress n نیالی

mature adj رسبدلی

maturity n پوخوالی

maul v حمله

maxim n متل

maximum adj اعظمي حد

may iv هیله

may-be adv شاید

mayor n ښاروال

maze n کرې ورې لارې

meadow n چمن

meager adj نرۍ

meal n جواری

mean iv معنا کول

mean adj تیټ

meaning n مقصد

meaningful adj له معنا ډک

meaningless adj بې معنا

meanness n نا تر سي

means n دارایي

meantime adv په ترڅ کې

measles n شرې

measure v حد ټاکل

measurement n اندازه

meat n غوښه

meatball n قیمه

M

mechanic *n* کسبګر	membership *n* غړيتوب
mechanism *n* ماشين دستګا	membrane *n* پرده
mechanize *v* ماشيني کول	memento *n* يادگار
medal *n* مډال	memo *n* يادانبتونه
medallion *n* لوي نښان	memoirs *n* يادانبت
mediate *v* منځګريتوب	memorable *adj* يادونې ور
mediator *n* منځګري	memorize *v* په يادول
medication *n* دوا	memory *n* حافظه
medicinal *adj* ګټور	men *n* وګړي
medicine *n* طب طبابت	menace *n* ويره
medieval *adj* د منځنيو پېړيو	mend *v* رغول
mediocre *adj* عادي	meningitis *n* ناروغي
mediocrity *n* منځنۍ حالت	mental *adj* دماغي
meditate *v* پلان جوړول	mentality *n* ذهنيت
meditation *n* تامل	mentally *adv* احساساتي
medium *adj* منځنۍ حالت	mention *v* ذکر کول
meek *adj* پوست	mention *n* ذکر
meekness *n* عاجزي	merchant *n* سوداګر
meet *iv* مخامخ کېدل	merciful *adj* زړه سواند
meeting *n* تن په تن جنګ	merciless *adj* بې رحمه
melancholy *n* وسواس	mercury *n* پاره
mellow *adj* پوخ	mercy *n* مهرباني
mellow *v* پخول	merely *adv* دومره
melodic *adj* موزيکي	merge *v* ضم کېدل
melody *n* خوږه نغمه	merit *n* ور والى
melon *n* خټکى	merit *v* کېدل
melt *v* ولي کېدل	mermaid *n* خيالي
member *n* غړى	merry *adj* خوښ

M

mesh n سوری	**migraine** n نیم سری
mess n پنده	**migrant** n کوچی
mess up v ضایع کول	**migrate** v بدل بدل
message n خبر	**mild** adj معتدل
messenger n استاخی	**mile** n میل
Messiah n مسیحا	**mileage** n بوتیندی‌گر
messy adj ود گد	**milestone** n خلی
metal n فلز	**militant** adj جنگیالی
metallic adj فلزي	**milk** n شیدې
meteor n کانې اسماني	**milky** adj پروري
method n طرز	**millennium** n زرکاله
meticulous adj وسواسي	**milligram** n گرام ملي
metric adj د مترسیستم	**millimeter** n متر ملي
metropolis n بنار لوي	**million** n میلون
mice n موږکان	**millionaire** n میلونر
microbe n میکروب	**mime** v کول مسخره
microphone n وونکی لور دغ	**mince** v کول میده
microscope n لید وور	**mincemeat** n غوښنه کوټلي
microwave n بین زره	**mind** v کول فکر یادول،
midair n انتن	**mind** n فکر دماغ،
midday n خابنت	**mind-boggling** adj ور منلو نه د
middle n منځنی	**mindful** adj لرونکی پام
middleman n منځگر	**mindless** adj فکره بی
midget n لویشتکی	**mine** n تونل
midnight n شپه نیمه	**mine** v کیندل کان
midsummer n پشکال	**mine** pro زما
midwife n دایي	**minefield** n ساحه ددماغ
mighty adj پیاوړی	**miner** n گر کار دکان

M

mineral *n* معدني مواد	miserable *adj* خوار
mingle *v* ګډېدل	misery *n* خواري
miniature *n* وړوکی	misfit *adj* نا برابر
minimize *v* لږول	misfortune *n* بد مرغي
minimum *n* وور بخي	misgiving *n* اندېښنه
miniskirt *n* کميس ډول يو	misguided *adj* غلطي
minister *n* ملا عيسوي	misinterpret *v* غلط تعبيرول
minister *v* کول اداره	misjudge *v* غلط قضاوت
ministry *n* کابينه،وزارت	mislead *v* کول لاري بې
minor *adj* لغ نابا جزیه	misleading *adj* غولوونکي
minority *n* لږوالی	mismanage *v* کول پروايي بې
mint *n* وبلنی	misprint *n* غلطي
minus *adj* پرتله	miss *v* پوهېدل نه
minute *n* شېبه	miss *n* پېغله
miracle *n* تريانوونکې	missile *n* ګولي
miraculous *adj* العاده حارق	missing *adj* وتلی لاسه له
mirage *n* سراب	mission *n* دله استاخو
mirror *n* هندار ه	missionary *n* مبلغات مذهبي
misbehave *v* کول چلند ناوړه	mist *n* لره
miscalculate *v* شمېرل غلط	mistake *iv* کول سهوه
miscarriage *n* ورونکي ناکار ه	mistake *n* سهوه
miscarry *v* کېدل ناکامه	mistaken *adj* وتلی خطا
mischief *n* خور	mister *n* ښاغلی
mischievous *adj* شيطان	mistreat *v* ټل تر
misconduct *n* رویه پده	mistreatment *n* اچونه کار په
misconstrue *v* پوهېدل غلط	mistress *n* مېرمن
misdemeanor *n* سلوک بد	mistrust *n* اعتباري بې
miser *n* خسیس	mistrust *v* کول نه ویسا

misty *adj* خړ	**moldy** *adj* چناسک
misuse *n* ناوړه استفاده	**mole** *n* تکی، خال
mix *v* سره اخبنل	**molecule** *n* ماليکول
mixed-up *adj* مشغولوالي	**molest** *v* ازارول
mixture *n* کډوله	**mom** *n* شببه
mix-up *n* روزل	**moment** *n* لږ وخت
moan *v* زګېروي	**momentous** *adj* مهم
moan *n* زګېروي	**monarch** *n* پاچا
mob *v* په ډله ورتلل	**monarchy** *n* پاچاهي
mob *n* پاربدلې ډله	**monastery** *n* شاهي دولت
mobile *adj* ګرځنده	**monastic** *adj* روحاني
mobilize *v* چمتو کول	**Monday** *n* دوشنبه
mock *v* ملنډې وهل	**money** *n* پيسې
mockery *n* ملنډې	**monitor** *v* مبصر
mode *n* دود	**monk** *n* څیله کې
model *n* نمونه	**monkey** *n* بیزو
moderate *adj* برابر	**monopolize** *v* څانته کول
moderation *n* اعتدال	**monopoly** *n* انحصار
modern *adj* اوسنی	**monotonous** *adj* لټ
modernize *v* عصري کول	**monotony** *n* يو شی والی
modest *adj* حياناک	**monster** *n* غټه بلا
modesty *n* حيا	**monstrous** *adj* ظالم
modify *v* بړلول	**month** *n* مياشت
module *n* برخه	**monthly** *adv* مياشتنی
moisten *v* نمجنول	**monument** *n* ياد ګار
moisture *n* رطوبت	**monumental** *adj* خلی
molar *n* زامنې غاښ	**mood** *n* وضع
mold *n* چناسې	**moody** *adj* بد خلقه

M

moon n سپوږمۍ	**motion** n پیشنهاد
moor v مراکشي سري	**motionless** adj بې حرکته
mop v غولی پاکوونکی	**motivate** v پارول
moral adj چلند	**motive** n خوځنده
moral n اخلاق	**motor** n ماشيني موټر
morality n فضلیت	**motorcycle** n ډپ ډبی
more adj ډېر زیات	**motto** n شعار
moreover adv برسېره پر دې	**mouldy** adj چناسک
morning n سهار	**mount** n غر
moron adj ډیر احمق سري	**mount** v ختل
morphine n سهار	**mountain** n غر
morsel n ګوله	**mountainous** adj غرنۍ
mortal adj تلونی	**mourn** v ويرکول
mortality n مرګ	**mourning** n غم
mortar n هاوان توپ	**mouse** n موږک
mortgage n ګروی	**mouth** n خوله
mortification n وژنه	**move** n بنـورونه
mortify v وژل	**move** v بنـورول
mosaic n موزک	**move back** v بېرته حرکت کول
mosque n مسجد	**move out** v خالي کول
mosquito n غوماشي	**movement** n حرکت
moss n خزه	**movie** n فلم
most adj خورا ډېر	**mow** v بوس خانه
mostly adv اکثره	**much** adv ډېر
moth n پتنګ	**mucus** n چوخړې
mother n مور	**mud** n خټه
motherhood n موروالی	**muddle** n ګډول
mother-in-law n خواښې	**muddy** adj خټين

M

muffle v نغاړل

muffler n دغاړې دشمال

mug n گیلوی

mug v برغل کول

mugging n برغل کونه

mule n کچر

multiple adj مضاعف

multiplication n ضرب

multiply v ضربول

multitude n ډله

mumble v بنگیدنه

mummy n مومیا شوی

munch v چیچل

munitions n تجهیزات

murder n وژل

murderer n وژونکی

murky adj تیاره

murmur v پس پسې کول

murmur n پس پسې

muscle n عضله

museum n موزیم

mushroom n مرخبزی

music n موسیقي

musician n سازنده

Muslim adj مسلمان

must iv باید

mustache n بریت

mustard n اوری

muster v را ټولول

mutate v بدلون

mute adj گونگ

mutilate v له پښو غورځول

mutiny n پورته کیدنه

mutually adv له دواړو خواوو

muzzle v کټپوز ور اچول

muzzle n زربوز، ورسک

my adj زما

myopic adj خرافاتي

myself pro زه پخپله

mysterious adj له سرو ډک

mystery n سر

mystic adj نا معلوم

mystify v وار خطاکول

myth n افسانه

N

nag *v* څورول

nagging *adj* څورول شوی

nail *n* نوک

naive *adj* ساده والی

naked *adj* لوڅ

name *n* نوم

namely *adv* په نامه

nanny *n* دايي / نيا

nap *n* ورين استر

napkin *n* دسمال

narcotic *n* مخدره مواد

narrate *v* کيسه ويل

narrow *adj* نرۍ

narrowly *adv* په څير

nasty *adj* ناوی

nation *n* اولس

national *adj* ملي

nationality *n* مليت

nationalize *v* ملي کول

native *adj* ځاني

natural *adj* طبيعي

naturally *adv* په طبيعي

nature *n* طبيعت

naughty *adj* شوخ

nausea *n* خوا ګرزي

nave *n* غولی

navel *n* دنامه غوټی

navigate *v* چلول

navigation *n* چلبدنه

navy *n* د جنګ نقشه

near *pre* نږدی

nearby *adj* په نږدې توګه

nearly *adv* تقريباً نږدې

nearsighted *adj* ناپوه

neat *adj* پاک

neatly *adv* په سوتره توګه

necessary *adj* ضروري

necessitate *v* ارايستل

necessity *n* ضرورت

neck *n* اورمبر

necklace *n* اورۍ

necktie *n* نکتايي

need *v* ارتيا درلودل

need *n* ارتيا

needle *n* ستن

needless *adj* بې ارتيا

needy *adj* ډبر ضروري

negative *adj* منفي

neglect *v* بې پروايي کول

neglect *n* بې پروايي

negligence *n* بې احتياطي

negligent *adj* بې پروا

negotiate *v* ګړبدل

N

negotiation *n* ګړبدنه	nicely *adv* په ښه ډول
neighbor *n* ګاونډي	nickel *n* نيكل
neighborhood *n* ګاونډيتوب	nickname *n* لقب
neither *adj* هيڅ	nicotine *n* نيكوټين
neither *adv* يو هم نه	niece *n* وبره
nephew *n* وراره	night *n* شپه
nerve *n* عصب	nightfall *n* ترہ غونی
nervous *adj* عصبي	nightgown *n* د خوب كالي
nest *n* خاله	nightingale *n* بلبل
net *n* جال	nightmare *n* خپسه
Netherlands *n* ندر ليند	nine *adj* نه ۹
network *n* شبكه	nineteen *adj* نولس ۱۹
neurotic *adj* عصاباني	ninety *adj* نوي ۹۰
neutral *adj* بې طرفه	ninth *adj* نهم
neutralize *v* بې طرف كول	nip *n* موښنه
never *adv* نه هيڅكله	nip *v* موښل
new *adj* نوی	nipple *n* د تي سر
newborn *n* نوی زېږد	nitpicking *adj* بحراني
newcomer *n* نوی راغلی	nitrogen *n* نايتروجن
newly *adv* نوی	no one *pro* هيڅ يو هم نه
newlywed *adj* نوي واده كړي	nobility *n* اشراف
news *n* خبر	noble *adj* شريف
newscast *n* نوی لنډيز	nobleman *n* شريف سړی
newsletter *n* نوی ليک	nobody *pro* هيڅوك
newspaper *n* ورځپانه	nocturnal *adj* د شپې
next *adj* راتلونكی	noise *n* خور
next door *adj* ننوتخی	noisy *adj* شورناك
nice *adj* ګلالی	nominate *v* ټاكل

N

none *pre* هیڅکله	notification *n* خبرتیا
nonetheless *c* په هر حال	notify *v* حبرول
nonsense *n* بې ځایه	notion *n* خیالي
nonstop *adv* پر له پسې	notorious *adj* رسوا
noon *n* غرمه	noun *n* نوم
noose *n* د رۍ کړۍ	nourish *v* روڅ ورکول
nor *c* نه	nourishment *n* روڅ ورکونه
norm *n* ټاکلي اندازه	novel *n* ناول
normal *adj* نورمال	novelist *n* ناول لیکونکی
normalize *v* منظم کول	novelty *n* نوی والی
normally *adv* په عادي توګه	November *n* نومبر
north *n* شمال	novice *n* نابلده
northern *adj* شمالي	now *adv* اوس
Norway *n* ناروی	nowhere *adv* هیچرې
nose *n* پوزه	noxious *adj* مضر
nosedive *v* کمو ل	nozzle *n* نلۍ
nostril *n* سرمی	nuance *n* لږ فرق
nosy *adj* د تورو مچ	nuclear *adj* ذروي
not *adv* نه	nude *adj* لوڅ
notable *adj* دیادونې وړ	nudism *n* د برېنډېدو نظریه
notably *adv* په تېره بیا	nudity *n* بر بنډتوب
notary *n* لیکونکی	nuisance *n* ربروونکی
notation *n* یادونه	null *adj* بې ارزښته
note *v* یادګېرنه	nullify *v* بې ارزښته کول
noteworthy *adj* د یاونې وړ	numb *adj* ویدول
noteworthy *n* یادداشت	number *n* شمېرنه
notice *n* خبر، پاملرنه	numbness *n* بې حسه والی
noticeable *adj* د پام وړ	numerous *adj* ګڼ سمبر

nun *n* راهبه
nurse *n* وروکپاله
nurse *v* وروکپالل
nursery *n* وروکتون
nurture *v* پالنه
nutrition *n* خواړه
nutritious *adj* مغذي
nutty *adj* زړی لرونکی

O

oak *n* څیړی
oar *n* د بیړی راشیل
oasis *n* رغیانه
oath *n* لوړه
obedience *n* مننه
obedient *adj* منوونکی
obese *adj* قوي
obey *v* منل
object *v* اعتراض کول
object *n* اعتراض
objection *n* نیوکه
objective *n* عیني
obligate *v* اړ کول
obligation *n* اړتیا

obligatory *adj* واجب
oblige *v* اړکول
obliged *adj* اړ
oblique *adj* کوږ
obliterate *v* تورل
oblivion *n* هېرول
oblivious *adj* هېربرجن
oblong *adj* اوږد وزمه
obnoxious *adj* ناوړه
obscene *adj* کرغېړن
obscenity *n* ناولتوب
obscure *adj* تیاره
obscurity *n* تتوالی
observation *n* لیدنه
observe *v* کتل
obsess *v* څورول
obsession *n* کړاو
obsolete *adj* زوړ
obstacle *n* خنډ
obstinacy *n* سر تنبګي
obstinate *adj* سر تنبه
obstruct *v* خنډ اچول
obstruction *n* خنډ
obtain *v* لاسته راوړل
obvious *adj* څرګند
obviously *adv* په څرګند ډول
occasion *n* وخت وار
occult *adj* پټ

occupant n نيوونکی	often adv ډېر ځلي
occupation n نيونه	oil n تيل
occupy v نيول	ointment n ملهم
occur v پيښېدل	okay adv صحيح
ocean n سمندر	old adj زوړ
October n اکتوبر	old-fashioned adj زوړ سينگار
ocurrence n ارزښت	olive n زيتون
odd adj تاک	olympics n اولمپيک
oddity n عجلب والی	omelette n خاګينه
odds n توپير	omen n شګون
odious adj خوا بدوونکی	ominous adj بد مرغه
odometer n اودو ميتر	omission n حذف
odor n بوي	omit v غورځول
of pre په	on pre پر
off adv جلا	once adv يو ځلي
offend v تبری کول	once c زر تر زر
offense n تبری	one adj يو
offensive adj تبری کوونکی	oneself pre پخپله
offer v تبری کول	ongoing adj جاري
offer n وراندېز	onion n پياز
offering n پخښنه	onlooker n نندارچي
office n دفتر	only adv يوازې
officer n منصبدار	onset n يرغل
official adj مامور	onslaught n کلکه حمله
officiate v لمونځ ور کول	onwards adv مخ په وراندې
offset v لبښته	opaque adj خړ
offspring n اولاد	open v خلاصول
off-the-record adj شخصي	open adj پرانستی

O

open up v اعلان کول	orangutan n وحشي سرى
opening n پرانسته	orbit n مدار
openness n خرگندوالی	orchard n د میوو باغ
opera n اوپرا	orchestra n ارکسترا
operation n عملیات	ordain v ټاکل
opinion n نظریه	ordeal n سخته تجربه
opinionated adj سر تنبه	order n ترتیب
opium n اپین	ordinarily adv په عادي ډول
opponent n چپ	ordinary adj متوسط
opportune adj ور	ore n کانی
opportunity n فرصت	organ n اله
oppose v مخالف کول	organism n ارگانبزم
opposite adj مخامخ	organist n ارگان
opposite adv مخامخ شوی	organization n اداره
opposite n ضد	organize v رغول
opposition n مخالفه ډله	orient n ختیځ
oppress v تبری کول	oriental adj شرقي
oppression n ظلم	orientation n اوردونه
opt for v انتخابول	oriented adj ریونده
optical adj په لید پوهنې	origin n سر چینه
optician n جوروونکي	original adj لومړنی
option n واک	originally adv په لمړی توگه
optional adj اختیاري	originate v نوی را ایستل
opulence n شتمني	ornament n گاڼه
or c یا	ornamental adj ولي
oracle n غیب وینه	orphan n یتیم
orally adv شفاهي	orphanage n مرستون
orange n نارنج	orthodox adj جزمي

ostrich *n* شتر مرغ	outlook *n* اورد ژوند
other *adj* بل	outmoded *adj* دتیري په توګه
otherwise *adv* مختلف	outpatient *n* غاروان بنرهب
otter *n* د اوبو پیشی	outperform *v* ماتول
ought to *iv* باید	outpouring *n* څرګندونه
ounce *n* اونس	output *n* محصول
our *adj* څمونږ	outrage *n* تېری
ours *pro* څمونږه	outrageous *adj* تند خويه
ourselves *pro* څمونږه خپله	outright *adj* ټول
oust *v* غورځول	outright *v* په ډانګ پیلي
out *adv* د باندي	outset *n* برید
outbreak *n* چاودنه	outshine *v* ډیر ځلیدبل
outburst *n* اور اخیستنه	outside *adv* د باندي
outcast *adj* رټنه	outsider *n* بیګانه
outcome *n* نتیجه	outspoken *adj* سپین
outcry *n* سورب ناره	outspoken *adj* سپین ویونکي
outdated *adj* نادوده	outstretched *adj* غوړول
outdo *v* اړول	outward *adj* په عامه توګه
outdoor *adv* باندي	outweigh *v* تیاره کول
outdoors *adv* بهر	oval *adj* شفايي
outer *adj* وتلی	ovation *n* هر کلی
outfit *n* اسباب	oven *n* تنور
outgoing *adj* وتونکی	over *pre* لور
outgrow *v* بې وخته لو یېدل	overall *adv* په ټولبزه توګه
outlast *v* ډیر پاینېت کول	overbearing *adj* کبر جن
outlaw *v* باغي	overboard *adv* په اوبو کي
outlet *n* سوری، مخرج	overcast *adj* اورو کب پټ
outlive *v* ډیر پاینېت کول	overcharge *v* زیات اخیستل

overcoat n کوټ

overcome v لاندبی کول

overcrowded adj شور ما شور

overdo v افراط

overdone adj شاباس

overdose n تر اندزي ډير

overdue adj ځندبدل

overestimate v اټکونه

overflow v تر څنډ اووختل

overhaul v کوزول

overlap v وبرول

overnight adv په شپه کې

overpower v لاندې کول

override v بې اثره کول

overrule v په ځټ کول

overrun v لوټول

oversee v څارل

overshadow v تباره

oversight n غلطي

overstate v مبالغه کول

overstep v

overtake v لاندې کول

overthrow v ورانول

overthrow n وران

overtime adv اضافه کاري

overturn v تباه کول

overview n خلاصه

overweight adj دروندوالې

overwhelm v لاندي کول

owe v مدیون

owing to adv ژر ادا کول

owl n کونک

own v شخصي

own adj ځانګرتوب

owner n څښتن

ownership n ملکټ

ox n غوبی

oxen n غوا

oxygen n اکسبجن

P

pace v کام کول

pace n کام

pacify v ارامول

pack v کبډي کول

package n پنډه کې

pact n ترون

pad n کونستر ګب

paddle v پار ووهونکب

padlock n کلپ

pagan adj مشرک

page n مخ ،صفحه

pail *n* ستل ،بوكه	**pantry** *n* د لوښو خونه
pain *n* درد	**pants** *n* پتلون
painful *adj* دردمن	**papacy** *n* د پاپ مقام
painless *adj* پې درده	**paper** *n* كاغذ
paint *v* رنګول	**paperclip** *n* ټومبونې
paint *n* رنګ	**paperwork** *n* ورځنادارۍ کار
paintbrush *n* د رنګولو برش	**parable** *n* کېسه
painter *n* رنګمال	**parachute** *n* پراشوت
painting *n* رنګونه	**parade** *n* رسم ګذشت
pair *n* جوړه	**paradise** *n* جنت ،
pajamas *n* د خوب کلې	**parallel** *n* موازي
pal *n* ارګ	**paralysis** *n* شل
palace *n* ماڼۍ	**paralyze** *v* شل کول
palate *n* تالو	**parameters** *n* د اندازې ور
pale *adj* رنګ الوتې	**paramount** *adj* ستر
paleness *n* پېکه توب	**paranoid** *adj* ډار ونکې
palm *n* کجورې ونه	**parasite** *n* طفېلي
palpable *adj* محسوس	**parcel** *n* پارسل
paltry *adj* سپک ورک	**parcel post** *n* پاسل استونه
pamper *v* په ناز لوپول	**parch** *v* ورېتول
pamphlet *n* رساله	**parchment** *n* د لېکلو څرمن
pan *n* کړاۍ	**pardon** *v* بښنل
pancreas *n* ترېخې	**pardon** *n* بښنه
pander *v* پروا توب	**parenthesis** *n* قوسونه
pang *n* څرېکه	**parents** *n* مور او پلار
panic *n* وبره	**parity** *n* مساوات
panorama *n* منظره	**park** *v* هوا خورې کول
panther *n* پړانګ	**park** *n* پارک

parliament *n* ولسي شورا	passionate *adj* قار
parochial *adj* پر سبمه	passive *adj* زغمونکي
parrot *n* توتي	passport *n* پاسپورت
parsley *n* دنپا	password *n* شفر
parsnip *n* ساراني گازره	past *adj* تېره
part *v* اخېستل برخه	paste *v* سرېښ کول
part *n* برخه	paste *n* سرېښ
partial *adj* پلوي	pasteurize *v* تعقېمول
participate *v* گډون کول	pastime *n* ساعت تېري
participation *n* گډون	pastor *n* کشبش
participle *n* صفت اسم	pastoral *adj* کشبشي
particle *n* ذره	pastry *n* پاستري
particular *adj* جلا	pasture *n* وښپانه
particularly *adv* مخصوصا	pat *n* په شا ټپونه
parting *n* بېلتون	patch *v* فېصله کول
partisan *n* طرفدار	patch *n* فېصله کول
partition *n* وېش	patent *n* خرگند
partner *n* شرېک بانی	patent *adj* خرگندوالي
partnership *n* گډون	paternity *n* پلاروالي
partridge *n* زرکه	path *n* لار
party *n* گوند،حزب	pathetic *adj* غبزه ټاک
pass *n* بربالي توب	patience *n* کالل
pass *v* پاس کول	patient *adj* کالونکي
pass around *v* د ډاډ ور	patio *n* انگر
pass away *v* ورور ورکېدل	patriarch *n* د کورنې مشر
passage *n* گودر	patrimony *n* مبراثب شتمنب
passenger *n* مسافر	patriot *n* وطن پالونکوب
passion *n* شهادت	patriotic *adj* وطن پالونکوب

patrol n گزمه	**peck** v په منښوکه وهل
patron n حامي، اتندوي	**peck** n په منښوکه وهل
patronage n ساتنه	**peculiar** adj ټاکلی
patronize v ساتل	**pedal** n پايډل
pattern n نمونه	**pedantic** adj کتابي ملا
pavement n هوار	**pedestrian** n پلی
pavilion n نندارتون	**peel** v پوستول
paw n خپر	**peel** n پوست
pawn v د شطرنج ګوتک	**peep** v چوپیدل
pawnbroker n ګروي وال	**peer** n جوړه
pay n ادا	**pelican** n ماهي خورک
pay iv ادا کول	**pellet** n ګولی
pay off v ګتور	**pen** n قلم
paycheck n ادا کونه	**penalize** v سزا ورکول
payee n اخبستونکي	**penalty** n سزا، جريمه
payment n تاديه	**penance** n توبه
payslip n د تنخا رسید	**penchant** n تمایل
pea n پلی	**pencil** n پنسل
peace n روغه	**pendant** n غوروالی
peaceful adj په روغه	**pending** adj ناتمامه
peach n شفتالو	**pendulum** n خورند
peacock n تاوس	**penetrate** v ورننوتل
peak n څوکه	**penicillin** n پنسلبن
peanut n مو پلی	**peninsula** n ټاپو وزمه
pear n ناک	**penitent** n توبه ګار
pearl n ملغلري	**penniless** adj مفلس
peasant n دهقان	**penny** n پوه انه
pebble n شګه	**pension** n تقاعد

P

پنځه ارخبز n **pentagon**

نا وبلې adj **pent-up**

خلک n **people**

مرچ n **pepper**

په هر pre **per**

ور کول v **perceive**

په سلو کې adv **percent**

په سلو کې n **percentage**

ادراک n **perception**

کړي کال adj **perennial**

پوره adj **perfect**

پوره توب n **perfection**

سوړی کېدل v **perforate**

سوړی n **perforation**

سر ته رسول v **perform**

تمامول n **performance**

عطر n **perfume**

شاید adv **perhaps**

ډار n **peril**

ډارونکې adj **perilous**

چاپېربال n **perimeter**

موده n **period**

تباه کېدل v **perish**

ورستېدونکې adj **perishable**

نا حقه لوړه n **perjury**

تل تر تله adj **permanent**

ډکول v **permeate**

اجازه n **permission**

منل v **permit**

ناوړه adj **pernicious**

مرتکب کېدل v **perpetrate**

ربړول v **persecute**

ټينګار v **persevere**

درېدل v **persist**

ټينګار n **persistence**

ټينګېدونکې adj **persistent**

نفر n **person**

ذاتي adj **personal**

شخصیت n **personality**

غړي n **personnel**

لید n **perspective**

خوله n **perspiration**

خوله کېدل v **perspire**

تشوبق v **persuade**

تشوبقول n **persuasion**

تشوبقي adj **persuasive**

اړه لرل v **pertain**

تړلي adj **pertinent**

خوړول v **perturb**

پخپل سر adj **perverse**

غلطه مانا کول v **pervert**

مرتتوالي adj **pervert**

نا امېدي n **pessimism**

منفي adj **pessimistic**

وبا n **pest**

خپه کول v **pester**

pesticide *n* حشره	physics *n* فزیک
pet *n* کورنی ځناور	pianist *n* پیانو غږونکی
petal *n* گلپاڼی	piano *n* پیانو
petite *adj* وړوکی	pick *v* پاکول، غوندول
petition *n* غوښتنه	pick up *v* اوچتول
petrified *adj* ډار وونکی	pickpocket *n* گنډکپ
petroleum *n* پترول	pickup *n* اوچتونه
petty *adj* کم، وړوکی	picture *n* عکس
pew *n* اوردہ چوکی	picture *v* انځورول
phantom *n* بلا	picturesque *adj* ښکلی
pharmacist *n* کمپوډر	pie *n* سمبوسه
pharmacy *n* درملتون	piece *n* ټوټه
phase *n* مرحله	piecemeal *adv* ټوټه ټوټه
pheasant *n* ساراېي چرگ	pier *n* ډکه
phenomenon *n* پیښنه	pierce *v* سوری کول
philosopher *n* فېلسوف	piercing *n* سوری کونکی
philosophy *n* فلسفه	piety *n* دینداري
phobia *n* ډار	pig *n* خوگ
phone *n* تېلېفون	pigeon *n* کوتره
phone *v* تېلېفون کول	piggy bank *n* د پیسو بکس
phoney *adj* ساختگي	pile *v* دلی کېدل
phosphorus *n* فاسفورس	pile *n* اړم
photo *n* عکس	pile up *v* بار
photocopy *n* نقل	pilfer *v* پټول
photography *n* عکاسي	pilgrim *n* مسافر
phrase *n* نیمگړی جمله	pilgrimage *n* زیارت
physically *adv* جسما	pill *n* مردکی
physician *n* طبیب	pillage *v* لوټ

P

pillar *n* ستنه	**placid** *adj* نرم
pillow *n* تکیه	**plague** *n* طاعون
pillowcase *n* د بالښت پوښ	**plain** *n* ساده ډوله
pilot *n* پیلوټ	**plain** *adj* ډبر والي
pimple *n* دانه	**plainly** *adv* ساده ډوله
pin *n* سنجاق	**plaintiff** *n* مدعي
pincers *n* نوسي	**plan** *v* تدبیرول
pinch *v* څورول	**plan** *n* تدبیر
pinch *n* څورونه	**plane** *n* اوار
pine *n* د زنغوزي ونه	**planet** *n* سباره
pineapple *n* اناناس	**plant** *v* نبالول
pink *adj* ګلابي	**plant** *n* نبات
pinpoint *v* په نښه کول	**plaster** *n* پلستر
pious *adj* پاک	**plaster** *v* پلسترول
pipe *n* شپیلندوی	**plastic** *n* پلستبک
pipeline *n* نل	**plate** *n* پشقاب
piracy *n* سمندري غلا	**plateau** *n* لوړه سطحه
pirate *n* ادبي غلا	**platform** *n* دربځ
pistol *n* تمانچه	**platinum** *n* پلاتین
pit *n* زري	**platoon** *n* دلګی
pitch-black *adj* تباره	**plausible** *adj* د مننې وړ
pitchfork *n* بناخی	**play** *v* لوبي کول
pitfall *n* لټ ، کروکب	**play** *n* لوبي
pitiful *adj* زړه سواندي	**player** *n* لوبغاړي
pity *n* زړه سوي	**playful** *adj* شوخ
placard *n* اعلان لپک	**playground** *n* لوبغالي
placate *v* کرارول	**plea** *n* د تورن دفاعبه
place *n* ځای	**plead** *v* دفاع

pleasant adj	په زړه پورې
please v	منل
pleasing adj	خوشالېدل
pleasure n	خوشالۍ
pleat n	چوڼ
pleated adj	چوڼ شوی
pledge v	ګروول
pledge n	ګروۍ
plentiful adj	پرېمانه
plenty n	پورہ
pliable adj	تغبر منونکی
pliers n	پلاس
plot v	نحشه کول
plow v	کولبه کول
ploy n	چل
pluck v	شکول
plug v	اعلان کول
plug n	پلګ
plum n	زردالو
plumber n	نل دوان
plumbing n	نل دواني
plummet v	شاول کو ل
plump adj	رډ
plunder v	تلا کول
plunge v	دنګبدونکی
plunge n	ډوببدنه
plural n	جمع
plus adj	د جمع اعلام+

plutonium n	پلوتونيم
pneumonia n	سبنه بغل
pocket n	جېب
poem n	نظم
poet n	شعر
poetry n	شاعرۍ
poignant adj	تند
point n	ټکی ، نمرہ
point v	اشارہ
pointed adj	نبغه
pointless adj	پڅ
poise n	انډول
poison v	زهر ورکول
poison n	زهر
poisoning n	زهر
poisonous adj	زهر جن
Poland n	پولند
polar adj	قطبي
pole n	پولندي
police n	پولبس
policeman n	ساتندوی
policy n	بيمه لبک
Polish adj	پولندي
polish n	پالش
polish v	ځلا ورکول
polite adj	مودپ
politeness n	ادب
politician n	سباست مدار

P

politics *n* سياست	**portent** *n* بد فال
poll *n* سر	**porter** *n* پنډی
pollen *n* دګل ګرده	**portion** *n* برخه
pollute *v* ناولې کول	**portrait** *n* څېره
pollution *n* ناپاکې	**portray** *v* عکس کښل
pomegranate *n* انار	**Portugal** *n* پرتګال
pomposity *n* برمر	**Portuguese** *adj* پرتګالي
pond *n* ډنډ	**pose** *v* ځان ښودل
ponder *v* فکر	**pose** *n* ځان ښونه
pontiff *n* اسقف	**posh** *adj* ډولي
pool *n* دبليارډلوبه	**position** *n* مقام
pool *v* ډنډ، حوض	**positive** *adj* مثبت
poor *n* غريب	**possess** *v* لرل
poorly *adv* په نسبتي	**possession** *n* ملکيت
popcorn *n* نبنې	**possibility** *n* امکان
Pope *n* پاپ	**possible** *adj* کېدونکي
poppy *n* خاشخاش	**post** *n* پايه
popular *adj* اسان	**post office** *n* پوسته خانه
popularize *v* شهرت ورکول	**postage** *n* د پوستي محصول
populate *v* ودانول	**postcard** *n* پوست کارد
population *n* نفوس	**poster** *n* اعلان
porcelain *n* چيني لوښي	**posterity** *n* نسل
porch *n* دالان	**postman** *n* پوسته رسونکي
porcupine *n* شکوپ	**postmark** *n* د پوستي نښه
pore *n* مسام	**postpone** *v* ځنډول
pork *n* د خوک غوښه	**postponement** *n* ځنډونه
porous *adj* ماسادام	**pot** *n* لوښي
portable *adj* سپک	**potato** *n* الو

P

potent *adj* قوي	precaution *n* مخکبني
potential *adj* پت قوت	precede *v* مخکبدل
pothole *n* سوري	precedent *n* وراندي والي
poultry *n* کورنۍ مرغان	preceding *adj* وراندي
pound *v* ټکول	precept *n* قانون
pound *n* شپول	precious *adj* گران
pour *v* توپول	precipice *n* کمر
poverty *n* نبستي	precipitate *v* لاندي غورځول
powder *n* پودر	precise *adj* درست
power *n* قوت	precision *n* درستي
powerful *adj* پياوري	precursor *n* شاتر
powerless *adj* بي زوره	predecessor *n* ورادبني
practical *adj* ملي	predicament *n* لالهندي
practice *n* عادت	predict *v* پیشگوپي وپل
practise *v* تمرپن	prediction *n* پیشگوپي
practising *adj* اغبزناک	predilection *n* خوښه
prairie *n* وينبانه	predisposed *adj* گرم
praise *v* ستاپلول	predominate *v* توافق لرل
praise *n* ستاپل	preempt *v* خند اچول
praiseworthy *adj* د ثنا ور	preface *n* سر لبک
prank *n* مستي	prefer *v* غوره گڼل
pray *v* دعا کول	preference *n* غوره توب
prayer *n* عبادت	prefix *n* مختارپ
preach *v* وعظ کول	pregnancy *n* امبندواري
preacher *n* خطیب	pregnant *adj* امبندواره
preaching *n* تبلیغ	prehistoric *adj* ما قبل التاریخ
preamble *n* سرپزه	prejudice *n* تعصب
precarious *adj* بي اتباره	preliminary *adj* لومړني

P

prelude n تمهيد

premature adj نا بالغه

premeditate v د مخه سنجول

premeditation n د مخه سوچ

premier adj صدر اعظم

premise n قضيه

premises n ودانۍ

premonition n احساس

preoccupation n د مخه نيونه

preparation n تياري

prepare v د مخه تيارول

preposition n د ربط توري

prerequisite n لازم

prerogative n امتياز

prescribe v توصيه

prescription n نسخه

presence n موجودیت

present adj حاضر

present v حاضر کول

presentation n سوغات

preserve v ساتل

preside v ریاست کول

presidency n ریاست

president n ولس مشر

press n تولنه، فشار

press v کیمندل، دربل

pressing adj بير گندۍ

pressure v فشارول

pressure n فشار

prestige n حیثیت

presume v گڼل

presumption n احتمالي

pretend v بهانه کول

pretense n ادعا

pretension n بهانه

pretty adj ښکلی

prevail v خپريدل

prevalent adj خپور

prevent v مخه نیول

prevention n بندیز

preventive adj بندونکی

preview n مخه لیدل

previous adj پخوانی

previously adv پخوا

prey n ښکار

price n بيه

pricey adj قيمتي

prick v چوخول

pride n کبر

priest n ملا

priestess n ملاگی

priesthood n ملايي

primacy n لومړي والي

primarily adv په اصل کې

prime adj غوره

primitive adj ساده

prince n	واكمن
princess n	شـهزادگۍ
principal adj	مدبر
principle n	لوی مشر
print v	چاپول
print n	چاپ
printer n	د چاپ ماشين
printing n	چاپونه
prior adj	پخانی
priority n	لومړی توب
prism n	منشور
prison n	جبل
prisoner n	بندي
privacy n	خلوت
private adj	شخصي
privilege n	امتياز
probability n	احتمال
probable adj	پنبدونكي
probe v	د جراحي مبل
probing n	پلټنه
problem n	كشاله
problematic adj	مشكوك
procedure n	كړنلار
proceed v	په مخ تلل
proceedings n	ازمبنت
proceeds n	گټه
process v	مرحله
process n	جريان

procession n	ډلبيز تګ
proclaim v	خرګندول
proclamation n	اعلاميه
procrastinate v	ټالول
procreate v	پيداكول
procure v	گټل
prod v	چوكول
prodigious adj	ډېر لوی
prodigy n	عجب
produce v	تولبدول
produce n	تولبد
product n	حاصل
production n	پيداوار
productive adj	گټور
profane adj	كفر وبل
profess v	اعتراف كول
profession n	كسب
professional adj	مسلكي
professor n	پوهاند
proficiency n	مهارت
proficient adj	ماهر
profile n	د نبم مخ تصوبر
profit v	گټه كول
profit n	گټه
profitable adj	گټور
profound adj	ژور پوه
program n	كړنلار
programmer n	پروگرامر

P

progress v ترقي كول	**prophet** n پيغمبر
progress n ترقي كول	**proportion** n تناسب
progressive adj مترقي	**proposal** n تجويز
prohibit v ستنول	**propose** v راندي كول
prohibition n مخنيوي	**proposition** n تجويز
project v پروژه	**prose** n نثر
project n پروژه	**prosecute** v پسي اخبستل
prologue n سريزه	**prosecutor** n څارنوال
prolong v اوږدول	**prospect** n ننداره
promenade n نخا	**prosper** v بربالي كېدل
prominent adj وتلي	**prosperity** n بربالتوب
promiscuous adj ګډوډ	**prosperous** adj بربالي
promise n وعده	**prostate** n را تول کر شوى
promote v پورته كول	**prostrate** adj نسكور
promotion n ترفع	**protect** v ساتل
prompt adj چټک	**protection** n دفاع
prone adj كوږ	**protein** n پروتين
pronoun n ضمير	**protest** v احتجاج كول
pronounce v تلفظ كول	**protest** n احتجاج
proof n ثبوت	**protocol** n پروتوكول
propaganda n تبليغات	**prototype** n اصلي نمونه
propagate v زياتول	**protract** v غزول
propel v شړل	**protracted** adj پراخ
propensity n تمايل	**protrude** v پراخول
proper adj وړ	**proud** adj مغرور
properly adv په مناسب ډول	**proudly** adv په غرور
property n بنه سلوک	**prove** v ثابتول
prophecy n پيشګويي	**proven** adj وچ وابنه

proverb n متل	**pudding** n پودېن
provide v تپارول	**puerile** adj چتپ
province n ولاېت	**puff** n پاستپ
provision n تپارې	**puffy** adj پوکونکپ
provisional adj موقتپ	**pull** v کشکول
provocation n لمسون	**pull ahead** v مخامخ کپدل
provoke v لمسول	**pull down** v ورانول
prowl v تلاش	**pull out** v ننوپستل
prowler n سپورپ	**pulley** n څرخه
proximity n خپلوپ	**pulp** n شپره
proxy n وکالت	**pulpit** n درپځ
prudence n سنجش	**pulsate** v غورځپدل
prudent adj هوښنپار	**pulse** n نپض
prune v پرپکول	**pulverize** v مبده کول
prune n اصلاح	**pump** v بمبه کول
prurient adj شپوانپ	**pump** n بمبه
pseudonym n جعلپ نوم	**pumpkin** n کدو
psychiatrist n عصبپ ډاکتر	**punctual** adj په وعدپ ټپنگ
psychic adj روحپ	**puncture** n پنچر
psychology n اروا پوهپ	**punish** v جزا ورکول
psychopath n دماغپ حلل	**punishable** adj د جزا ور
puberty n پلوغ	**punishment** n جزا
public adj عام	**pupil** n پوه
publication n نشرېه	**puppet** n نانځکه
publicity n اعلان	**puppy** n کوچنپ سپپ
publicly adv په عمومپ ډول	**purchase** v رانپول
publish v عامول	**purchase** n رانپول
publisher n ناشر	**pure** adj صاف

P

puree n صافي كول

purgatory n اعراف

purge n پاكي

purge v پاكول

purification n تصفیه

purify v پاكول

purity n مبنځل

purple adj ارغواني

purpose n پلان

purposely adv په قصدي ډول

purse n بټوه

pursue v نبول، تعقبول

pursuit n پسې كېدنه

pus n زوه

push v زور وركول

pushy adj جابر

put iv ابښودل

put aside v ساتل

put away v ضایع كول

put off v ټالول

put out v ځندول

put up v نغول

put up with v كالل

putrid adj خوسا

puzzle n ارپانول

pyramid n هرمه

Q

quagmire n جبه

quail n مرز

quake v لرزېدل

qualify v قبدول

quality n مقام

qualm n وسواس

quandery n لالهندي

quantity n مقدار

quarrel v کبله كول

quarrel n کبله

quarrelsome adj جګره مار

quarry n ښکار

quarter n څلورمه برخه

quarters n کور جورونه

queen n ملكه

queer adj عجیب

quell v لاندي كول

quench v وژل

quest n ښکار

question v پوښتنه

question n پوښتنه

questionable adj مشكوك

questionnaire n پوښتنلیک

queue n كوثب

quick adj چتک

quicken *v* ژوند وركول	rebellion *n* بغاوت
quickly *adv* په بيره	rebound *v* بېرته راګرځېدل
quicksand *n* لمدي شګې	rebuff *v* مخ نيونه، ردول
quiet *adj* غلې	rebuff *n* منع كول
quietness *n* چپتيا	rebuild *v* بيا ودانول
quilt *n* برستن	rebuke *v* ملامتول
quit *iv* ترك كول	rebuke *n* شرمول
quite *adv* ببخي	rebut *v* ردول
quiver *v* لړزېدل	recall *v* رابلل
quiz *v* ازموېل	recant *v* پښېمان كېدل
quotation *n* نقل	recap *v* خلاصه
quote *v* رانقلول	recapture *v* بيانيول
quotient *n* وېش	recede *v* په شت كېدل
	receipt *n* رسيد
	receive *v* نيول
	recent *adj* تازه
R	reception *n* مبلمه پالنه
	receptionist *n* مبلمه پالوونكی
	receptive *adj* موندونكی
rear *n* شت	recess *n* تفربح
rear *adj* سموالی	recession *n* تركول
reason *v* دليل	recharge *v* تازه
reason *n* دليل	recipe *n* نسحه
reasoning *n* دليل	reciprocal *adj* متقابل
reassure *v* ارامول	recital *n* بيان
rebate *n* تپتونه	recite *v* بيانول
rebel *v* باغي كېدل	reckless *adj* بې باكي
rebel *n* باغي كېدل	reckon *v* شمېرل

---

reckon on v اعتماد کول	**rectangle** n مستطیل
reclaim v پبا ادعا کول	**rectangular** adj مستطیل شکله
recline v کږبدل	**rectify** v سمول
recluse n صوفي	**rector** n د پوهنتون رئیس
recognition n پیژندنه	**rectum** n اندرنه
recognize v پیژندل	**recuperate** v پورته کبدل
recollect v را په زړه کبدل	**recur** v په یاد کبدل
recollection n حافظه	**recurrence** n ستنبدنه
recommend v ستایل	**recycle** v خوندي کول
recompense v تاوان ورکول	**red** adj سور
recompense n تاوان ورکونه	**redden** v سور کبدل
reconcile v پخلا کول	**redeem** v بیا اخیستل
reconsider v بیا کتل	**redemption** n خلاصونه
reconstruct v بیا ودانول	**red-hot** adj ډیر قوي
record v ثبتول	**redo** v خور ورمه
record n ثبت، خوندي	**redouble** v غبرګول
recorder n ثبتونکی	**redress** v سمول
recording n نمونه	**reduce** v کمول
recount n حال وینه	**redundant** adj ډیر زیات
recoup v تاوان اخیستل	**reed** n شپیلی
recourse v مرسته کول	**reef** n ګاره
recourse n مرسته	**reel** n سکاټلبندي نخا
recovery n نوی کول	**reelect** v بیا ټکل
recreate v بیا پیداکول	**reenactment** n بدلون
recreation n بیا پیداپنبت	**reentry** n دوباره کتنه
recruit v جلبول	**refer to** v سلا مشوره کول
recruit n نوي عسکر	**referee** n منصف
recruitment n استخدام	**reference** n مرجع

refill v ببا ډکول	regeneration n بیا زیږیدنه، نوی
refinance v اقتصادی	regent n د پاچا نایب
refine v چنل	regime n رژبم
refinery n تصفیه خانه	regiment n کنډک
reflect v ښکاره کول	region n سبمه
reflection n فکر	regional adj سبمه ایز
reflexive adj گرامر لازمی	register v ثبتبدل
reform v سمول	registration n نوم لبکنه
reform n سم	regret v خوشبنې
refrain v ډډه کول	regret n
refresh v ببا تازه کول	regrettable adj د خواشبنې وړ
refreshing adj ببا تازه والې	regularity n سمون
refrigerate v بخول	regularly adv په منظم ډول
refuel v ببا ډکول	regulate v سمول
refuge n سبب	regulation n قاعده
refugee n مهاجر	rehabilitate v ببا ودانول
refund v ببرته ورکول	rehearsal n تمرېن
refund n ببرته ورکونه	rehearse v تمرېن کول
refurbish v ستنول	reign v پاچاهي کول
refusal n انکار کونه	reign n عصر
refuse v رده ول	reimburse v ببا ادا کول
refuse n رده ونه	reimbursement n ادا کونه
refute v غلط ثابتول	rein v ملونه
regal adj شاهانه	rein n کبزه کول
regard v په خبر کتل	reindeer n گاوزه
regarding pre په باره کې	reinforce v تقوبه کول
regardless adv بې پامه	reinforcements n تقوبه کونه
regards n درناوې	reiterate v زباتول

R

reject v نه منل	**relocate** v منتقل کېدل
rejection n نه منه	**relocation** n منتقل کېدنه
rejoice v خوشاله کول	**reluctant** adj بې مېنې
rejoin v بیا بو ځای کېدل	**reluctantly** adv په بې مېلي
rejuvenate v پیا تازه کول	**rely on** v باور کول
relapse n بیا ککړېدل	**remain** v پاتې کېدل
related adj وبل شوې	**remainder** n پاتې شونکې
relationship n خپلوې	**remaining** adj پاتې شونې
relative adj خپنې	**remains** n باقي پاتې
relative n موصول	**remake** v کتل
relax v سپاله	**remark** v نبنه کول
relaxation n دمه نېونه	**remark** n نبنه
relaxing adj ستړیاوالی	**remarkable** adj فوق العاده
relay v بدلول	**remarry** v بیا واده کول
release v اېله کول	**remedy** v درمل کول
relegate v شړل	**remedy** n درمل
relent v نرمېدل	**remember** v یادول
relentless adj بې رحمه	**remembrance** n یاد
relevant adj ور	**remind** v ور په یادول
reliable adj باورې	**reminder** n یادونه
reliance n باور	**remission** n بښنه
relic n مقدسات	**remit** v بښل
relief n مرسته	**remittance** n وربښنه
religion n دېن	**remnant** n پاتې
religious adj دېنې	**remodel** v بیا جوړول
relinquish v لاس اخېستل	**remorse** n افسوس
relish v خوند	**remorseful** adj پښېمان
relive v بیا پیدا کېدل	**remote** adj لرې

R

removal *n* بې ځايه کېدنه	replica *n* ورته
remove *v* بې ځايه کول	replicate *v* کټ مټ کول
remunerate *v* ادا کول	reply *v* ځواب ورکول
renew *v* نوي کول	reply *n* ځواب
renewal *n* نوي توب	report *v* خبرول
renounce *v* پرېښودل	report *n* راپور
renovate *v* جوړول	reportedly *adv* په فرضي ډول
renovation *n* جوړونه	reporter *n* خبريال
renowned *adj* نامتو	repose *v* تکيه کول
rent *v* درز	repose *n* تکيه
rent *n* کرايه	represent *v* ښودل
reorganize *v* بيا جوړول	repress *v* بندول
repair *v* ترميمول	repression *n* فشار
reparation *n* ترميم	reprieve *n* ټالول
repatriate *v* کور ته تلل	reprint *v* بيا چاپول
repay *v* ادا کول	reprint *n* بيا چاپول
repayment *n* ادا کونه	reprisal *n* برغمل
repeal *v* لبري کول	reproach *v* سپکول
repeal *n* ابستنه	reproach *n* سپکونه
repeat *v* بيا وبل	reproduce *v* بيا تولېدول
repel *v* تر شا کول	reproduction *n* بيا زېږونه
repent *v* توبه کول	reptile *n* خزنده
repentance *n* توبه	republic *n* جمهوريت
repetition *n* تکرار	repudiate *v* نه منل
replacement *n* په ځای کول	repugnant *adj* نا وړه
replay *n* ځواب ورکول	repulse *v* پورې وهل
replenish *v* بيا ډکول	repulse *n* پورې وهنه
replete *adj* موړ	repulsive *adj* پېړي کونکې

R

reputation *n* شهرت	**resort** *v* ورتلل
reputedly *adv* په فرضي ډول	**resounding** *adj* لوړ
request *v* غوښتنه کول	**resource** *n* توښه
request *n* غوښتنه	**respect** *v* عزت کول
require *v* غوښتل	**respect** *n* عزت
requirement *n* اړتیا	**respectful** *adj* محترم
rescue *v* ژغورل	**respective** *adj* خان خانې
rescue *n* ژغورنه	**respiration** *n* سا اخیستنه
research *v* څېړنه کول	**respite** *n* ټالونه
research *n* څېړنه	**respond** *v* ځوابول
resemblance *n* ورته والی	**response** *n* ځواب
resemble *v* ورته والی	**responsibility** *n* مسولیت
resent *v* خپه کېدل	**responsible** *adj* مسول
resentment *n* کرکه	**responsive** *adj* ځواب ورکونکې
reservation *n* ساتنه	**rest** *v* پاتې کول
reserve *v* ساتل	**rest** *n* پاتې
reservoir *n* د اوبو ذخیره	**rest room** *n* تشناب
reside *v* اوسېدل	**restaurant** *n* خورن ځای
residence *n* کور	**restful** *adj* ارام ورکونکې
residue *n* پاتې شونې	**restitution** *n* ورستوونه
resign *v* استعفا ورکول	**restless** *adj* نا ارام
resignation *n* استعفا	**restoration** *n* بیا تولیدونه
resilient *adj* غزېدونکې	**restore** *v* په ځټ کول
resist *v* ټېنګار کول	**restrain** *v* خان ساتل
resistance *n* ټېنګار	**restraint** *n* ډیډه
resolute *adj* کلک	**restrict** *v* ابسارول
resolution *n* پرېکړه	**result** *n* نتیجه
resolve *v* بیلول	**resumption** *n* له سره نیونه

R

resurface v په بادبدل	reverse n خت
resurrection n د قیامت ورخ	reversible adj نسکوروالی
resuscitate v بیا ژوندي کول	revert v ستنبدل
retain v ساتل	review v بیا کتل
retaliate v بدله اخیستل	review n دسره کتنه
retaliation n بدله	revise v کره کول
retarded adj پخوالی	revision n بیاکتنه
retention n ساتنه	revive v بیا سبک اخبستل
retire v شاته کبدل کبدل	revoke v لری کول
retirement n شاته کبدنه	revolt v بلوا کول
retract v ببرته ننوتل	revolt n بلوا
retreat v په شا کبدل	revolting adj وبروونکپ
retreat n په شا کبدنه	revolve v خرخبدل
retrieval n بیا غوښتنه	revolver v خرخپ تمانچه
retrieve v موندل	revue n ملندپ
retroactive adj	revulsion n ناخاپپ
return v راگرخبدل	reward v بدله ورکول
return n راگرخبدنه	reward n بدله
reunion n بیا بو ځای کبدنه	rewarding adj بدله ورکونکپ
reveal v ښکاره کول	rheumatism n روماتبزم
revealing adj ښکاروالپ	rhyme n قافیه
revel v چرچپ کول	rhythm n وزن
revelation n خرگندونه	rib n پوښتی
revenge v غچ اخبستل	ribbon n رشمه
revenge n غچ	rice n وربجپ
revenue n فایده	rich adj ښتمن
reverence n درناوپ	rid of iv نجات حاصلول
reversal n بدلون	riddle n غلبپل

R

ride iv	سوربدل
ridge n	دغونډپو لړ
ridicule v	ربشخند وهل
ridicule n	ملنډي
ridiculous adj	ربشخند
rifle n	توپک
rift n	چاک
right adv	په مناسب ډول
right adj	نغ، وړ
right n	سموالي
rigid adj	ټينګ
rigor n	شدت
rim n	ژۍ، څنډه
ring iv	کړۍ کول
ring n	ګوتمۍ، احاطه
ringleader n	ډله مشر
rinse v	کنګالول
riot v	بلوا کول
riot n	بلول
rip v	شکول
rip apart v	ماتول
rip off v	غولول
ripe adj	پوخ
ripen v	پخېدل
rise iv	پورته کېدل
risk v	خطر کې اچول
risk n	خطر
risky adj	خطر ناک

rite n	دستور
rival n	سيالي کول
rivalry n	سيالي
river n	سيند
rivet v	مېخ کول
riveting adj	مېخ کونه
road n	سړک
roam v	چتې ګرزېدنه
roar v	غړمبېدل
roar n	غوربدنه
roast v	وربتول
roast n	وربته
rob v	لوټا
robber n	غل
robbery n	غلا
robe n	جامې
robust adj	قوي
rock n	پرښه
rocket n	توغنډپ
rocky adj	ډبربن
rod n	سبخ
rodent n	چک وهونکپ
roll v	کولول
romance n	د الانو کبسه
roof n	بام
room n	کوټه، چانس
roomy adj	ارت
rooster n	چرګ

R

root n ريښه	**rudimentary** adj بنبادي
rope n رسۍ	**rug** n غټه
rosary n تسپې	**ruin** v ورانې کول
rose n ګلاب	**ruin** n ورانې کول
rosy adj ګلابي	**rule** v امر چلول
rot v خوسا کېدل	**rule** n قانون
rot n خوساکېدنه	**ruler** n واکمن، امبر
rotate v څرخول	**rum** n شراب
rotation n څرخ	**rumble** v غورېدل
rotten adj زرزست	**rumble** n غورهار
rough adj زبر	**rumor** n انګازه
round adj غونډارې	**run** iv منډه وهل
roundup n پنډونه	**run away** v تښتېدل
rouse v پاڅول	**run into** v وهل
rousing adj پاڅونه	**run out** v پاې ته رسول
route n لار	**run over** v ټوټه ټوټه کول
routine n ورځنۍ کار	**run up** v تولول
row v څمڅې وهل	**runner** n سبال
row n شور ما شور	**rupture** n چاودنه
rowdy adj پتنه ګر	**rupture** v چول
royal adj شاهانه	**rural** adj کلیوالي
royalty n پاچاهي	**ruse** n ټګي
rub v سولول	**rush** v تلوار کول
rubber n ربړ	**Russia** n روس
rubbish n خزلې	**Russian** adj روسان
ruby n لعل	**rust** v زنګ کول
rude adj شډل	**rust** n زنګ
rudeness n شډلوالي	**rustic** adj شډل

R

بنـدونکی rust-proof *adj*

زنگ وهلي rusty *adj*

بې رحمه ruthless *adj*

جودر rye *n*

S

ورانكاري كول sabotage *v*

تخريب sabotage *n*

ابستل، رخصتول sack *v*

بوجی، جوال sack *n*

دبنې دود sacrament *n*

قرباني sacrifice *n*

ددين سپكاوې sacrilege *n*

خپه sad *adj*

خپه كول sadden *v*

زين saddle *n*

ظالم شهواتي sadist *n*

خپګان sadness *n*

خوندي safe *adj*

ساتل safeguard *n*

ساتنه safety *n*

بېرې چلول sail *v*

بادوان sail *n*

بادواني بېرۍ sailboat *n*

مانو sailor *n*

پير saint *n*

سلاته salad *n*

تنخواه salary *n*

لبلام sale *n*

بازاري چكر sale slip *n*

دوكاندار salesman *n*

لارې saliva *n*

لوپه خوفه saloon *n*

مالګه salt *n*

مالګين salty *adj*

خلاصونه salvation *n*

ورته same *adj*

نمونه sample *n*

پاكول sanctify *v*

منظورول sanction *v*

مننه sanction *n*

پاكوالي sanctity *n*

جومات sanctuary *n*

شګه sand *n*

څپلۍ sandal *n*

ربګ مال sandpaper *n*

سېندوېچ sandwich *n*

معقول sane *adj*

معقولبت sanity *n*

شېن saphire *n*

پېغور sarcasm *n*

د پېغور sarcastic *adj*

sardine *n* خبنتپ	scan *v* په غور کتل
satanic *adj* شېطاني	scandal *n* تور لګونه
satellite *n* چوپړی	scandalize *v* تور لګول
satire *n* ملنډي	scapegoat *n* د قرباني ګډوری
satisfaction *n* قناعت	scar *n* داغ
satisfactory *adj* د تسل وړ	scarce *adj* لږ
satisfy *v* راضي کول	scarcely *adv* په لږوالي
saturate *v* ډکول	scarcity *n* لږوالي
Saturday *n* خالي	scare *v* ډارول
sauce *n* چکنپ	scare *n* ډار
saucepan *n* ارکاره	scare away *v* ویره ول
saucer *n* نالبکپ	scarf *n* زروکی
savage *adj* وحشي	scary *adj* ډارونکپ
savagery *n* وحشت	scatter *v* پاشل
save *v* ساتل	scenario *n* د فلم کېسه
savings *n* خوندپ	scene *n* پرده، ننداره
savior *n* بچونکپ	scenic *adj* د نندارې
savor *v* خوند	scent *n* بوبول
saw *iv* اره کول	sceptic *adj* بل ډول
saw *n* متل	schedule *v* پروگرام جوړول
say *iv* وبل	schedule *n* تقسیم اوقات
saying *n* متل	scheme *n* پلان، جدول
scaffolding *n* خوازه	schism *n* جلا کېدنه
scald *v* ابشول	scholar *n* پوه
scale *v* اندازه کول	scholarship *n* سکالرشپ
scale *n* پوستکپ، وېش	school *n* ښوونخپ
scalp *n* د سر پوستکپ	science *n* پوهه
scam *n* لوچک	scientific *adj* علمپ

S

ساينس پوه n **scientist**	اړول، کړول v **screw**
بباتي n **scissors**	پيچ n **screw**
لنډې وهل v **scoff**	پيچ تاو n **screwdriver**
ښکنځل کول v **scold**	سرسري ليکل v **scribble**
ښکنځل کبدل n **scolding**	لاسي لېک n **script**
سکوټر n **scooter**	ملاتفه n **scroll**
غابه n **scope**	مينل v **scrub**
وچول v **scorch**	ضمير n **scruples**
پور n **score**	وسواسي adj **scrupulous**
شمېرل v **score**	په څېر کتنه n **scrutiny**
،کرکه کول v **scorn**	لاس اچول v **scuffle**
د کرکې adj **scornful**	مجسمه جوړونه n **sculpture**
لرم n **scorpion**	سمندر n **sea**
لوچک n **scoundrel**	سمندري غذا n **seafood**
ژرژر ګرځېدل v **scour**	سگ لاهو n **seal**
په متروکه وهل n **scourge**	بخی n **seam**
څارندوې n **scout**	بې درزه adj **seamless**
ثبت والی adj **scrambled**	درزې n **seamstress**
ټوټه n **scrap**	پلټل v **search**
ټوټه کول v **scrap**	لټونه n **search**
پاکول v **scrape**	ساحل n **seashore**
ګروول v **scratch**	سمندري ناروغ adj **seasick**
پاکې n **scratch**	موسم n **season**
بغارې وهل v **scream**	موسمي adj **seasonal**
بغارې n **scream**	مساله n **seasoning**
چغې وهل v **screech**	د ناستې ځای n **seat**
پرده، جالی n **screen**	په سېټ ناستې adj **seated**
پرده نيول v **screen**	بېلبدل v **secede**

secluded adj کوبنه کېدنه	seize v نبول، لاندي کول
seclusion n کوبنه توب	seizure n نبونه
second n ثانیه	seldom adv غوره
secondary adj ثانوي	select v خونبول
secrecy n پټوالی	selection n خونبونه
secret n راز	self-concious adj شواره
secretary n منشي	self-esteem n وربا
secretly adv په پنه	self-evident adj روڼ
sect n فرقه	self-interest n خان ستاینه
section n برخه	selfish adj بې فکره
sector n قطاع	selfishness n غوره والب
secure v خوندي کول	self-respect n مغرور
secure adj ساتلب	sell iv خرخول
security n ساتنه	seller n خرخونکب
sedate v چپ	sellout n سپارل
sedation n بلوا	semblance n شکل
seduce v بې لاري کول	semester n سمستر
seduction n غولونکی	seminary n مدرسه
see iv لېدل	senate n د مشرانو جرګه
seed n زرب	senator n سناتور
seedless adj بې تخمه	send iv لېرل
seedy adj ناپاکي	sender n لېرونکب
seek iv لټول	senile adj بوڈا
seem v ښکارېدل	senior adj مشر
see-through adj روڼ	seniority n مقام
segment n برخه	sensation n احساس
segregate v بېلول	sense v حس کول
segregation n بېلتون	sense n تمیز، عقل

S

senseless *adj* بې حسه	session *n* غونډه
sensible *adj* هوښيار	set *n* ابنودنه
sensitive *adj* حساس	set *iv* ابنودل
sensual *adj* جسمي	set about *v* پيل کول
sentence *v* پربکړه	set off *v* پيل کبدل
sentence *n* جزا، جمله	set out *v* الوتکې ته ختل
sentiment *n* احساس	set up *v* لرى
sentimental *adj* نرې زړی	setback *n* تر شا کبدنه
sentry *n* پېره دار	setting *n* ابنسوونه
separate *v* بېلتون	settle *v* رسول، اداکول
separate *adj* بېل	settle down *v* سباله
separation *n* جلاوالى	settle for *v* د تجزېى له پاره
September *n* سپتمبر	settlement *n* استوګنه، بانډه
sequel *n* اثر	settler *n* لومړۍ کبدل
sequence *n* لړ	setup *n* مرکب
serene *adj* صاف	seven *adj* اووه
serenity *n* ارامي	seventeen *adj* اوولس
sergeant *n* دلګى مشر	seventh *adj* اووم
series *n* سلسله	seventy *adj* اويا
serious *adj* جدي، تینګ	sever *v* پرې کول
seriousness *n* جدي توب	several *adj* ېو څو
sermon *n* وعظ	severance *n* شکونه
serpent *n* مار	severe *adj* کلک، شدېد
serum *n* سبرم	severity *n* کلکوالى
servant *n* نوکر	sew *v* ګنډل
serve *v* نوکري کول	sewage *n* ناولې اوبه
service *n* کار	sewer *n* ګنډونکى
service *v* کار کول	sewing *n* ګنډنه

S

sex n جنس	**shattering** adj تس نس والي
sexuality n جنسي	**shave** v خربل
shabby adj زاړه	**she** pro هغه دا (بنځه)
shack n کوډله	**shear** iv پري کول
shackle n ځولنې	**shed** iv خپره
shade n سبوری، تتوالی	**sheep** n پسه
shadow n سبوری، تتوالی	**sheets** n څادر
shady adj سبورن	**shelf** n رپ
shake iv رپردول	**shell** n کاسه
shaken adj رپردونه	**shellfish** n کونب کبر
shaky adj خوځند	**shelter** v ساتل
shallow adj ګوګ	**shelter** n سر پټونی
sham n مر مر تلل	**shelves** n المارۍ
shambles n مسلح	**shepherd** n شپون
shame v شرمول	**shield** v ساتل
shame n شرم	**shield** n ډال سپر
shameful adj شرم ناک	**shift** n بدلون، بانه
shameless adj بې شرمه	**shift** v بدلول
shape v جوړول	**shine** iv څلبدل
shape n بڼه	**shiny** adj ځلاند
share v برخه	**ship** n بېرۍ
share n پاله، کره کپ	**shipment** n ازادونه
shareholder n ونډه وال	**shipwreck** n ماته بېرۍ
shark n ټګ	**shirk** v ډډه کول
sharp adj تبره، نغ	**shirt** n کمبس
sharpen v تبره کول	**shiver** v لرزېدل
sharpener n تیره کونکي	**shiver** n لرزېدنه
shatter v تس نس کول	**shock** v لرزه

S

shock n سترى، ولى	**shouting** n غالمغال
shocking adj ناوره	**shove** v تبل وهل
shoddy adj پلمه گر	**shove** n مندل
shoe n پينې	**shovel** n چارى
shoelace n غوټه کونه	**show** iv ښودل
shoepolish n د بتانو رنگ	**show off** v باټو
shoot iv وشتل، وار کول	**show up** v سپکول
shoot down v وژل	**showdown** n جگره
shop v سودا اخبستل	**shower** n څيه
shop n دوکان	**shrapnel** n بمې گولې
shoplifting n غلا	**shred** v ربښکى کول
shopping n خربدارى	**shred** n ربښکى
shore n ارم	**shrewd** adj زگ
short adj لند، پاتي	**shriek** v چغې وهل
shortage n کمى	**shriek** n چغې
shortcoming n عيب	**shrine** n روضه
shortcut n لنديز	**shrink** iv غونجېدل
shorten v لنډول	**shroud** n کفن
shorthand n لند ليک	**shrouded** adj دپوى پلى
shortlived adj ناپوره	**shrub** n بوټى
shortly adv دستي	**shrug** v اورې څنډل
shorts n لنډ	**shudder** n لرزه
shortsighted adj لنډ پارى	**shudder** v لرزبدل
shot n ډز، ستن	**shuffle** v گډوډول
shotgun n ښکارى ټوپک	**shun** v لرې کول
shoulder n اوږه	**shut** iv بندول
shout v چغې وهل	**shut off** v بنده ول
shout n چغې	**shuttle** v تلل او راتلل

S

shy *adj* شرمناک

shyness *n* شرم

sick *adj* ناروغ

sicken *v* ناروغول

sickening *adj* هیبتناکه

sickle *n* لور

sickness *n* رنځ

side *n* اړخ

sidestep *v* مخه نیول

sidewalk *n* ځنګلاره

sideways *adv* غیر مستقیم

siege *n* کلابندي

siege *v* ابسارول

sift *v* غلبیلول

sigh *n* اوسیلی

sigh *v* اوسیلی کول

sight *n* لید

sightseeing *v* سیاحت کول

sign *v* نښه کول

sign *n* نښه، رمز

signal *n* اشاره

signature *n* لاس لیک

significance *n* اهمیت

significant *adj* مهم

signify *v* نښیل

silence *n* چوپتیا

silence *v* کرارول

silent *adj* غلی

silhouette *n* نیم مخی

silk *n* ریښم

silly *adj* ساده

silver *n* سپین زر

silversmith *n* زرگر

silverware *n* کاچوغي

similar *adj* ورته

similarity *n* ورته والی

simmer *v* خوټیدل

simple *adj* ساده

simplicity *n* ساده توب

simplify *v* ساده کول

simply *adv* په ساده ډول

simulate *v* بنوول

simultaneous *adj* یو ځای

sin *v* گناه کول

sin *n* گناه

since *c* راهسې

since *pre* راپه دیخوا

since then *adv* په دې شان

sincere *adj* اصلي

sincerity *n* اخلاص

sinful *adj* گناه گار

sing *iv* بدلې ویل

singer *n* سندر غاړی

single *n* بواځی

single *adj* ځانګړی، یو

singlehanded *adj* بواځبوالی

singleminded *adj* باوري

singular *adj* مفرد

sinister *adj* شوم

sink *iv* ډوبېدل

sink in *v* ننوتل

sinner *n* گناه گار

sip *v* غړپ كول

sip *n* غړپ

sir *n* بناغلي

siren *n* د خطر زنگ

sirloin *n* بوټۍ

sissy *adj* كمرزوري

sister *n* خور

sister-in-law *n* نږبنه

sit *iv* كبنېناستل

site *n* ځای

sitting *n* تن په تن جنگ

situated *adj* محلي

situation *n* حالت

six *adj* شپږ

sixteen *adj* شپاړلس

sixth *adj* شپږم

sixty *adj* شپېته

sizable *adj* لر زبات

size *n* اندازه

size up *v* ټاكل

skeleton *n* خاكه ، سكلېت

skeptic *adj* شكمن

sketch *v* خاكه جوړول

sketch *n* خاكه

sketchy *adj* ساده

ski *v* دردنگ

smoothness *n* بنويوالى

smother *v* حفه كول

smuggler *n* قاچاق ورونكى

snail *n* اوبنېكى

snake *n* مار

snapshot *n* فوري عكس

snare *v* لومه نيول

snare *n* لومه

snatch *v* الوزول

sneak *v* خان ايستل

sneeze *v* پرنجېدل

sneeze *n* پرنجېدل

sniff *v* سوغول

sniper *n* غلا كول

snitch *v* پټول

snooze *v* سترگې پټول

snore *v* پرېشان ول

snore *n* خربدل

snow *v* واوره ورېدل

snow *n* واوره ورېدل

snowfall *n* واوري وريا

snowflake *n* خپركى

snub *v* تر ټل

snub *n* ترټنه

soak v خیشتول	**soldier** n سپاهي
soak in v ډوبیدل	**sold-out** adj خرڅلاو
soak up v جذب کول	**sole** n تله
soar v خوا ته ختل	**sole** adj تلل شوي
sob v سلګي وهل	**solely** adv تش
sob n سلګی	**solemn** adj مذهبي
sober adj سپما غري	**solicit** v زاري کول
so-called adj فرضي	**solid** adj کلک
sociable adj اجتماعي	**solitary** adj یواز ې
socialism n سوشیالبزم	**solitude** n یوازېتوب
socialist adj کمونست	**soluble** adj ویلي کېدونکی
socialize v اجتماعي	**solution** n محلول
society n ټولنه	**solve** v حل کول
sock n جورابه	**solvent** adj محلل
sod n شنیلی	**somber** adj تیاره
soda n سوډا	**some** adj څه اندازه
sofa n ګټکمی	**somebody** pro یو څوک
soft adj نرم پوست	**someday** adv مهم شخص
soften v نرمول	**somehow** adv په کومه لاره
softly adv په نرمی	**someone** pro یو څوک
softness n نرمي	**something** pro یو څه
soggy adj خیشت	**sometimes** adv ځینې وختونه
soil v خیرنول	**someway** adv په یوه لاره
soil n داغ پلمونی	**somewhat** adv یو څه
soiled adj خاوره	**son** n ځوي
solace n ډاډ ساتل	**song** n سندره
solar adj لمریز	**son-in-law** n زوم
solder v لیم کول	**soon** adv ژر

S

soothe v خاموش	**spacious** adj اورد
sorcerer n جادو گر	**spade** n چاری
sorcery n جادو	**Spain** n زيا تول
sore n درد	**span** v فاصله
sore adj دردمند	**span** n اوردوالی، توټه
sorrow n خفگان	**Spanish** adj هسپانوي
sorrowful adj له غمه ډک	**spank** v د ژبې ټکونه
sort n صنف يا ډول	**spanking** n پوره
sort out v بيل بيل كول	**spare** v بشپړول، تكميلول
soul n خوټبدل	**spare** adj مكمل
sound n شور، غالمغال	**spare part** n اضافي پرزې
sound v شور كول	**sparingly** adv پاملرنې سره
soup n بنـوروا	**spark** n ځلا
sour adj تريخ	**spark off** v د بم چاودنه
source n بنسټ	**sparkle** v ځلول
south n جنوبي قطب	**sparrow** n مرغي
southbound adv د جنوب سرحد	**sparse** adj نرى
southeast n جنوب ختيځ	**spasm** n كمبدنه
southern adj جنوبي	**speak** iv خبرې كول
southerner n جنوبي	**speaker** n ويوونكى
southwest n جنوب لوېديځ	**spear** n اشاره
souvenir n ځاي	**spearhead** v منظمول
sovereign adj سلطنتي	**special** adj ځانګړى
sovereignty n لوروالي	**specialize** v ځانګړى كول
sow iv سهيلي قطب	**specialty** n ځانګړتيا
spa n لمبدنه	**species** n درجه
space n ازادي	**specific** adj درست
space out v فاصله ساتل	**specimen** n مثال

S

speck n ټوټه	**spirit** n خوټېدل
spectacle n ښرګند	**spiritual** adj روحي
spectator n لیدونکي	**spit** iv د کباپ سیخ
speculate v حیراني	**spite** n کینه
speculation n نظریه	**spiteful** adj کینه ور
speech n کلام	**splash** v شیندل
speechless adj تندر وهلی	**splendid** adj ځلاند
speed iv سرعت	**splendor** n ځلاند
speed n سرعت	**splint** n مزری
speedily adv تېزي	**splinter** n نری اوږده دره
speedy adj تېز	**splinter** v ترازه بېلول
spell iv معنی کول	**split** n چاودلی
spell n معنی	**split** iv چول
spelling n معنی کونه	**spoil** v تالا کول
spend iv مصرفول	**spoils** n تالان
spending n مصرفېدنه	**sponge** n سپنج
sperm n سپرم	**sponsor** n ذمه وار
sphere n ساحه	**spontaneity** n بدهت
spice n علاقه	**spontaneous** adj پخپله
spicy adj ګرم	**spooky** adj سیوري
spider n غنه	**spool** n څرخ
spiderweb n د غني خاله	**spoon** n کاشقه
spill iv لوبدل	**spoonful** n یوه کاشقه
spill n لوبدنه	**sporadic** adj تیت و پرک
spin iv څرخول، چورلول	**sport** n بدني روزنه
spine n وروسته	**sportman** n ورزش کار
spineless adj خواشینوونکی	**sporty** adj لباسي
spinster n مجرد	**spot** v داغ لګول

S

spot n خال، نښه	**stab** n پرهار
spotless adj بې داغه	**stability** n ثبات
spotlight n ترهِ رڼا	**stable** adj ټینگ
spouse n میره	**stable** n غوجل
sprain v اوبنـتل	**stack** v پر ځای ولاړ
sprawl v شواړ	**stack** n کوټ
spray v مندکی	**staff** n ګروپ
spread iv توپیر، پوښ	**stage** n صحنه، ستیج
spring iv ټوپ وهل، کریدل	**stage** v دریځ
spring n لښته	**stagger** v رنگ بنگ کېدل
sprinkle v شیندل	**staggering** adj حیرانونکي
sprout v تبغ وهل	**stagnant** adj درېدلی
spruce up v سینگار کول	**stagnation** n لتي
spur v پونده کول	**stain** v داغ کول،
spur n نوکه، څوکه	**stain** n رټه کول
spy v څارل	**stair** n زینه
spy n جاسوس	**staircase** n د زینې پاڼکی
squalid adj خیرن	**stairs** n زینه
squander v بخایه خرڅول	**stake** n موری، ستن
square adj څلور ګوتیز	**stake** v برید ټاکل
square n مربع	**stale** adj باسي
squash v نری غاړی کډو	**stalemate** n بندیز لګونه
squeak v چغبدل	**stalk** v خپ خپ تلل
squeaky adj چغنده	**stalk** n ډنډ
squeamish adj کارجن	**stall** n غوجل
squeeze v کښپکښنل	**stall** v درول
squirrel n موږک	**stammer** v ترى ترى کېدل
stab v سوری کول	**stamp** v اوره کول

stamp n ختنه	**stationery** n قرطاسیه
stampede n تپنبته	**statistic** n احسایوي
stand iv دربدل	**statue** n مجسمه
stand n دربدنه	**status** n دریځ، موقف
stand for v دلالت کول	**statute** n قانون، منشور
stand up v ودربدل	**staunch** adj قوي
standardize v معیاري	**stay** v پاتې کېدل
standing n نبغ	**stay** n مخه نیول
standpoint n نظر	**steady** adj ثبات، ټینګ
standstill adj ټال	**steak** n بوټی
staple v اساسي	**steal** iv غلا کول
staple n اساسي برخه	**stealthy** adj غلا
stapler n ستپلر	**steam** n براس
star n ستورک	**steel** n پولاد
starch n بت	**steep** adj ستوغ
starchy adj ډیر تشریفاتي	**stem** n ډډ
stark adj په ځیر کتنه	**stem** v را ولاړېدل
start v پیل کول	**stench** n ډوزمه
start n پیل	**step** n قدم، پل، مرحله
startle v زیري کول	**step out** v پر مختګ
startled adj زیري ورکونه	**step up** v اصلاح کول
starvation n لوږه	**stepbrother** n میري زی
starve v لوږه ګالل	**step-by-step** adv قدم په قدم
state n حالت، دریځ	**stepdaughter** n پرکتی
state v موقف	**stepfather** n پلندر
statement n وینا	**stepladder** n زینه
station n اډه	**stepmother** n میره
stationary adj ځای په ځای	**stepsister** n ناسکه خور

S

stepson *n* پرکټی	**stingy** *adj* کنجوس
sterile *adj* شنډ	**stink** *iv* ورم کول
sterilize *v* تغقیم کول	**stink** *n* ورم
stern *n* سخت	**stinking** *adj* بوین
stern *adj* ثابت	**stipulate** *v* ترون کول
sternly *adv* په تینگه	**stir** *v* لرل، خوځول
stew *n* وبشنه	**stir up** *v* تاو راتاو
stewardess *n* میلمه پال	**stitch** *n* ټک
stick *n* لنبته	**stock** *v* ډډ
stick *iv* ټومبدل	**stock** *n* ببرا، احمق
stick around *v* انتظار کول	**stocking** *n* اورده جرابه
stick out *v* زغم	**stockroom** *n* ګودام
stick to *v* وفا دار پاتي کیدل	**stoic** *adj* صبر ناک
sticker *n* ستېکر	**stomach** *n* ګېده
sticky *adj* لوند	**stone** *n* کاڼی
stiff *adj* شخ	**stone** *v* تیره ویشتل
stiffen *v* شخول	**stool** *n* کتکی
stiffness *n* کلکوالی	**stop** *v* ټالول
stifle *v* خپه کول	**stop** *n* ټال
stifling *adj* شدید	**stop by** *v* نا څاپي درېدنه
still *adj* ولاړ	**storage** *n* ساتنځی
still *adv* بې حرکته	**store** *v* انبارول
stimulant *n* پاروونکی	**store** *n* ذخیره
stimulate *v* پارول	**stork** *n* لګ لګ
stimulus *n* محرک	**storm** *n* توپان
sting *iv* چیچل	**stormy** *adj* توپاني
sting *n* نېش وهل	**story** *n* کیسه، نقل
stinging *adj* سخت	**stove** *n* ایشتوب

straight adj سم	**stretcher** n تسکیره
straighten out v سیده کیدل	**strict** adj درست
strain v خرابول	**stride** iv اوردہ گامونه
strain n خراب	**strife** n جگړه
strained adj خراب شوی	**strike** n وهل
strainer n غلبیل	**strike** iv لګېدل، اچول
strait n تنگ	**strike out** v ختمول
stranded adj معیاري	**strike up** v ساز غږول
strange adj قوي	**striking** adj د پام وړ
stranger n قویتر	**string** n تار، مزی
strangle v خپه کول	**stringent** adj تینگ
strap n سمه	**strip** n بربنډ
strategy n تګلاره	**strip** v بربنډېدل
straw n پروړه	**stripe** n لیکه
strawberry n څمکنی توت	**striped** adj لیکې
stray adj سرگردان	**strive** iv هاند کول
stray v لاره ورکول	**stroke** n گذار، وار
stream n ویاله، روانب	**stroll** v قدم وهل
street n کوڅه	**strong** adj غبنتلی
streetcar n واگون	**structure** n جوړښت
streetlight n د کوڅې څراغ	**struggle** v غبنتلی
strength n توان	**struggle** n کوشش
strengthen v تینگوالی	**stub** n سته، کونده
strenuous adj تکړه	**stubborn** adj ارم
stress n زور، فشار	**student** n زده کوونکی
stressful adj زورور	**study** v مطالعه
stretch n غزېدنه	**stuff** n اومه مواد، اصل
stretch v غزول	**stuff** v توک وهل

stuffing *n* د ډکولو مواد

stuffy *adj* تر بوخته

stumble *v* ښوئېدل

stun *v* بې هوښه کول

stupendous *adj* مشهور

stupid *adj* بېرا

stupidity *n* حماقت

sturdy *adj* مزی

stutter *v* توری کښدل

style *n* ډول

subdue *v* برې موندل

subdued *adj* بې خونده

subject *v* اهل، رعیت

subject *n* تر لاس لاندي

sublime *adj* د برم خاوند

submerge *v* ډوبول

submissive *adj* منونکی

submit *v* تسلیمول

subpoena *v* جلبول

subpoena *n* اخطار لیک

subscribe *v* لاس لیک کول

subscription *n* بسپنه

subsequent *adj* ورورستنی

subsidiary *adj* کومکي

subsidize *v* مرسته کول

subsidy *n* مالي مرسته

subsist *v* پایېدل

substance *n* جوهر

substantial *adj* تومنه

substitute *v* بدل

substitute *n* بدلون

subtitle *n* وروکی اعنوان

subtle *adj* نازک

subtract *v* لرول

subtraction *n* لرونه

suburb *n* د ښار شا و خوا

success *n* برې

successful *adj* په بریالی توګه

successor *n* خلف

succulent *adj* اوبلن

succumb *v* غاړه ایښودل

such *adj* داسې

suck *v* رودل

sucker *adj* ودونکی

sudden *adj* ناڅاپي

suddenly *adv* ناڅاپه

sue *v* عریضه کول

suffer *v* کالل

suffer from *v* تکلیف کې اخته

suffering *n* درد

sufficient *adj* کافي

sugar *n* بوره

suggest *v* تجویز کول

suggestion *n* تجویز

suggestive *adj* اشاره کوونکی

suicide *n* ځان وژنه

S

suit n غوښتنه	superstition n خرافات
suitable adj ور	supervise v څارل
suitcase n بکس	supervision n څارنه
sullen adj تغمه ناک	supper n د ماښام ډوډۍ
sulphur n ګوګړ	supple adj نه ماتېدووکی
sum n اندازه	supplier n برابروونکی
sum up v لندول	supplies n رسونه
summarize v خلاصه	supply v بشپړول
summary n لنډیز	support v ساتل
summer n اوړی	supporter n ملا ساتوونکب
summit n څوکه	suppose v ګڼل
summon v بلل	supposing c فرضآ
sumptuous adj ګران	supposition n فرضیه
sun n لمر	suppress v ځپل
sunburn n لمر وهلی	supremacy n پورته والی
Sunday n یکشنبه	supreme adj ستر
sundown n لمر پربواته	sure adj یقیني
sunken adj ډوب	surely adv په یقیي توګه
sunny adj پتاوی	surf v اضافي قیمت
sunrise n لمر خاته	surface n مخ
sunset n لمر لوېده	surge n بوره
superb adj برم لروونکی	surgeon n جراح
superfluous adj پالتو	surgical adv د جراحي
superior adj لوړ	surname n د کورنۍ نوم
superiority n لوړ والی	surpass v لوروالي
supermarket n لوی پلورنځی	surplus n پاتب شونب
superpower n لوی طاقت	surprise v نا څا په یخای
supersede v ځاي نیونه	surprise n ارین

S

surrender v غاړره ایښودنه	sweat v خولې کول
surrender n سپارل	sweater n خوله کوونکی
surround v چاپېرول	Sweden n سویس
surroundings n احط کوا	Sweedish adj سویس
surveillance n څارنه	sweep iv جارو کول
survey n سروی	sweet adj خوږ
survival n پیاښت	sweeten v خوږول
survive v پیاښت	sweetheart n معشوقه
susceptible adj ور	sweetness n خوږوالی
suspect v تور لګول	sweets n خواږه
suspect n تورن	swell iv پړسېدل
suspend v ځندول	swelling n پړسوب
suspense n امید	swift adj ګړندی
suspension n ټال	swim iv لامبو وهل
suspicion n شک	swimmer n لامبوزن
suspicious adj شکمن	swimming n لامبل
sustain v ساتل	swindle v غلول
sustenance n خواړه	swindle n شوکمار
swallow v تېرول	swindler n دوکه باز
swamp n جبه	swing iv زنګېدل
swamped adj سیلاب	swing n زنګېدا، ټال
swan n قاز	Swiss adj سویسي
swap v مبادله کول	switch v لنبته
swap n مبادله	switch n تنی
swarm n سیل	switch off v پند
sway v څنګېدل	switch on v چالان
swear iv لوړه کول	Switzerland n سویزرلاینډ
sweat n خولې	swivel v چورلکه

swollen *adj* پړسېدلی
sword *n* توره
swordfish *n* يو ډول ماهي
syllable *n* هجا
symbol *n* ننبه
symbolic *adj* ايز ننبه
symmetry *n* تناظر
sympathize *v* خواخوږي کول
sympathy *n* خواخوږي
symphony *n* تال
symptom *n* علامه
synagogue *n* يهودانو جومات
synchronize *v* برابرول
synod *n* د کليسا جرګه
synonym *n* مترادف
synthesis *n* ترکيب
syphilis *n* اتسک
syringe *n* يو ډول پېچکاري
syrup *n* شربت
system *n* نظام
systematic *adj* منظم

T

table *n* مېز
tablecloth *n* مېز پوښ
tablespoon *n* کاشوقه
tablet *n* دره، ګولۍ
tack *n* مېخ
tackle *v* نيول
tact *n* وخت پېژندنه
tactful *adj* مهارت
tactical *adj* چالباز
tactics *n* جګړه وهنه
tag *n* تکټ
tail *n* لکۍ
tail *v* لکۍ
tailor *n* ګنډونکی
tainted *adj* ناولي شوي
take *iv* نيول
take apart *v* برخه اخيستل
take away *v* لاره نيول
take back *v* بېرته راتلل
take in *v* داخل ته تلل
take out *v* بهر ته تلل
take over *v* وظيفه بدلول
tale *n* کيسه
talent *n* استعداد
talk *v* خبرې

S
T

talkative adj کپاو	**tasty** adj خوندور
tall adj اورد	**tax** n تور لګول
tame v روړدی	**tea** n چای
tangent n مماس	**teach** iv ښوودل
tangerine n کینو	**teacher** n ښوونکی
tangible adj واقعي	**team** n ډله
tangle n سره، اوښتل	**teapot** n چائینک
tank n تانک	**tear** iv اوښکه، غوخول
tanned adj خورورکونه	**tear** n اوښکه
tantamount to adj برابر	**tearful** adj ژراند
tantrum n ناخاپي غصه	**tease** v څیرل
tap n چوښکه	**teaspoon** n کاشوقه
tap into v چوښکول	**technical** adj فني
tap into n چوښکونه	**technicality** n تخنیکي
tape recorder n تیپ ریکارډر	**technician** n تخنیکګر
tapestry n چکن شوپ پرده	**technique** n اصول
tar n قیر	**technology** n تیکنالوژي
tarantula n غوندی	**tedious** adj ستومانوونکی
tardy adv سوست	**tedium** n ستریا
target n نښان، څلی	**teenager** n جوریي
tariff n ګمرکي تعرفه	**teeth** n غاښ
tarnish v پیکه کېدل	**telegram** n تلګرام
tartar n د غاښونو منګ	**telepathy** n تیلي پتي
task n کار	**telescope** n تلسکوپ
taste v خوند ورکول	**televise** v خپرونه
taste n خوند ورکول	**television** n تلوزیون
tasteful adj خوندور	**tell** iv بیانول
tasteless adj بې خونده	**teller** n بیانوونکی

T

telling *adj* اغېزناک	terms *n* تبرشوی
temper *n* برابرول	terrace *n* چوتره
temperature *n* درجه حرارت	terrain *n* عسکر سیمه
tempest *n* سخت توپان	terrestrial *adj* مځکنی
temple *n* شقیقه	terrible *adj* خطرناکه
temporary *adj* لنډ مهال	terrific *adj* ډاروونکی
tempt *v* لمسول	terrify *v* سخت ډارول
temptation *n* لمسون	terrifying *adj* وبره
tempting *adj* لسوونکی شی	territory *n* سیمه
ten *adj* لس	terror *n* ډېره وبره
tenacity *n* تینګار	terrorism *n* مجبورول
tenant *n* اجاره دار	terrorist *n* ډا اچوونکی
tendency *n* هڅه	terrorize *v* وبره اچوونکی
tender *adj* نازک، تنکی	terse *adj* لنډه مجزه خبره
tenderness *n* نرمي، پام	test *v* ازموینه
tennis *n* یو ډول لوبه ده	test *n* ازموینه
tenor *n* سمت	testament *n* وصیت
tense *adj* ترنګلی	testify *v* تصدیق کول
tension *n* تشنج	testimony *n* شاهدي
tent *n* خیمه	text *n* متن
tentacle *n* ښکر	textbook *n* درسي کتاب
tentative *adj* ازمایښتي	texture *n* جوړښت
tenth *n* لسم	thank *v* کورودانې
tenuous *adj* نری	thankful *adj* ممنون
tepid *adj* ترمر	thanks *n* شکر کښنل
term *n* موده	that *adj* په لاندې ډول
terminate *v* درول	thaw *v* ویلي کېدل
terminology *n* اصطلاحات	thaw *n* ویلي کېدل

T

theater n نندارچي	**thirty** adj دېرش
theft n غلا	**this** adj دغه
theme n موضوع	**thorn** n اغزی
themselves pro هغوي په خپله	**thorny** adj اغزن
then adv په غه وخت کې	**thorough** adj بشپړ
theologian n الهياتو پوه	**those** adj هغوي
theology n دينيات	**though** c که څه هم
theory n تيوري	**thought** n فکر
therapy n طبابت	**thoughtful** adj مفکر
there adv هلته	**thousand** adj زر
therefore adv ځکه نو	**thread** v تار
thermometer n ترمامیټر	**thread** n تار
these adj دغه	**threat** n تهدید
thesis n تيسس	**threaten** v ډارول
they pro دوي	**three** adj درې
thick adj پنډ، پړبړ	**thresh** v ټکول، غوبلول
thicken v ډبلول	**threshold** n درشل، شروع
thickness n پنډوالی	**thrifty** adj سپموونکی
thief n غل	**thrill** v پارول
thigh n ورون	**thrill** n پارول
thin adj نری، سپک	**thrive** v بډای کېدل
thing n شی	**throat** n ستونی
think iv فکر کول	**throb** n دربېدل
thinly adv لږ	**throb** v دربېدل
third adj دريمه برخه	**throne** n تخت
thirst v تنده	**throng** n غونډه
thirsty adj تږی	**through** pre د منځ څخه
thirteen adj ديارلس	**throw** iv غورځول

T

throw away v	ضایع کول
throw up v	قی کول
thumb n	غټه ګوته
thumbtack n	ګل تبخی
thunder n	تالنده
thunderbolt n	بریښنا
thunderstorm n	جم جګړه
Thursday n	پنجشنبه
thus adv	په دې ډول
thwart v	مایل
thyroid n	په عرض
tickle v	تخبدل
tickle n	تخول
ticklish adj	تخبدونکی
tidal wave n	توپاني څپه
tide n	څپه
tidy adj	پکول
tie v	تړل
tie n	نبکتايي
tiger n	پړانګ
tight adj	کلک
tighten v	کلکول
tile n	پخي خښتي
till adv	تر هغه وخته
till v	شودیاره کول
tilt v	کږول
timber n	الوار
time n	وخت

time v	وخت تاکل
timeless adj	تل
timely adj	پر وخت
times n	وخت
timetable n	مهال وېش
timid adj	شرمندوکی
timidity n	ډار
tin n	ډله
tiny adj	ډېر کوچنی
tiptoe n	پنډو څوکب
tired adj	ستړی ستومانه
tiredness n	ستړي والي
tiresome adj	ستومانوونکب
tissue n	نسج
title n	سرلیک
to pre	ته
toad n	غټه چنګاښ
toast v	تودول
tobacco n	تمباکو
today adv	نن
toe n	د پنډب ګوته
together adv	سره یو ځای
toil v	کار کول
toilet n	لمباښی
token n	نښه
tolerable adj	دزغملو وړ
tolerance n	زغم
tolerate v	زغمل

T

toll n ټلۍ وهل	**torture** v شکنجه کول
toll v ټلۍ وهل	**torture** n شکنجه
tomato n رومي	**toss** v اچونه
tomb n مرستون	**total** adj ټول
tombstone n شناخته	**totalitarian** adj ټولواک کې پر خوا
tomorrow adv سبا	**totality** n مجموع
ton n ټن	**touch** n سپک ګذار
tone n رنګ ورکول	**touch** v لمس کول
tongs n نوسۍ	**touch up** v ترمیم کول
tongue n ژبه	**touching** adj اغېز ناک
tonic n غاړیزه	**tough** adj کلک
tonight adv نن شپې	**toughen** v کلکوالی
tonsil n بغوټ	**tour** n ګرځنت
too adv همداسې	**tourism** n د سياحت ډله
tool n جوړول	**tourist** n ګرځندوي
tooth n غاښ	**tournament** n مسابقه
toothache n د غاښ درد	**tow** v کشول
toothpick n غاښ پاکی	**tow truck** n دوه ترکونه
top n چور لنډۍ	**towards** pre لوري ته
topic n موضوع	**towel** n خان وچونی
topple v غورځول	**tower** n خلی
torch n مشعل	**towering** adj ډېر لوړ
torment v عذاب ورکول	**town** n ښارګی
torment n عذاب	**toxic** adj زهر جن
torrent n سېل	**toxin** n زهرناک
torrid adj تکند	**toy** n لوبتکه
torso n تنه	**trace** v ننبه کول
tortoise n شمشتۍ	**track** n پل

T

track v منډ ه اخیستل	transcribe v نقلول
traction n غونجېدنه	transfer v انتقال ورکول
tractor n تراکتور	transfer n بدلونه
trade n تجارت	transform v اړول
trade v راکړه ورکړه	transformation n بدلون
trademark n تجارتي نښه	transfusion n وینه ورکونه
trader n تاجر	transient adj څو ورځنی
tradition n دود	transit n وړنه
traffic n ورل راورل	transition n تېربدنه
traffic v ورنه راورنه	translate v ژباړل
tragedy n وېرجنه کسه	translator n ژباړونکی
tragic adj وېرجن	transmit v استول
trail v لیکه	transparent adj روڼ
trail n راکبنل	transplant v نیالول
trailer n تره	transport v ورل راورل
train v روزل	trap n په تلک نیول
trainee n برخوال	trash n بې ارزښته
trainer n روزونکی	trash can n د کسافت بیلر
training n روزنه	traumatic adj د تقسیم ور
trait n څانګري نښه	traumatize v خفه
traitor n درغل	travel v سفر کول
trajectory n تګ کرښه	traveler n سفر کوونکی
tram n دکوڅې ګاډی	tray n پتنوس
trample v دربونه	treacherous adj درغل
trance n پربښاني	treachery n درغلي
tranquility n ارامي	tread iv پښه اېښودل
transaction n چلونه	treason n درغلي
transcend v بریالي کول	treasure n پاسره کول

treasurer n خزانه دار	**trip** n اوچت گام، چکر
treat v خوښي	**trip** v تېر وتل
treat n خبري اترې	**triple** adj درې گوني کول
treatment n چال چلند، سلوک	**tripod** n درې پښيز
treaty n تړون	**triumph** n بری
tree n ونه	**triumphant** adj برياليتوب
tremble v رپېدبدل	**trivial** adj پې ارزښته
tremendous adj ډېر لوي	**trivialize** v وروکيکول
tremor n رپېد	**trolley** n لاس رپر
trench n لښتی ويستل	**troop** n فوج
trend n مخه	**trophy** n د بري نښان
trendy adj فيشني	**tropic** n ناکراري
trespass v لاس اچول	**tropical** adj پراس لرونکی
trial n ازمايښتي	**trouble** n ناکراري
triangle n مثلث	**trouble** v رېروونگی
tribe n قبيله	**trousers** n پرتوگ
tribulation n کړاو	**truce** n موقتي روغه
tribunal n محکمه	**truck** n جنسي تبادل
tribute n باج	**trucker** n موټر وان
trick v غولول	**trumped-up** adj غلط
trick n چل، تېر ايستنه	**trumpet** n بنکر
trickle v څڅېدل	**trunk** n مواصلاتي
tricky adj څڅېدنه	**trust** v باور کول
trigger v ماشه	**trust** n باوزل
trigger n ماشه	**truth** n رښتيا
trim v سوتره	**truthful** adj رښتيني
trimester n ترې مبتر	**try** v کوښښ کول
trimmings n داس گانه	**tub** n نبانک

tuberculosis *n*	نری رنځ
Tuesday *n*	سه شنبه
tuition *n*	ښوونه
tulip *n*	خاټول
tumble *v*	لوېدنه
tummy *n*	پړپوتنه
tumor *n*	تومور
tumult *n*	اله گوله
tumultuous *adj*	چغندک
tuna *n*	ټونا
tune *n*	سورول
tune *v*	سورول
tune up *v*	موټر جوړول
tunic *n*	بلوز
tunnel *n*	تونل
turbine *n*	څرخ
turbulence *n*	اله گوله
turf *n*	چم
Turk *adj*	پیل مرغ
Turkey *n*	ترکي
turmoil *n*	زوږ
turn *n*	گرځېدل
turn *v*	گرځېدل
turn back *v*	بېر ته گرځېدل
turn in *v*	داخل ته تلل
turn off *v*	بند ول
turn off *v*	بند ول
turn out *v*	جمع کېدل

turn over *v*	دولت لگول
turn up *v*	تهیه کول
turret *n*	وړوکې مناره
turtle *n*	شمشتي
tusk *n*	يو ډول لوبه ده
tutor *n*	کورنی ښوونکی
tweezers *n*	نوسی
twelfth *adj*	دولسم
twelve *adj*	درجن ۱۲
twentieth *adj*	شلم
twenty *adj*	شل۲۰
twice *adv*	دوه ځله
twilight *n*	شپېدي
twin *n*	غبر گون
twinkle *v*	ځلا
twist *v*	غړل، پیچل
twist *n*	غړنه، پېچنه
twisted *adj*	خراب شوی
twisted *n*	خراب
two *adj*	دوه
tycoon *n*	لوي تجار
type *n*	ټاپه، مارکه
type *v*	مارکه کول
typical *adj*	ځانگړی
tyranny *n*	استبدادي نظام
tyrant *n*	مستبد

T

U

ugliness *n* بدرنګتوب

ugly *adj* بدرنګه

ulcer *n* ناسور

ultimate *adj* وروستنی

ultimatum *n* وروستی ټکی

ultrasound *n* الترا سوند

umpire *n* منځګړی

unable *adj* ناوړه

unanimity *n* همفکري

unarmed *adj* بی وسلې

unassuming *adj* کمین

unattached *adj* بې کوژدې

unavoidable *adj* د نه پربنسودلو

unaware *adj* نا خبره

unbearable *adj* نه زغمبدونکی

unbeatable *adj* لور

unbelievable *adj* د نه منلو وړ

unbiased *adj* بې طرفه

unbroken *adj* پرله پسې

unbutton *v* تڼی خلاصول

uncertain *adj* نا معلوم

uncle *n* کاکا

uncomfortable *adj* نا ارامه

uncommon *adj* کله کله

unconscious *adj* بې حسه

uncover *v* لوڅول

undecided *adj* زړه نا زړه

undeniable *adj* رببستنی

under *pre* لاندې

undercover *adj* پټ لټون

underdog *n* بایلونکی

undergo *v* زغمل

underground *adj* د څمکې لاندې

underlie *v* بنسټ جوړول

underline *v* تاکید کول

underlying *adj* موندیز

underneath *pre* کوز

underpass *n* زیرزمینې

understand *v* پوهول

understandable *adj* د پهپدو وړ

understanding *n* پوهه

undertake *v* په غاړه اخیستل

underwear *n* جانګی

underwrite *v* پیمه وال

undeserved *adj* نا وړ

undesirable *adj* نا غوښتی

undisputed *adj* پې شخړې

undo *v* بېرته کول

undoubtedly *adv* بې شکه

undress *v* لڅول

undue *adj* بې قانونه

unearth *v* رابرسېره کول

uneasiness *n* نا ارامي

uneasy *adj*	نا ارامه
uneducated *adj*	نا لوستی
unemployed *adj*	بې کاره
unemployment *n*	بې کاري
unending *adj*	نه ختمېدونکی
unequal *adj*	نا برابر
unequivocal *adj*	ښکاره
uneven *adj*	نا هوار
uneventful *adj*	بې پېښې
unexpected *adj*	نا څاپه
unfailing *adj*	نه کمېدونکی
unfair *adj*	چلي
unfairly *adv*	په در غلۍ
unfairness *n*	خیانت
unfaithful *adj*	بې وفا
unfamiliar *adj*	نا اشنا
unfasten *v*	پرانیستل
unfavorable *adj*	نا وړه
unfit *adj*	نا وړ
unfold *v*	سپړل
unforeseen *adj*	نا څاپه
unforgettable *adj*	نه هېرېدوکی
unfounded *adj*	بې بنسټه
unfriendly *adj*	نا مهربان
unfurnished *adj*	بې سامانه
ungrateful *adj*	نا شکره
unhappiness *n*	غم
unhappy *adj*	خفه
unharmed *adj*	تڼ غوړ
unhealthy *adj*	نا غوړ
unheard-of *adj*	اصلي
unhurt *adj*	تڼ غوړ
unification *n*	یو ځای کېدنه
uniform *n*	یو شان
uniformity *n*	یو شان توب
unify *v*	یو کول
unilateral *adj*	یو اړخیز
union *n*	یو والی
unique *adj*	بې ساری
unit *n*	یکه
unite *v*	یو کول
unity *n*	اتحاد
universal *adj*	عمومي
universe *n*	نړۍ
university *n*	پوهنتون
unjust *adj*	بې انصافه
unjustified *adj*	بې بنسټه
unknown *adj*	نا معلوم
unlawful *adj*	پټ قانونه
unless *c*	که چېرې
unlike *adj*	بدل
unlikely *adj*	ناشونی
unlimited *adj*	بې بریده
unload *v*	بار کوزول
unlock *v*	پرانستل
unlucky *adj*	بد مرغه

U

unmarried *adj* بې واده	**until** *pre* تر څو چې
unmask *v* بې څبرې کول	**untimely** *adj* بې وهخته
unmistakable *adj* بې غلطی	**untrue** *adj* نا رښتیا
unnecessary *adj* بې لزومه	**unusual** *adj* غیر عادي
unnoticed *adj* نا څرګند	**unveil** *v* ښکاره کول
unoccupied *adj* تش	**unwillingly** *adv* بې ارادې
unofficially *adv* غیر رسمي	**unwind** *v* سپرل
unpleasant *adj* بې خونده	**unwise** *adj* ناپوه
unplug *v* قطعه ارتباط	**unwrap** *v* خلاصول
unpopular *adj* بې شهرته	**upbringing** *n* روزنه
unprofitable *adj* چتي	**upcoming** *adj* را تلونکی
unprotected *adj* نا ساتلی	**update** *v* عصري کېدل
unravel *v* خلاصول	**upgrade** *v* اوچتول
unreal *adj* غیر واقعي	**upheaval** *n* لوړه
unrealistic *adj* غیر متحمل	**uphill** *adv* پرسوب
unreasonable *adj* نا معقول	**uphold** *v* نیول
unrelated *adj* نا تړلی	**upholstery** *n* د کوټې فرش
unreliable *adj* بې اعتماده	**upkeep** *n* څارنه
unrest *n* نا ارامي	**upon** *pre* دپاسه
unsafe *adj* نا خوندي	**upper** *adj* پورتنی
unselfish *adj* سخي	**upright** *adj* ولاړ
unstable *adj* سست	**uprising** *n* پورته کېدنه
unsteady *adj* نا منظم	**uproar** *n* غوغا
unsuccessful *adj* نا بریالی	**uproot** *v* له بیخه ویستل
unsuitable *adj* نا مناسب	**upset** *v* نسکور
unsuspecting *adj* نا معلوم	**upside-down** *adv* د نقل تمري
unthinkable *adj* له اټکله لرې	**upstairs** *adv* پورته منزل
untie *v* فیصله کول	**uptight** *adj* ترینګلي

U

upturn *n* اړول	**V**
upwards *adv* پورته خوا	
urban *adj* ښاري	**vacancy** *n* تش ځای
urge *n* هیله	**vacant** *adj* نا نیول شوی
urge *v* هیله لرل	**vacate** *v* تشول
urgency *n* اهمیت	**vacation** *n* رخصتي
urgent *adj* بیر ګرندی	**vaccinate** *v* خال وهل
urinate *v* متیازې کول	**vaccine** *n* واکسین
urine *n* متیازې	**vacillate** *v* ریبدل
urn *n* جګ چائینک	**vagrant** *n* چتي
us *pro* مور	**vague** *adj* نا څرکند
usage *n* دود	**vain** *adj* بې کاره
use *v* استعمالول	**vainly** *adv* بې ګټې
use *n* استعمال	**valiant** *adj* اتل مېرنی
used to *adj* ګټور	**valid** *adj* سم
useful *adj* ګټور	**validate** *v* اعتبار ور
usefulness *n* ګټورتوب	**validity** *n* اعتبار
useless *adj* بې ګټې	**valley** *n* دره
user *n* غړی	**valuable** *adj* ارزښتنک
usher *n* محکمه	**value** *n* ارزښت
usual *adj* عادي	**valve** *n* د زړه ورخ
usurp *v* غصبول	**vampire** *n* بې وفا ښخه
utensil *n* اساب	**vandal** *n* بر بري
uterus *n* زبلانځی	**vandalism** *n* د علم
utmost *adj* زښت ډېر	**vandalize** *v* خراب
utter *v* بشیره	**vanish** *v* له منځه تلل
	vanity *n* بې ګټېتوب

vanquish v بری موندل	**venture** n بی زړه
vaporize v بړاس کول	**verb** n فعل
variable adj بد لبدونکی	**verbally** adv شفاهي
varied adj اوبنتی	**verbatim** adv ټکي په ټکي
variety n تنوع	**verdict** n پربکون
various adj قسم قسم	**verge** n لګبدل
varnish v څلا ورکول	**verification** n رښتیا کرنه
varnish n څلوونکی	**verify** v رښتیاکول
vary v اوبنتل	**versatile** adj اوبنتونکی
vase n گلدانی	**verse** n مصرع
vast adj ستر	**versed** adj ماهر
veal n د خوسي غوښه	**version** n ژباړه
veer v مخه اړول	**versus** pre ضد
vegetable v تنکی کدو	**vertebra** n دملابند
vegetation n زرغونوالی	**very** adv زښت زیات
vehicle n گاډی	**vessel** n لوښي
veil n پرده	**vest** n واسکټ
vein n رده	**vestige** n پل
velocity n ګړندیتوب	**veterinarian** n بېطار
velvet n بخمل	**veto** v نه منل
venerate v لمانځل	**viaduct** n ددرې پل
vengeance n کسات	**vibrant** adj خوځند
venison n هوسۍ غوښه	**vibrate** v لړزبدل
venom n زهر	**vibration** n زنګبدنه
vent n موری	**vice** n ناېب
ventilate v هوا بدلول	**vicinity** n نژدهوالی
ventilation n د هوا بدلون	**vicious** adj بد
venture v زړه کول	**victim** n جار

V

victimize *v* جارول

victor *n* ور

victorious *adj* بریالی

victory *n* بری

view *n* لیدنه

view *v* لیدل

viewpoint *n* دنظر ټکی

vigil *n* د اختر شپه

village *n* کلی

villager *n* کلیوال

villain *n* بدی

vindicate *v* ځان سپینول

vindictive *adj* انتقامی

vinegar *n* سرکه

vineyard *n* د انگورو باغ

violate *v* ماتول

violence *n* زور

violent *adj* زورور

violet *n* چنیابی

violin *n* سریندہ

viper *n* ټرگ

virgin *n* پیغله

virginity *n* پیغلتوب

virile *adj* نر

virility *n* نارینتوب

virtually *adv* په حقیقت کی

virtue *n* ښه والی

virtuous *adj* ښه

virulent *adj* زهر ناک

virus *n* زهر

visibility *n* څرکندتیا

visible *adj* څرگند

vision *n* لیدل

visit *n* کتنه

visit *v* کتل کول

visitor *n* کتونکی

visual *adj* د لیدنی

visualize *v* ښکاره کیدل

vital *adj* د ژوند

vitality *n* ژوندون

vitamin *n* ویتامین

vivacious *adj* ژوندی

vivid *adj* تازه

vocabulary *n* قاموس

vocation *n* بلنه

vogue *n* دود

voice *n* وبل

void *adj* تش، خالی

volatile *adj* الوتونکی

volleyball *n* والی بال

voltage *n* ولتیج

volume *n* توک، جلد

volunteer *n* خپل خوښی

vomit *v* قی کول

vomit *n* قی

vote *v* راپه کول

vote *n* رايه

voting *n* ټاکنه

vouch for *v* ملاتړ

voucher *n* سند

vow *v* نذر کول

vowel *n* غږيز

voyage *n* ساه

voyager *n* مسافر

vulgar *adj* شډل

vulgarity *n* شډلتبا

vulnerable *adj* کېدونکی

vulture *n* لوت مار

W

wafer *n* کمر بند

wag *v* ښندول

wage *n* برخه اخيستل

wagon *n* واګون

wail *v* وير کول

wail *n* وير

waist *n* نرۍ ملا

wait *v* انتظار

waiter *n* کول

waiting *n* انتظار

waive *v* ډډه کول

wake up *iv* ويښېدل

walk *v* قدم وهل

walk *n* چلند

walkout *n* اعتصاب

wall *n* دېوال وزمه

wallet *n* بټوه

walnut *n* غوز

walrus *n* سمندري نولی

waltz *n* والس نڅا

wander *v* لالهنده

wanderer *n* چکر وهونکی

wane *v* وروکی کېدل

want *v* لټول

war *n* جګړه

ward *n* ساتل

warden *n* ساتوندوۍ

wardrobe *n* کالبو الماري

warehouse *n* ګودام

warfare *n* مبارزه

warm *adj* تړم

warm up *v* تړمول

warmth *n* تړموالی

warn *v* خبرول

warning *n* خبرداری

warp *v* کږول

warped *adj* کوروالی

warrant *v* واک ورکول

warrant *n* امر	**wax** *n* موم ژاوله
warranty *n* تضمین	**way** *n* لار، سرک
warrior *n* توربالی	**way in** *n* لار اوروده
warship *n* جنگي بیړۍ	**way out** *n* غیر معمولي
wart *n* غوټه	**we** *pro* مونږ
wary *adj* پام کونکی	**weak** *adj* کمزوري
wash *v* وینځل	**weaken** *v* کمزوری کول
washable *adj* د وینځلو وړ	**weakness** *n* کمزورتیا
wasp *n* غومبسه	**wealth** *n* شتمني
waste *v* توبول	**wealthy** *adj* بډایي
waste *n* شاړه	**weapon** *n* وسله
wasteful *adj* ضایع کونکی	**wear** *n* اغوستنه، جامه
watch *n* څوکۍ	**wear down** *v* غوڅول، خوړل
watch *v* څارل	**wear out** *v* خرابیدل، یخیدل
watch out *v* خبرداره کیدل	**weary** *adj* ستړی
watchful *adj* وښ	**weather** *n* هوا
water *n* اوبه	**weave** *iv* اوبدل
water *v* لندول	**web** *n* وبب پاڼه، شبکه
water down *v* اوبلنول	**web site** *n* انترنتي پاڼه
waterfall *n* ابشار	**wed** *iv* واده شوی
waterheater *n* اوبه ګرمونکي	**wedding** *n* واده
watermelon *n* هندوانه	**wedge** *n* پاڼه
watertight *adj* سر پیچلی	**Wednesday** *n* چهارشنبه
watery *adj* اوبلن	**weed** *n* واښه
watt *n* واټ	**weed** *v* للونل
wave *n* غورځنګ	**week** *n* اونۍ
waver *v* رپیدل	**weekly** *adv* اوونبز
wavy *adj* څپاند	**weep** *iv* ژړل

W

weigh *v* تلل	**whether** *c* یا
weight *n* وزن	**which** *adj* کوم
weird *adj* عجيب	**while** *c* هغه وخت کې
welcome *v* هر کلي کول	**whim** *n* هوس
welcome *n* ښه راغلی	**whine** *v* شکایت
weld *v* کوشبر کول	**whip** *v* شړ کول، جړ کول
welder *n* کوشبر کوونکی	**whip** *n* چوکه
welfare *n* ښېګڼه	**whirl** *v* چورلول
well *n* څا	**whirlpool** *n* گرداو
well-known *adj* مشهور	**whiskers** *n* ژويو بريتونه
well-to-do *adj* شتمن	**whisper** *v* پس پسي کول
west *n* لويديځ	**whisper** *n* پس پس
westbound *adv* سفر لويديځ ته	**whistle** *v* شپيلي کول
western *adj* غربي	**whistle** *n* شپيلي
wet *adj* لوند	**white** *adj* سپين
whale *n* نهنگ	**whiten** *v* سپينول
wharf *n* ډکه	**whittle** *v* تورل
what *adj* هغه چې	**who** *pro* څوک
whatever *adj* هر څه چې	**whoever** *pro* څوک چې
wheat *n* غنم	**whole** *adj* بشپړ
wheel *n* اربه	**wholehearted** *adj* رښتونی
wheelbarrow *n* لاس گاډی	**wholesale** *n* غونډ پلورنه
when *adv* کله	**wholesome** *adj* گټور
whenever *adv* په هر ساعت کې	**whom** *pro* کوم ته چې
where *adv* چېرته	**why** *adv* ولې
whereabouts *n* چېري	**wicked** *adj* بد کاري
whereas *c* حال دا چې	**wickedness** *n* بدي
wherever *c* په کوم ځای کې	**wide** *adj* پراخ

W

widely *adv* لبرې	windpipe *n* غاړه غاښه
widen *v* ارتول	windy *adj* بادیز
widespread *adj* خپور	wine *n* انګوروشراب د
widow *n* کونډه	winery *n* زبر خانه
widower *n* کونډ	wing *n* وزر
width *n* پلنوالی	wink *n* سترګک
wife *n* ښځه	wink *v* سترګک وهل
wiggle *v* خوځېدل	winner *n* ګټوونکی
wild *adj* بدیایي	winter *n* ژمی
wild boar *n* وحشي پيشو	wipe *v* پاکول
wilderness *n* دښت	wire *n* فلزي, مزی
wildlife *n* ځناور	wireless *adj* بې تاره
will *n* اراده, اختيار	wisdom *n* حکمت
willfully *adv* قصداً	wise *adj* بنه
willing *adj* راضي	wish *v* هیله کول
willingly *adv* په خوښه	wish *n* هیله
willingness *n* خوښه	wit *n* پوهېدل
willow *n* وله	witch *n* کوډګره
wily *adj* زګ	witchcraft *n* کوډې
wimp *adj* خپوني	with *pre* سره
win *iv* ګټل	withdraw *v* بېرته اخیستل
win back *v* دوباره حاصلول	withdrawal *n* لاس اخیستنه
wind *n* باد	withdrawn *adj* غلی
wind *iv* تاوول، ګرځول	wither *v* مراوچ کول
wind up *v* کرکی خلاصول	withhold *iv* بندول
winding *adj* کوږ ووږ	within *pre* دننه
windmill *n* بادي ژرنده	without *pre* پې له
window *n* کرکۍ	withstand *v* ټینګار کول

W

witness *n* شاهد	**worm** *n* چینجی
witty *adj* څیرک	**worrisome** *adj* خوروونکی
wives *n* ښځې	**worry** *v* تشویش کول
wizard *n* کوډ ګر	**worry** *n* تشویش
wobble *v* ګوډ ور تلل	**worse** *adj* ډېر بد
woes *n* ویر	**worsen** *v* ډېر خرابول
wolf *n* لېوه	**worship** *n* لمانځنه
woman *n* ښځه	**worst** *adj* تر ټولو بد
womb *n* زیلانس	**worth** *adj* ارزښت
women *n* ښځې	**worthless** *adj* بې ارزښته
wonder *v* اریانېدل	**worthwhile** *adj* کوښښ
wonder *n* حیرانۍ	**worthy** *adj* ور
wood *n* لرګی	**would-be** *adj* ممکن
wooden *adj* لرګین	**wound** *n* ټپ
wool *n* وړۍ	**wound** *v* زخمي کول
woolen *adj* وړین	**woven** *adj* کتل شوی
word *n* کلمه	**wrap** *v* پېچل
wording *n* وینا	**wrap up** *v* مکمل کول
work *n* دنده	**wrapping** *n* د کاغذ کثوړه
work *v* کار، زیار	**wrath** *n* قهر
work out *v* حل کول	**wreath** *n* غړوشکه
workable *adj* کار وړ	**wreck** *v* ړنګول
workbook *n* درسي کتاب	**wreckage** *n* ړنګ
worker *n* کار ګر	**wrench** *n* پانه
workshop *n* د کار ځی	**wrestle** *v* غبر نیول
world *n* نړۍ	**wrestler** *n* پالوان
worldly *adj* دنیوي	**wrestling** *n* غبر
worldwide *adj* نړیوال	**wretched** *adj* خواشینی

W

wring *iv* پېچل	
wrinkle *v* گونجه کېدل	
wrinkle *n* گونجه	
wrist *n* دلاس بند	
write *iv* لیکل	
write down *v* لیکل	
writer *n* لیکوال	
writhe *v* له دردہ تاوېدل	
writing *n* لیک	
written *adj* لیکل شوی	
wrong *adj* غلط	

X

X-mas *n* ایکس ماس
X-ray *n* ایکس ری

Y

yam *n* خواره کچلان
yard *n* یارډ
yarn *n* تار
yawn *n* اړمی
yawn *v* اړمی ایستل
year *n* کال
yearly *adv* کلنی
yearn *v* هیله من
yeast *n* خمیره
yell *v* چغې وهل
yellow *adj* ژېړ
yes *adv* هو
yesterday *adv* پرون
yet *c* تر اوسه
yield *v* حاصل ورکول
yield *n* حاصل
yoke *n* ژغ
yolk *n* ژېړ
you *pro* تاسې
young *adj* ځوان
youngster *n* وروکی
your *adj* ستاسې
yours *pro* ستاسې خپل
yourself *pro* ته پخپله
youth *n* ځواني

youthful *adj* ځلمی

Z

zap *v* وژل
zeal *n* شوق
zealous *adj* لبوال
zebra *n* ګوره خر

zero *n* صفر
zest *n* خوندور
zinc *n* جست
zipper *n* ځنګیر
zone *n* سیمه
zoo *n* ژوبڼ
zoology *n* ژوپوهنه

Pashto-English

Bilingual Dictionaries, Inc.

Abbreviations

English - Pashto

a - article - د تعریف حرف

adj - adjective - صفت

adv - adverb - قید

c - conjunction - د وصل توری

e - exclamation - ندایی الفاظ

n - noun - اسم

pre - preposition - د ربط توری

pro - pronoun - ضمیر

v - verb - فعل

اثرناک impressive *adj*

اجاره lease *n*

اجاره دار tenant *n*

اجاره کول hire *v*

اجاره کوونکی lessee *n*

اجازه leave, permission *iv*

اجازه لیک License *n*

اجازه ورکول let in, admit *v*

اجبار constraint *n*

اجتماعي sociable *adj*

اجتماعي socialize *v*

اجرا fulfillment *n*

اجرا کول do *iv*

اجراء behavior *n*

اجرائیه executive *n*

اجوره fee *n*

اچول emit, exert, hurl *v*

اچونه toss *v*

احاطه coverage *n*

احتجاج protest *n*

احتجاج کول protest *v*

احتراق combustion *n*

احترام کول look for *v*

احتمال probability *n*

احساس emotion, feeling *n*

احساسا تي bizarre *adj*

I

ابتکار innovation *n*

ابدي everlasting *adj*

ابشار waterfall *n*

اپندیسآیټ appendicitis *n*

اپین opium *n*

اتحاد unity *n*

اتحادیه corporation *n*

اتحادیه federal *adj*

اتسک syphilis *n*

اتشبازي fireworks *n*

اتفاقي casual *adj*

اتل champion, hero *n*

اتل مبرنی valiant *adj*

اتلتوب heroism *n*

اتلسم eighteen *adj*

اتله heroin *n*

اتم eighth *adj*

اتموسفیر atmosphere *n*

اتموسفیري atmospheric *adj*

اته eight *adj*

اتوم atom *n*

اتومي atomic *adj*

اتپا eighty *adj*

اثر sequel *n*

احساساتي mentally adv	ادا pay n
احساساتي emotional adj	ادا كول pay, remunerate iv
احساسول feel iv	ادا كونه repayment n
احساوي statistic n	ادادره كوونكى manager n
احط كوا surroundings n	اداره organization n
احمق idiot n	اداره كول manage, minister v
اخترع invention n	اداره كوونكى mastermind n
اخترع كول invent v	اداره كوونكى mastermind v
اخترع كوونكى creative adj	اداري administer v
اختلاف discouraging adj	ادب courtesy n
اختيارول appropriate adj	ادبي literate adj
اختياري optional adj	ادبيات literature n
اخر last adj	ادبي غلا pirate n
اخطار caution n	ادراك perception n
اخطار ليك subpoena n	ادعا pretense, claim n
اخلاص sincerity, demeanor n	ادعا كول allege v
اخلاقي demeaning adj	اذان كول crow v
اخلاقي ethics n	اراده will n
اخور manger n	ارام comfortable adj
اخور crib n	ارام دپاره lean on v
اخيستل confiscate v	ارام كول chill out v
اخيستوونكى buyer n	ارام وركونكب restful adj
اخبري extreme adj	ارامچي armchair n
اخبستل expropriate v	ارامول pacify, reassure v
اخبستنه excerpt n	ارامي calm, serenity n
اخبستوونكب payee n	ارايش جورول make up for v

wheel *n* اربه	European *adj* اروپایی
roomy, ample *adj* ارت	astonish, astound *v* اریانول
avenue *n* ارت سرک	astonishing *adj* اریانوونکی
freeway *n* ارت بسکلی واټ	wonder *v* اریانبدل
allied *adj* ارتباط	surprise *n* ارین
artery *n* ارتباطي	yawn *n* ارومی
commit *v* ارتکاب کول	yawn *v* ارومی ایستل
enlarge, widen *v* ارتول	pal *n* ارگ
enlargement *n* ارتونه	organist *n* ارگان
amplifier *n* ارتوونکی	organism *n* ارگانبزم
genetic *adj* ارثي	admiration *n* ارپان پاتپ کبدنه
inexpensive *adj* ارزان	puzzle *n* ارپانول
devalue *v* ارزانه کول	fantastic *adj* ارپانوونکپ
cost *iv* ارزښت	amazement *n* ارپاني
cost, value *n* ارزښت	independent, free *adj* ازاد
worth *adj* ارزښت	acquit, free *v* ازادول
evaluate *v* ارزښت ټاکل	shipment *n* ازادونه
appraisal *n* ارزښت ټاکنه	freedom, liberty *n* ازادپ
valuable *adj* ارزښتنک	liberate, molest *v* ازدول
crater *n* ارشیند	tentative *adj* ازمایشتپ
purple *adj* ارغواني	trial *n* ازماینتي
saucepan *n* ارکاره	test *n* ازموینه
orchestra *n* ارکسترا	quiz, test *v* ازموپل
saw *iv* اره کول	proceedings *n* ازمبنبت
psychology *n* اروا پوهي	horse *n* اس
Europe *n* اروپا	utensil *n* اساب

insinuation n اساره	talent n استعداد
basis n اساس	resignation n استعفا
mainly adv اساسا	resign v استعفا وركول
basic adj اساسي	colonial adj استعماري
staple v اساسي	use n استعمال
staple n اساسي برخه	use v استعمالول
constitution n اساسي قانون	imply v استنباط
catalog n اساسي لست	transmit v استول
catalog v اساسي لست	inhabitant n استوگن
capital letter n اساسي مكتوب	settlement n استوگنه، پانډه
fundamental adj اساسي	apartment n استوگنځى
easy, popular adj اسان	Jewish adj اسراييلي
foolproof adj اسانه	litigate v اسره كول
facilitate v اسانول	pontiff n اسقف
outfit, appliance n اسباب	Islamic adj اسلامي
aspirin n اسپرين	horizon n اسمان
mare n اسپه	diving n اسماني
mission n استاځو ډله	meteor n اسماني كاڼي
envoy n استاځى	heavenly, blue adj اسماني
tyranny n استبدادي نظام	diarrhea n اسهال
exploit n استثمار	bond n اسير
exception n استثنا	innuendo n اشارتآ رسول
exceptional adj استثنايي	hint, signal, spear n اشاره
deserving adj استحقاق موندل	hint, insinuate v اشاره كول
enrollment n استخدام	suggestive adj اشاره كوونكى
lining n استر	tip n اشاره وركول

cook n اشپز	profess v کول اعتراف
appetite n اشتها	confessor n کونکی اعتراف
appetizer n ور اشتها	walkout n اعتصاب
nobility n اشراف	reckon on v کول اعتماد
insist v اصرار	confidential adj اعتمادي
idiom n اصطلاح	purgatory n اعراف
terminology n اصطلاحات	maximum adj حد اعظمي
amendment n اصلاح	proclamation n اعلامبه
step up v کول اصلاح	declaration, poster n اعلان
initial, sincere adj اصلي	plug, open up v کول اعلان
mainland n خاوره اصلي	placard n لبک اعلان
authenticity n اصليتوب	announce v اعلانول
prototype n نمونه اصلب	announcer n اعلانوونکی
technique n اصول	thorny adj اغزن
overtime adv کاري اضافه	thorn n اغزی
spare part n پرزي اضافي	entice v کول اغوا
surf v قيمت اضافي	wear n اغوستنه
address n اضافي	effective, telling adj ناک اغبز
emergency n حالت اضطراري	effectiveness n اغبزناکب
extremist adj سپري اطرفب	effect n اغبزه
credit, validity n اعتبار	affect v کول اغبزه
validate v ور اعتبار	overdo v افراط
moderation n اعتدال	myth n افسانه
object n اعتراض	remorse n افسوس
challenge v کول اعتراض	lift off v ختل افقي
challenge n کول اعتراض	lift-off n ختنه افقي

افقي horizontal *adj*	الوتکه aeroplane *n*
اقتباس کول adopt *v*	الوتکي ته ختل set out *v*
اقتدار authoritarian *adj*	الوتل fly *iv*
اقتصادي economical, frugal *adj*	الوتونکی flier *n*
اقليم climate *n*	الوتونکب volatile *adj*
اقليمي climatic *adj*	الوزول snatch *v*
اکتوبر October *n*	الوهبت divinity, deity *n*
اکثره mostly *adv*	امپراتور emperor *n*
اکسل axle *n*	امپراتورب empire *n*
اکسبجن oxygen *n*	امپريالبزم imperialism *n*
اکشاف development *n*	امتحان examination *n*
اکټ کونکی actress, actor *n*	امتحانول examine *v*
الترا سوند ultrasound *n*	امتباز prerogative *n*
الجبر algebra *n*	امر warrant *n*
الحاد at *pre*	امر چلول rule *v*
الفبا alphabet *n*	امر ورکول command *v*
الکولي څنباک booze *n*	امربکايي American *adj*
الماری closet, shelves *n*	امساک frugality *n*
الماس diamond *n*	امکان eventuality *n*
المان Germany *n*	املا ويل dictate *v*
المونيم aluminum *n*	امنيت bail out *v*
اله device, organ *n*	اموخته کول accustom *v*
اله ګوله tumult *n*	امونيا ammonia *n*
الهياتو پوه theologian *n*	امبد suspense *n*
الو potato *n*	امبد expectancy, hope *n*
الوار timber *n*	امبل garland *n*

pregnant adj امېندواره	engine n انجن
pregnancy n امېندواري	bible n انجيل
anatomy n اناتومي	biblical adj انجيلي
pomegranate n انار	engineer n انجنر
pineapple n اناناس	inch n انچ
store v انبارول	devastation n انحراف
choice, election n انتخاب	monopoly n انحصار
choosy adj انتخاب شوی	deal iv اندازه
choose, opt for iv انتخابول	size, deal, sum n اندازه
campaign v انتخابي مبازره	gauge, scale v اندازه کول
web site n انترنتي پانه	limb n اندام
wait v انتظار	anxious adj اندېښنمن
waiting n انتظار	apprehensive adj اندېښنمن
hang on v انتظار کول	anxiety n اندېښنه
await v انتظار ویستل	mankind n انسان
criticism n انتقاد	manpower n انساني قوت
criticize v انتقاد کول	gratuity n انعام
critique n انتقادي نظر	flu n انفلو انز
demise n انتقال	influenza n انفلوانزا
transfer v انتقال ورکول	gestation n انکشاف
alien n انتقال ورکول	atheist, denial n انکار
hand down v انتقالول	deny, disclaim v انکار کول
hit back v انتقام	refusal n انکار کونه
vindictive adj انتقامي	develop v انکشاف ورکول
midair n انتن	diagram n انځور
antibiotic n انتي بيوتيک	depict, picture v انځورول

202

rectum *n* اندره	dehydrate *v* اوبو كموالى
poise *n* اندول	irrigate *v* اوبول
crony *n* اندیوال	opera *n* اوپرا
girlfriend *n* اندپواله	high *adj* اوچت
rumor *n* انګازه	trip *n* اوچت ګام
English *adj* انګرېزي	hoist, pick up *v* اوچتول
England *n* انګلستان	pickup *n* اوچتونه
howl *v* انګلل	odometer *n* اودو ميتر
howl *n* انګولا	fire *v* اور
patio, court *n* انګر	fire, firefighter *n* اور
assumption *n* انګبرنه	outburst *n* اور اخیستنه
disappear *v* اه نظره پټېدل	flammable *adj* اور اخبستونكى
subject *v* اهل	combustible *n* اور ايستوونكي
domesticate *v* اهلي كول	match *n* اور لګيت، ګوګر
importance *n* اهميت	curiosity *n* اور وژنه
arson *n* او ر اچونه	barely *n* اوربشب
plane *n* اوار	neck *n* اورمبږ
gossip, hearsay *n* اوازه	overcast *adj* اورو كب پټ
gossip *v* اوازه كول	mustard *n* اورک
knit, weave *v* اوبدل	hear, listen *iv* اوربدل
succulent *adj* اوبلن	audience *n* اوربدنه
dilute, water down *v* اوبلنول	listener *n* اوربدونكي
water *n* اوبه	currently, now *adv* اوس
intake *n* اوبه خور	iron *n* اوسپنه
waterproof *adj* اوبه نه جذبونكى	lately *adv* اوسنى
waterheater *n* اوبه ګرموونكي	modern *adj* اوسنى

اوسېدل reside, be v	اوردہ چوکۍ pew, bench n
اوسېدو کوټه living room n	اوردہ لار way in n
اوسپلی۔ sigh n	اوردہ موده long-term adj
اوسپلی۔ کول sigh v	اوردہ گامونه stride iv
اولاد offspring n	اوردوالی longitude n
اولس nation n	اوردوالی، توټه span n
اولسوالی۔ coup n	اوردول lengthen, prolong v
اولمپیک olympics n	اوردونه orientation n
اومه رېبنم floss n	اوردې جرابې hose n
اومه مواد stuff n	اوږه shoulder n
اونس ounce n	اوږۍ۔ necklace n
اونۍ۔ week n	اوږۍ خندل shrug v
اوولس seventeen adj	اوښ camel n
اووم seventh adj	اوښتل sprain, vary v
اوونبز weekly adv	اوښتونکی versatile adj
اووه seven adj	اوښتونې immutable adj
اوږه flour n	اوښتی varied adj
اوږه کول grind, stamp iv	اوښتۍ بنه masquerade v
اورونکۍ chopper n	اوښکه tear iv
اورۍ summer n	اوښکه tear n
اورد lengthy, long adj	اوښکۍ۔ snail n
اورد ژوند outlook n	اوښۍ brother-in-law n
اورد کوټ cassock n	اوپا seventy adj
اورد والی length n	ایرلینډ Ireland n
اورد وزمه oblong adj	ایرلینډي Irish adj
اوردہ جرابه stocking n	ایسارول beset, besiege iv

castaway n ایسته غورځول	later adv ارخیز
boiler n ایشولو لوښی	enforce, oblige v ارکول
stove n ایشتوب	exact adj ارکول
boil v ایشېدل	crowbar, lever n ارم
X-ray n ایکس رې	stubborn adj ارم
X-mas n ایکس ماس	pertain v اره لرل
loose v ایله	insurrection n ارو دور
Italian adj ایټالوي	convert, alter, distort v ارول
italics adj ایټالوي ژبه	upturn n ارول
Italy n ایټالیا	screw v ارول، کړول
bear n ایږ	distortion n ارونه
donation n اینبل	compulsion n اریستنه
implant v اینبول	link v اریکه
deem, estimate v اټکلول	cut off v اریکه قطع کول
estimation n اټکلونه	boycott v اریکې شلول
approximate adj اټکلي	grayish adj ابرن
overestimate v اټکونه	embers n ابرې
station n اډه	extinct adj ابرې شوې
framework n اډونه	restrict, siege v ابسارول
obliged adj اړ	dislodge, extract v ابستل
obligate v اړ کول	repeal n ابستنه
necessitate v اړایستل	discard v ابسته غورځول
obligation, need n اړتیا	scald v ابشول
need v اړتیا درلودل	release v ابله کول
lack v اړتیا لرل	drifter n ابله گرد
aspect, facet, side n اړخ	faith n ابمان،وفا

fig n اېنځُر	imposition n بارونه
put, set iv اېنبودل	bazaar, fair n بازار
set n اېنبودنه	sale slip n بازاري چکر
setting n اېنبوونه	stale adj باسي
granddad n آبا	garden n باغ
appeasement n آسآن	gardener n باغوان
	outlaw v باغي
	rebel v باغي کېدل
	rebel n باغي کېدل
ب	bean n باقلي
	remains n باقي پاتې
tribute n باج	grow up v بالغ کېدل
carelessness n باحتياطي	crossword n بالمقابل الفاظ
breeze, wind n باد	crossfire n بالمقابل ډزې
lord n بادار	cushion n بالښت
sail n بادوان	cushion v بالښت
sailboat n بادواني بېړۍ	roof n بام
windmill n بادي ژرنده	attic n بامبوټۍ۔
windy adj باديز	outdoor adv باندې
burden, charge n بار	aboard adv باندې.
dump v بار چپه کول	bamboo n بانکس
unload v بار کوزول	chalet n بانډه
dump n بارچپه	reliance n باور
barracks n باركونه	trust, rely on v باور کول
gunpowder n باروت	confidant n باوري
burden, charge v بارول	reliable adj باوري

باوزل trust n	بخنښل forgive, absolve v
باید must, ought to iv	بخنښنه apology n
بایسکل bicycle n	بخی seam n
بایلونکی underdog n	بخی وهل stitch v
بایلوونکی loser n	بد bad, vicious adj
باتو show off v	بد اخلاقه dissolute adj
باتپ وهل brag v	بد بویه fetid adj
بانه eyelash n	بد بین cynic adj
باید have to v	بد بيني cynicism n
ببوزپ ،پکي fan n	بد خلقه moody adj
بت starch n	بد خوا malevolent adj
بت پرستي idolatry n	بد سلوک misdemeanor n
بته goose n	بد فال portent n
بچت earnings n	بد کاري wicked adj
بچول fend v	بد لمني adultery n
بچونکپ savior n	بد لبدونکی variable adj
بحث consultation n	بد مرغه ominous, unlucky adj
بحث کول argue v	بد مرغي misfortune n
بحث کونه fallout n	بد مرغپ extremities n
بحران crisis n	بد نيتي malign v
بحراني nitpicking adj	بد هضمي indigestion n
بحراني critical adj	بد خپنپ راتلل detestable adj
بخت fortune, luck n	بد گماني disbelief n
بختور lucky adj	بد گڼل disapprove v
بخشش bonus n	بدخوپه disagreeable adj
بخمل velvet n	بدرنگتوب ugliness n

ب

ugly *adj* بدرنگه	برابر tantamount to *adj*
convoy, escort *n* بدرگه	برابرو arrange *v*
lump together *v* بدشکله	برابرول synchronize, fit *v*
delinquent *adj* بدعمله	برابرول temper *n*
insolent *adj* بدغونی	برابرونکي adjustment *n*
substitute *v* بدل	برابروونکی supplier *n*
interchange *n* بدلزل	برابربدل coincide *v*
retaliation, reward *n* بدله	براپرول adjust *v*
retaliate *v* بدله اخیستل	برانشیت bronchitis *n*
reward *v* بدله ورکول	براندي brandy *n*
rewarding *adj* بدله ورکونکي	بربریت barbarism *n*
barter, relay *v* بدلول	بربند strip *n*
shift *v* بدلول	بربندول expose *v*
change, mutate *v* بدلون	بربندبدل strip *v*
shift, reversal *n* بدلون	برتانوي British *adj*
change, transfer *n* بدلونه	برجسته کول emboss *v*
sing *iv* بدلې وبل	برچه bayonet *n*
blackmail *v* بدنامول	برخه segment, section, part *n*
sport *n* بدني روزنه	برخه اخیستل take apart *v*
spontaneity *n* بدهت	برخه اخبستل wage *n*
wickedness *n* بدي	برخوال collaborator *n*
wild *adj* بدیايي	برس brush *n*
feud *n* بدۍ	برسبره beside *pre*
villain *n* بدۍ	برسبره پر دۍ moreover *adv*
vandal *n* بر بري	برطانوپ Britain *n*
nudity *n* بر بندوتوب	برعکس contrary *adj*

electricity n برق	prosperous adj برپالي
electric adj برقي	pass n برپالي توب
blessing n بركت	prosper v برپالي كېدل
bless v بركت وركول	prosperity n برپالبتوب
fertile adj بركتي	cramp, flare n بربښ
glory n برم	mail n بربنباليک
majestic adj برم لرونکی	dazzling adj بربنبېدونکی
superb adj برم لروونکی	goat n بزه
gorgeous adj برم ناک	farmer n بزګر
drill n برمه	bus n بس
bureaucrat n بروکريټ	enough adv بس
conquest, triumph n برى	subscription n بسپنه
attain, conquer v برى موندل	donate v بسپنه وركول
transcend v بريالي كول	donor n بسپنه وركونکب
triumphant adj برياليتوب	biscuit n بسكوټ
mustache n بريت	whole, thorough adj بشپړ
attack n بريد	integrity n بشپړتيا
bound adj بريد	accomplish v بشپړكول
margin, outset n بريد	utter v بشپړه
attack v بريد كول	absolute adj بشپړه
attacker n بريد كوونکی	loaf n بشپړه ډوډۍ
stake v بريد ټاكل	supply v بشپړول
lightning n بريښنا	integration n بشپړونه
electronic adj بريښناپي	human adj بشر
burger n برگر	humankind n بشر
victory n برې	scream n بغارې

بغاري وهل scream v	بمبه كول pump v
بغاوت rebellion n	بمې گولې shrapnel n
بغوټ tonsil n	بند articulation, joint n
بغير له فراغته ingratitude n	بند ول turn off v
بقا eternity n	بندر harbor n
بكس suitcase n	بنده ول shut off v
بكتريا bacteria n	بندول break off, withhold v
بل else adv	بندونكې preventive adj
بل other adj	بندي captive n
بل ﺩول sceptic adj	بندي خانه jail n
بلا phantom n	بندي كول detain, imprison v
بلاربوالى conception n	بنديز لگول blockade v
بلاربېدل conceive v	بنديز لگونه blockade n
بلبل nightingale n	بندې prisoner n
بلدتيا informality n	بندې ساتل confinement n
بلل summon v	بندېدل go out v
بلنه calling, vocation n	بندېز prevention n
بله دا چې either adv	بنسټ foundation, source n
بلوا revolt n	بنسټ اېښودنه institution n
بلوا كول revolt, riot v	بنسټ اېښودل escalate v
بلوز blouse, tunic n	بنسټ جوړول underlie v
بلول kindle v	بنډل bundle n
بلول riot n	بنډل كول bundle v
بم bomb n	بنگبدل buzz n
بم چول bomb v	بنگبدل buzz v
بمبه pump n	بنگبدنه mumble v

بنبادي rudimentary *adj*	بیا نول acquaint *v*
بهاندي اوبه current *adj*	بیالوژیکي biological *adj*
بهانه pretension *n*	بیان recital *n*
بهانه کول feign, pretend *v*	بیانول recite, tell *v*
بهر outdoors *adv*	بیانوونکی teller *n*
بهر ته تلل take out *v*	بیخ bottom *n*
بهرني ناروغ outpatient *n*	بیده asleep *adj*
بهبدل flow *v*	بیر beer *n*
بهبدنه flow *n*	بیرغ banner *n*
بوتل bottle *n*	بیروکراسي bureaucracy *n*
بوجی، جوال sack *n*	بیزو ape, monkey *n*
بودیجه budget *n*	بیل بیل کول sort out *v*
بوره sugar, surge *n*	بیلجیم Belgium *n*
بوس خانه mow *v*	بیلر barrel *n*
بوک (کوهان) hump *n*	بیمه insurance *n*
بوکس box *n*	بیه bid *n*
بوکه bucket *n*	بیه ټاکل appraise, bid *v*
بوی odor *n*	بټوه purse, wallet *n*
بوین stinking *adj*	بخایه خرخول squander *v*
بوټی bush, shrub *n*	بډای کبدل thrive *v*
بوډا senile *adj*	بډاپ wealthy *adj*
بور بوره کی cyclone *n*	بډل fog *n*
بوبول scent *n*	بډوډی kidney *n*
بی وسلی unarmed *adj*	براس steam *n*
بي خونده subdued *adj*	براس کول vaporize *v*
بیا را گرځبدنه comeback *n*	براس کبدل evaporate *v*

tropical *adj* بېراس لرونکی	insignificant *adj* بې ارزښته
quilt *n* بريستن	nullify *v* بې ارزښته کول
modify *v* بړلول	baseless *adj* بې اساسه
pander *v* بروا توب	mistrust *n* بې اعتباري
grimace *n* بروستوب	discredit *v* بې اعتباري
grim *adj* بروسوالی	distrust *v* بې اعتباري کول
excuse *v* ببنل	deceptive *adj* بې اعتماده
pardon, remit *v* ببننه	irresistible *adj* بې اعتنايي
remission, pardon *n* ببننه	unjust *adj* بې انصافه
carriage *n* بګی	deceitful *adj* بې ايمانه
backyard *n* بڼ	needless *adj* بې ارتيا
feather *n* بڼکه	cheeky *adj* بې باکه
countenance *n* بڼه	reckless *adj* بې باکي
wise *adj* بڼه	unlimited *adj* بې بريده
disguise *v* بڼه بدلول	unjustified *adj* بې بنسته
deface *v* بڼه ور خرابول	disfigure *v* بې بڼې کول
remove *v* بی څاپه کول	customer *n* بې پار
precarious *adj* بې اتباره	indiscreet *adj* بې پامه
disunity *n* بې اتفاقي	regardless *adv* بې پامه
invalidate *v* بې اثره کول	bottomless *adj* بې پايه
disrespect *n* بې احترامه	endless *adj* بې پايه
negligence *n* بې احتياطي	highly *adv* بې پايه
impolite *adj* بې ادبه	intrepid *adj* بې پروا
discourtesy *n* بې ادبي	indifference *n* بې پروايي
unwillingly *adv* بې ارادي	mismanage *v* بې پروايي کول
manslaughter *n* بې اردي وژنه	disuse *n* بې پروا‌پ کول

بې ریا candid *adj*	بې پنبې uneventful *adj*
بې زوره powerless *adj*	بې تاره wireless *adj*
بې زره coward *n*	بې تخمه seedless *adj*
بې زره توب dismay *n*	بې تعصبه impartial *adj*
بې زره کول demoralize *v*	بې تکل توب indecision *n*
بې ساری unique *adj*	بې تناسبي imbalance *n*
بې سامانه unfurnished *adj*	بې تهذیبه crass *adj*
بې سرحده boundless *adj*	بې تیاری ویل improvise *v*
بې شرمه shameless *adj*	بې حالي coma *n*
بې شکه undoubtedly *adv*	بې حده ژور ځنډ abyss *n*
بې شمبره countless *adj*	بې حرکته immobile, still *adj*
بې شهرته unpopular *adj*	بې حسه indifferent *adj*
بې صبره impatient *adj*	بې حسه والی numbness *n*
بې صبري impatience *n*	بې خوبي insomnia *n*
بې ضرره harmless *adj*	بې خونده tasteless, insipid *adj*
بې طرف کول neutralize *v*	بې خوندي banality *n*
بې طرفه disinterested *adj*	بې خوندي bored *adj*
بې عقل کول fool *v*	بې داغه spotless *adj*
بې عقله dope *n*	بې دردي apathy *n*
بې عقله کول dope *v*	بې درزه seamless *adj*
بې عقلي craziness *n*	بې دلیله illogical *adj*
بې عیبه impeccable *adj*	بې دنیي atheism *n*
بې عببي flawless *adj*	بې ربطه impertinent *adj*
بې غلطی unmistakable *adj*	بې رحمه cruel, ruthless *adj*
بې غمه کول ease *v*	بې رحمي atrocity *n*
بې فکره careless *adj*	بې رحمي ferocity *n*

بې وخته لو يېدل outgrow v	بې قابو کېدل let go v
بې وسلې کول disarm v	بې قاعده abnormal adj
بې وسلې والي disarmament n	بې قاعده گي abnormality n.
بې وسې helpless adj	بې قاعدي irregular adj
بې وفا disloyal adj	بې قانونه undue adj
بې وفا نسخه vampire n	بې قانوني anarchy n
بې وفايي disloyalty n	بې قيمته invaluable adj
بې وهخته untimely adj	بې کار jobless adj
بې خايه irrational adj	بې کاره aimless adj
بې خايه اېنسودل misplace v	بې کاري laziness n
بې خايه extravagance n	بې کوژدې unattached adj
بې خايه کول dislocate v	بې لارې astray v
بې خايه کېدنه removal n	بې لارې کول mislead v
بې څبرې کول unmask v	بې لزومه unnecessary adj
بې ډوله grotesque adj	بې له except pre
بې گناه inexperienced adj	بې له خدايه godless adj
بې گناهي innocence n	بې له دې besides pre
بې گټې vainly adv	بې معنا brutality n
بې گټې useless adj	بې معنا meaningless adj
بې گټپتوب vanity n	بې مهارته incompetent adj
ببا ، له سره anew adv	بې مېنې reluctant adj
ببا اخيستل redeem v	بې هوښه کول stun v
ببا ادا کول reimburse v	بې هډوکو bone n
ببا پیدا کېدل relive v	بې واده unmarried adj
ببا پیداکول recreate v	بې واره کول embarrass v
ببا پیدابنست recreation n	بې وخته زيږېدنه abortion n

refresh v ببا تازه کول	minimum n ببخي وور
refreshing adj ببا تازه والی	quite adv ببخي
reproduce v ببا تولبدول	deserted adj ببدباپي
restoration n ببا تولبدونه	turn back v ببر ته گرځبدل
remodel v ببا جوړول	withdraw v ببرته اخیستل
reprint v ببا چاپول	replace v ببرته په ځاي کول
reprint n ببا چاپول	move back v ببرته حرکت کول
reproduction n ببا زپرونه	come back v ببرته راتلل
resuscitate v ببا ژوندي کول	get back v ببرته راگرځبدل
revive v ببا سبک اخبستل	undo v ببرته کول
retrieval n ببا غوښتنه	retract v ببرته ننوتل
reconsider v ببا کتل	give back v ببرته ورکول
hindsight n ببا کتنه	refund n ببرته ورکونه
relapse n ببا ککړبدل	bring back v ببرته ورل
remarry v ببا واده کول	beret n ببره خولۍ
rebuild v ببا ودانول	distasteful adj ببزاره
repeat v ببا وپل	aversion n ببزاري
reelect v ببا ټکل	gorilla n ببزو
refill, refuel v ببا ډکول	hysterical adj ببسدتیا
rejoin v ببا پو ځاي کبدل	hysteria n ببسدي
reunion n ببا پو ځاي کبدنه	veterinarian n ببطار
scissors n ببانچ	flute n ببکر
revision n بباکتنه	separate adj ببل
explain v ببانول	discord n ببل والي
recapture v ببانیول	parting n ببلتون
invoice n ببجک	separate v ببلتون

ب
پ

بېلول resolve v	پاتې کېدل remain, stay v
بېلونه amputation n	پاچا king, monarch n
بېلېدل differ, secede v	پاچاهي monarchy n
بيمه لېک policy n	پاچاهې royalty n
بيه price n	پاچاهي کول reign v
بير ګندۍ pressing adj	پاچايي kingdom n
بير ګرندۍ urgent adj	پادرنګ cucumber n
بيرا، احمق stock n	پادري clergyman n
بيرناک hasty adj	پار ووهونکې paddle v
بيرۍ ship n	پارسل parcel n
بيرۍ چلول sail v	پارک park n
بيګار grandstand n	پاره mercury n
بيګارول impress v	پارول thrill n
بيګانه outsider n	پارول enthuse, excite v
	پارونکې exciting adj
	پارونه inspiration n
پ	پاروونکی stimulant n
	پاربدل ferment n
	پاربدلی elated adj
پاپ Pope n	پاربدلې ډله mob n
پاتې remnant n	پاربدنه fuss n
پاتې rest n	پاس above pre
پاتې شونکې remainder n	پاس کول pass v
پاتې شوني leftovers n	پاسپورت passport n
پاتې شونې remaining adj	پاسترۍ pastry n
پاتې کول rest v	پاستب puff n

hoard v پاسره	attendance n پاملرنه
treasure n پاسره کول	attend, care v پاملرنه کول
parcel post n پاسل استونه	sparingly adv پاملرنې سره
crayon n پاستل	considerate adj پاملرونکي
disseminate v پاشل	wedge, wrench n پانه
chaste, clean adj پاک	investment n پانگه اچونه
clear-cut adj پاک صاف	investor n پانگه اچوونکي
cleanser n پاک کوونکي	residue n پانب شونې
clearness n پاکوالی	completion n پای
sanctity n پاکوالب	consequence n پایله
cleanse, purify v پاکول	subsist v پایبدل
pick v پاکول،غوندول	rouse v پاڅول
eraser n پاکونکی	rousing adj پاڅونه
cleaner n پاکوونکی	arise iv پاڅبدل
chastity n پاکي	blade n پاڼه
purge, scratch n پاکب	end n پاب
superfluous adj پالتو	end v پاب ته رسول
polish n پالش	post n پابه
nurture v پالنه	pedal n پابدل
share n پاله ،کره کب	furry adj پت لرونکی
wrestler n پالوان	fur n پت لرونکب
beware v پام ساتل	petroleum n پترول
amusing adj پام غلطول	jeans, pants n پتلون
behold iv پام کول	rowdy adj پتنه گر
wary adj پام کونکی	tray n پتنوس
mindful adj پام لرونکی	butterfly n پتنگ

پته address v	پر له اچول huddle v
پتې، کارت card n	پر له پسې nonstop adv
پچه lottery n	پر مختګ advance n
پچه کښل conscript n	پر مختګ ahead pre
پخانې prior adj	پر مخکب ورل doze v
پخپل سر perverse adj	پر مخکب ورنه doze n
پخپله oneself pre	پر وخت timely adj
پخلا کول reconcile v	پر ځای lieu n
پخلاکوال conciliate v	پر ځای کونه compliance n
پخلاوالی conciliatory adj	پر ځای ولاړ stack v
پخلنځی bakery, cuisine n	پراخ protracted, wide adj
پخوا before adv	پراخه جاده boulevard n
پخوا formerly adv	پراخوالی magnitude n
پخوا له پخوا beforehand adv	پراخول protrude v
پخوانی background n	پراشوت parachute n
پخوانی زمانب antiquity n	پرانستل unlock v
پخوانب previous adj	پرانستنه inauguration n
پخول bake, cook v	پرانسته opening n
پخونکی fries n	پرانستی open adj
پخښنه offering n	پرانیستل inaugurate v
پخب خښتي tile n	پرتله minus adj
پخبدل ripen v	پرتمین magnificent adj
پدل unlike adj	پرتوګ trousers n
پده رویه misconduct n	پرتګال Portugal n
پدې څول hereby adv	پرتګالب Portuguese adj
پر on pre	پرتب ویل babble v

abdicate v پرینسودل	dew, frost n پرخه
boulder, rock n پرنبه	curtain, veil n پرده
leave out v پرنسودل	scene n پرده ،نندارہ
gland n پرګی	screen v پرده نیول
sever v پری کول	extraneous adj پردي
derelict adj پری اینبي	faint adj پرکال
clipping n پری شوي ټوټه،	blackout n پرکالتوب
discontinue iv پری کول	faint n پرکالتوب
cut n پري کونه	faint v پرکاله کېدل
cut iv پري کېدل	dock v پرکول
breakdown n پري وتنه	stepdaughter n پرکتی
snore v پرېشان ول	consecutive adj پرله پسې
chagrin n پرېشاني	headway n پرمختک
drop off v پرېشاني ورل	sneeze v پرنجبدل
intersect, prune v پرېکول	sneeze n پرنجبدل
verdict n پرېکون	clot n پرند
determination n پرېکړه	bite, stab n پرهار
determine v پرېکړه کول	protocol n پروتوکول
liquidation n پرېکړون	protein n پروتبن
filling n پرېمانه	project v پروژه
plentiful adj پرېمانه	project n پروژه
excess n پرېماني	yesterday adv پرون
decline v پرېبوتل	hay, straw n پروړه
decline n پرېبوتنه	indoctrinate v پروگرامر
diameter n پربر	schedule v پروگرام جوړول
trance n پرېبنباني	programmer n پروگرامر

angel *n* پربښته	plaster *n* پلستر
angelic *adj* پربښته دوله	plaster *v* پلسترول
renounce *v* پربښودل	plastic *n* پلستبک
abandonment *n* پربښودنه	shoddy *adj* پلمه ګر
eyelid *n* پزراله	broad *adj* پلن
whisper *n* پس پس	stepfather *n* پلندر
murmur *n* پس پسپ	breadth *n* پلنوالی
murmur *v* پس پسپ کول	width *n* پلنوالی
diabolical *adj* پساتپ	kitchen *n* پلنځی
sheep *n* پسه	ligament *n* پله
aside *adv* پسیدا	plutonium *n* پلوتونپم
prosecute *v* پسپ اخپستل	puberty *n* پلوغ
pursuit *n* پسپ کېدنه	partial *adj* پلوپ
plate *n* پشقاپ	search *v* پلتل
midsummer *n* پشکال	inquiry, probing *n* پلتنه
buzzard *n* پکه بابنه	find out *v* پلتنه کول
tidy *adj* پکول	inspector *n* پلتونکی
vestige, track *n* پل	investigation *n* پلتنه
platinum *n* پلاتپن	plug *n* پلاګ
father *n* پلار	lentil *n* پلیـ
paternity *n* پلاروالپ	pedestrian *n* پلی
pliers *n* پلاس	dismount *v* پلی کېدل
hand out *v* پلاس تقسپمول	Thursday *n* پنجشنپه
blueprint, design *n* پلان	puncture *n* پنچر
meditate *v* پلان جوړول	switch off *v* پند
scheme *n* پلان، جدول	penicillin *n* پنسلبن

پنیر cheese n	په بحر کې afloat adv
پنځلس fifteen adj	په بدل instead adv
پنځم fifth adj	په برابره توګه conversely adv
پنځه five adj	په بربنډه بنه barely adv
پنځه ارخبز pentagon n	په بریالی توګه successful adj
پنځوس fifty adj	په بشپړه توګه entirely adv
پنډ والی density n	په بل دین شوی convert n
پنډ، پړپړ thick adj	په بل ځای کې elsewhere adv
پنډه luggage n	په بې مېلې grudgingly adv
پنډه کی baggage n	په بېړه hastily adv
پنډه ټوټه chunk n	په بېړه سره instantly adv
پنډوالی thickness n	په پام سره gingerly adv
پنډوالې compression n	په پای کې eventually adv
پنډونه roundup n	په پای کې end up v
پنډې porter n	په پراخه پیمانه broadly adv
په of pre	په پوره توګه completely adv
په ابتدايي توګه chiefly adv	په پته confident adj
په اجاره ورکول lease v	په پنبه وهل kick v
په احمقانه ډول idiotic adj	په پنه secretly adv
په اسانې easily adv	په ترځ کې meantime adv
په اصلي بنه initially adv	په ترځ کې during pre
په اصیل کې primarily adv	په تقدیر کې doomed adj
په اوبو کې overboard adv	په تلک نیول trap n
په اور وژنه holocaust n	په تلوار hurriedly adv
په اوردو along pre	په تواضع humbly adv
په باره کې concerning pre	په توپک وېشتنه gunshot n

په ترلب توګه closely adv	په رښتبا سره actually adv
په تبره بيا notably adv	په زوره غږ کول clamor v
په تبزی راتلل burst into v	په زياته پيمانه dearly adv
په جلا ډول asunder adv	په زړه پورې appealing adj
په جنګ اچول embroil v	په زباته اندازه further adv
په جوکار frame v	په زپروالي grossly adv
په حقبقت کې virtually adv	په ساده ډول simply adv
په خاپورو تلل crawl v	په سفر تلل fare n
په خاطر behalf (on) adv	په سلو کې percent adv
په خپل سر arbitrary adj	په سلو کې percentage n
په خوښه willingly adv	په سوتره توګه neatly adv
په خوښۍ joyfully adv	په سبټ ناستب seated adj
په خبال کب conjure up v	په شا backwards adv
په خبر کتل regard v	په شا کبدل retreat v
په دار ځړول crucify v	په شا کبدنه retreat n
په در غلی unfairly adv	په شا ټپونه pat n
په دوکه حاصلول worn-out adj	په شپه کب overnight adv
په دې شان since then adv	په شدت forcibly adv
په دې ورځو کب nowadays adv	په شوريزه توګه noisily adv
په دې ډول thus adv	په صحيح توګه alright adv
په ډبکه پاسول hitch up v	په صحيح ډول literally adv
په رسمي ډول formally adv	په طبيعي naturally adv
په روغه peaceful adj	په عادلا نه توګه justly adv
په روکه frankly adv	په عادي توګه normally adv
په رومانب fluently adv	په عادي ډول ordinarily adv
په رښتبا honesty n	په عامه توګه outward adj

په عرض thyroid n	په لاندي ځول that adj
په عمومي ځول publicly adv	په لرګي وهل club v
په عین حال کې meanwhile adv	په لست کې نبول enlist v
په غاړه اخیستل assume v	په لمړي توګه originally adv
په غاړه اخیستل undertake v	په لید پوهني optical adj
په غرور proudly adv	په لیکه درول array n
په غصه irate adj	په لږوالي scarcely adv
په غه وخت کې then adv	په لېکه درول align v
په غور کتل scan v	په متروکه وهل lash, flog v
په غبېر کې نبول entail v	په مخ تلل proceed v
په غبېر نبول hug, cling v	په مخه تلل go away v
په غبېر نبول hug n	په مخه ورتګ come across v
په فرضي ځول reportedly adv	په مناسب توګه duly adv
په فعاله توګه busily adv	په مناسب ځول properly adv
په فکر کې اچول puzzling adj	په منظم ځول regularly adv
په قار furiously adv	په مینه loving adj
په قصدي ځول purposely adv	په مښوکه وهل peck v
په کار اچونه mistreatment n	په مښوکه وهل peck n
په کتار abreast adv	په مبنځ کې amid, among pre
په کلکه earnestly adv	په ناز لوبول cater to v
په کلکه توګه hardly adv	په نامه namely adv
په کوتک وهل bludgeon v	په نرمي softly adv
په کوم باندي چې whereupon c	په نوبت کول alternate v
په کوم ځاې کې wherever c	په نورماله معیار substandard adj
په کومه لاره somehow adv	په نږدې توګه nearby adj
په کې in pre	په نښه کول locate v

پـه خـنـئـیـر تـړل chain v	پـه نبستي poorly adv
پـه خـیـر narrowly adv	پـه هـر per pre
پـه خـیـر کتنه stark adj	پـه هـر حـال however c
پـه خـبـر کتنه scrutiny n	پـه هـر سـاعـت کې whenever adv
پـه خـبـر والـې harshly adv	پـه هـر ډول anyhow pro
پـه خـرگند ډول expressly adv	پـه هکله about pre
پـه خـرگند ډول obviously adv	پـه همدې ډول as c
پـه خـنگ کې alongside pre	پـه هـبـله تـوب hopefully adv
پـه څـټ کـول overrule v	پـه واسطه in depth adv
پـه څـټ کـبـدل recede v	پـه واقعي تـوگه clearly adv
پـه ډانگ پـیـلـي outright v	پـه وچـه ایسـار landlocked adj
پـه ډلـه ورتللـ mob v	پـه وسـلـه سـنـبـال arm v
پـه بـنـه تـوگه fine adv	پـه وعـدې تـیـنگ punctual adj
پـه بـنـه ډول nicely adv	پـه وړانـدې تـلل come forward v
پـه گـرنـدپـتـوب activation n	پـه یادول commemorate v
پـه بـاد کـبـدل recur v	پـه یقـیـي تـوگه surely adv
پـه بـادبـدل resurface v	پـه یـوه لاره someway adv
پـوخ mellow, ripe adj	پـه یـوه وخـت کـې concurrent adj
پـوخ سـړې elderly adj	پـه تـراپ تلل gallop v
پـوخـوالـی maturity n	پـه ټوکو jokingly adv
پـودر powder n	پـه ټولبزه تـوگه overall adv
پـودبـن pudding n	پـه تـیـنگه sternly adv
پـور debt, score n	پـه ځـان غـره arrogant adj
پـور ادا کـول liquidate v	پـه ځـان مبـن egoist n
پـور کـوونکی creditor n	پـه ځـای کـې سـاتـل bolster v
پـور ه ول borrow v	پـه ځـاې کـول replacement n

پور ورکول lend iv	پوسته خانه post office n
پورتنی upper adj	پوسته رسونکی postman n
پورته خوا upwards adv	پوستول peel v
پورته کول promote v	پوکونکی puffy adj
پورته کېدل recuperate v	پوکنی bubble n
پورته کېدنه mutiny n	پوکی hiss v
پورته منزل upstairs adv	پولاد steel n
پورته والی supremacy n	پولادي livid adj
پوره complete, perfect adj	پولند Poland n
پوره plenty n	پولندی pole n
پوره پوهول fathom out v	پولندی Polish adj
پوره توب perfection n	پولبس police n
پوره خوشالي delightful adj	پونده heel n
پوره کول complete v	پونده کول spur v
پوره کېدنه expiration n	پوه aware adj
پوروری debtor n	پوه scholar, pupil n
پوري وتل ferry n	پوهاند professor n
پوري خوا beyond adv	پوهنتون university n
پوري وهل repulse v	پوهنځی college n
پوري وهنه impulse n	پوهه knowledge n
پوري وهونکی impulsive adj	پوهول understand v
پوزه nose n	پوهېدل comprehend v
پوست gentle, meek adj	پوټ خولی dumb adj
پوست کارد postcard n	پور flat, layer n
پوست یا خوبه iron v	پوښ bedspread, lid n
پوستکی، وپښ scale n	پوښ ورکول cover up v

clothing n پوښاک	پیمه وال v underwrite
questionnaire n پوښتنلبک	پینه کول v botch, darn
question v پوښتنه	پیوند n annexation
question n پوښتنه	پیتی n load
inquire v پوښتنه کول	پیتی ورل v load
rib n پوښتی	پټ adj covert, hidden
onion n پیاز	پټ قوت adj potential
chalice, cup n پیاله	پټ کښېناستل v lurk
mighty adj پیاوړی	پټ لتون adj undercover
survival n پیاښت	پټاخی n firecracker
survive v پیاښت	پترول n gasoline
sunny adj پیتاوی	پټوالی n secrecy
creation n پیداښت	پټول v conceal, hide
money n پیسب	پټی n bandage
apron n پیش بند	پټی ایښودل v bandage
kitten n پیشنگوری	پخ adj pointless, blunt
cat n پیشو	پخوالی adj retarded
lurid adj پیکه	پړانگ n panther, tiger
tarnish v پیکه کېدل	پړسوب n bulge, swelling
beginning n پیل	پړسوبوالی adj bloated
initiate, start v پیل	پړسېدل iv swell
commence v پیل کول	پړسېدلی adj swollen, baggy
start v پیل کول	پړک n flash
beginner n پیل کوونکی	پړی، رسی n cord
begin iv پیل کېدل	پښ n blacksmith
Turk adj پیل مرغ	پنبه n foot

پېچل complicate v	پښه ايښودل tread iv
پېچلى intricate adj	پښو څوکې tiptoe n
پېداكول procreate v	پښې feet n
پېداوار production n	پښې لوڅې barefoot adj
پیر saint n	پښېدونكې probable adj
پېره دار sentry n	پښېمان remorseful adj
پېروې milky adj	پښېمان كېدل recant v
پېروې cream n	پښېماني contrition n
پېرې كونكې repulsive adj	پښېمانېدل degrade v
پېژند پاڼه label n	پنه irrigation n
پېژند ګلوې acquaintance n	پنې shoe n
پېژندل know iv	پۍ ارزښته trivial adj
پېژندنه recognition n	پۍ درده painless adj
پېژندنې astronomic adj	پۍ شخړې undisputed adj
پېژندوې familiar adj	پۍ قانونه unlawful adj
پېسې funds n	پۍ كوره homeless adj
پېش بنې foresight n	پۍ له without pre
پېش بنې كول forecast iv	پيا ادعا كول reclaim v
پېش نظر foreground n	پيا تازه كول rejuvenate v
پېش ګوپې كېدل foretell v	پيانو piano n
پېشنهاد motion n	پيانو غږونكې pianist n
پېشګوپې prediction n	پياورې gladiator n
پېشګوپې وپل predict v	پياورې powerful adj
پېغلتوب maiden n	پېچ screw n
پېغله maid, virgin n	پېچ تاو screwdriver n
پېغمبر prophet n	پېچكاري injection n

ت

تائید n assertion

تابعیت n citizenship

تابوت n casket, coffin

تاج n crown

تاج یبنسودل v crown

تاجر n businessman

تادیه کول v defray

تادیه n payment

تار n fiber, thread

تار، مزی n string

تاریخ n chronicle

تاربخ n history

تاربخ پوه n historian

تازه adj fresh, recent

تازه adj vivid

تازه کول v freshen

تازه والی n freshness

تازب n hound

تازب سپي n greyhound

تاسب pro you

تاک adj odd

تاکید کول v underline

تال n symphony

تالا کول v spoil

پیغور adj ironic

پیغور n sarcasm

پبکه توب n paleness

پیل n elephant

پیل کول v set about

پیل کبدل، راوتل v set off

پیلوټ n pilot

پبنسل n pencil

پبنده n mess

پبوند n graft

پبوندکول v graft

پبرۍ n century

پبنبه n event, episode

پبنسوول v desert

پبنب n imitation

پبنب کول v imitate

پبنبدل v occur

پبنبدونکی adj impending

spoils *n* تالان	تبی disk *n* تبی
thunder *n* تالنده	cover *n* تپت
palate *n* تالو	bleak, gloomy *adj* تت
meditation *n* تامل	blurred *adj* تتوالی
stir up *v* تاو راتاو	obscurity *n* تتوالی
disadvantage *n* تاوان	dealer *n* تجار
recoup *v* تاوان اخیستل	industry *n* تجارت
recompense *v* تاوان ورکول	commercial *adj* تجارتي
recompense *n* تاوان ورکونه	trademark *n* تجارتي نښه
fiery *adj* تاوجن	advertising *n* تجارتي اعلانونه
peacock *n* تاوس	connive *v* تجاهل کول
wind, bend *iv* تاوول	infraction *n* تجاوز
compile *v* تألیفول	experience *n* تجربه
chalk *n* تباشیر	analysis *n* تجزیه
overturn *v* تباه کول	insistence *n* تجزیه کول
perish *v* تباه کبدل	analyze *v* تجزیه کول
dissolution *n* تباهي	deluxe *adj* تجمل
feverish *adj* تبجن	luxury *n* تجمل
hectic *adj* تبجن	munitions *n* تجهیزات
fumigate *v* تبخبر کول	connote *v* تجویز ورکول
ax, hatchet *n* تبر	suggest *v* تجویز کول
comment *n* تبصره	proposal *n* تجویز
comment *v* تبصره کول	guild *n* تحادیه
preaching *n* تبلیغ	instigate *v* تحریکول
propaganda *n* تبلیغات	inquisition *n* تحقیقات
fever *n* تبه	decompose *v* تحلیل کول

throne *n* تخت	تر منځ *pre* between
armpit *n* تخرګ	تر منځ راتللو *v* intervene
sabotage *n* تخریب	تر هغه وخته *adv* till
benefit *n* تخفه	تر ټل *v* mistreat, snub
benefit *v* تخفه ورکول	تر ټنه *v* censure
germ *n* تخم	تر ټولو بد *adj* worst
technicality *n* تخنیکي	تر ټولو ښه *adj* best
technician *n* تخنیکګر	تر ټولو ښه سړی *n* best man
tickle *n* تخول	تر څنډ اووختل *v* overflow
tickle *v* تخبدل	تر څو چې *pre* until
ticklish *adj* تخبدونکی	ترازه بلبول *v* splinter
devise *v* تدبیر کول	تراکتور *n* tractor
plan *n* تدبیر	ترانه *n* anthem
plan *v* تدبیرول	ترتیب *n* order
gradual *adj* تدریجي	ترتیبول *v* incline
evolution *n* تدریجي تکامل	ترتب والې *adj* armed
overdose *n* تر اندزې ډیر	تردد *n* hesitation
yet *c* تر اوسه	تردې وخته *adv* hitherto
laden, loaded *adj* تر بار لاندې	ترشوالی *n* austerity
interpret *v* تر جمه کول	ترفع *n* promotion
mesmerize *v* تر دم لاندې کول	ترقې کول *v* progress
repel *v* تر شا کول	ترقې کول *n* progress
setback *n* تر شا کېدنه	ترک کول *iv* quit
dependent *adj* تر لاس لاندې	ترکاڼ *n* carpenter
inundate *v* تر لاندې کېدل	ترکاڼي *n* carpentry
head for *v* تر لري سر	ترکول *n* check up

Turkey n تركي	vacancy n تش خأى
combination n تركيب	void adj تش، خالي
thermometer n ترماميتر	entrepreneur n تشبت كونكب
touch up v ترميم كول	basin n تشت
reparation n ترمبم	diagnose v تشخيص كول
repair v ترمبمول	identify v تشخيصول
tense adj ترنگلى	induce v تشديقول
nightfall n تره غونى	descriptive adj تشريحي
cornet n تروم	account for v تشربع كول
trimester n تري مبتر	formality n تشربفات
miracle n تريانوونكب	consist v تشكيلبدل
bitter, sour adj تريخ	bathroom n تشناب
uptight adj ترينگلي	tension n تشنج
lower adj تريو	emptiness n تشوالب
condemnation n ترتنه	deflate, empty v تشول
chisel n تربنخ	exhausting adj تشونه
pancreas n تربخب	worry n تشويش
litter n تزكره	worry v تشويش كول
shatter v تس نس كول	persuade v تشوبق
shattering adj تس نس والب	encourage v تشوبقول
rosary n تسپب	persuasion n تشوبقول
stretcher n تسكيره	persuasive adj تشوبقي
continuity n تسلسل	coincidence n تصادف
calm down v تسلي وركول	coincidental adj تصادفي
deliver, submit v تسليمول	assent v تصديق
blank, empty adj تش	testify v تصديق كول

certificate *n* تصدیق نامه	تعمیر casino *n*
certify *v* تصدیقول	sterilize *v* تغقیم کول
clarification *n* تصدیقول	sullen *adj* تغمه ناک
documentation *n* تصدق نامه	conversion *n* تغیر
affirm *v* تصدقول	fluctuate *v* تغیر خورل
clearance *n* تصفیه	pliable *adj* تغیر منونکب
clarify *v* تصفیه کول	contrast *n* تفاوت
purification *n* تصفیه	recess *n* تفریح
refinery *n* تصفیه خانه	annotation *n* تفسیر
intention *n* تصمیم	annotate *v* تفسیر لیکل
classify *v* تصنیف	detail *n* تفصیل
delusion *n* تصور	detail *v* تفصیل ورکول
imagine *v* تصور کول	pension *n* تقاعد
envisage *v* تصورکول	holiness *n* تقدس
approbation *n* تصویب	nearly *adv* تقریباً نردب
image *n* تصویر	schedule *n* تقسیم اوقات
illustration *n* تصویر	divide *v* تقسیمول
warranty *n* تضمین	reinforce *v* تقویه کول
complimentary *adj* تعارفي	reinforcements *n* تقویه کونه
definition *n* تعریف	repetition *n* تکرار
define *n* تعریف کول	intend *v* تکل کول
prejudice, bias *n* تعصب	suffer *v* تکلیف کب اخته
look after *v* تعقبول	energetic *adj* تکړه
pasteurize *v* تعقیمول	pillow, repose *n* تکیه
educational *adj* تعلیمي	repose *v* تکیه کول
baptism *n* تعمید غسل	ever, always *adv* تل

timeless *adj* تل	tobacco *n* تمباکو
permanent *adj* تل تر تله	icon *n* تمثال
blissful *adj* تل خوشاله	illustrate *v* تمثیل کول
immorality *n* تل ژوندی	allergic *adj* تمثیلي
immortality *n* تل یادونکي	exercise, practise *n* تمرین
plunder *v* تلا کول	exercise *v* تمرین کول
prowl *v* تلاش	rehearse *v* تمرین کول
atone *v* تلافي کول	crocodile *n* تمساح
telescope *n* تلسکوپ	prelude *n* تمهید
pronounce *v* تلفظ کول	sense *n* تمبز، عقل
go, hike *iv* تلل	meeting *n* تن په تن جنگ
shuttle *v* تلل او راتلل	proportion *n* تناسب
sole *adj* تلل شوي	symmetry *n* تناظر
sole *n* تله	salary *n* تنخواه
rush, hurry *v* تلوار کول	impetuous *adj* تند
television *n* تلوزیون	blast *n* تند باد
fad, longing *n* تلوسه	austere *adj* تند خویه
mortal *adj* تلونی	cranky *adj* تند مزاجه
telegram *n* تلگرام	speechless *adj* تندر وهلی
handgun *n* تماچه	thirst *v* تنده
feelings, impact *n* تماس	forehead *n* تندی
contact *v* تماس نیول	frown *v* تندي تربو کول
look into *v* تماشه کول	depreciation *n* تنزیل
performance *n* تمامول	deign *v* تنزیل کول
pistol *n* تمانچه	demote *v* تنزیل ورکول
propensity *n* تمایل	loom *v* تنسته

management *n* تنظیم ادارہ	predominate *v* توافق لرل
adjustable *adj* تنظیمولو	capability *n* توان
hatred *n* تنفر	can *iv* توان
breathing *n* تنفس	can *v* توان موندل
breathe *v* تنفس کول	influential *adj* توانا
vegetable *v* تنکی کدو	repentance *n* توبه
fjord *n* تنکي	repent *v* توبه کول
pillar, torso *n* تنه	penitent *n* توبه ګار
oven *n* تنور	globe *n* توپ
variety *n* تنوع	cannon *n* توپ خانه
strait *n* تنگ	hurricane, storm *n* توپان
bankruptcy *n* تنگ لاسي	stormy *adj* توپاني
chasm *n* تنگه درہ	tidal wave *n* توپاني څپه
canyon *n* تنگه ژورہ درہ	artillery *n* توپخانه
airtight *adj* تنگه کوڅهٔ	gun *n* توپک
defile *v* تنگي	rifle *n* توپک
to *pre* ته	penance *n* توپه
yourself *pro* ته پخپله	different *adj* توپیر
threat *n* تهدید	discrepancy *n* توپیر
imminent *adj* تهدیدووکي	diversity *n* توپیر
calumny *n* تهمت لګونه	discriminate *v* توپیر کول
blame, convict *v* تهمتي کول	distinguish *v* توپیر ورکول
turn up *v* تهیه کول	diversify *v* توپیرورکول
equilibrium *n* توازن	parrot *n* توتي
adaptable *adj* توافق	attention *n* توجه
adapt *v* توافق کول	intend *adj* توجه کول

ت

تود fervent *adj*	تولېدول generate *v*
تودول toast *v*	تولېدونکی generator *n*
تور black *adj*	تومن lukewarm *adj*
تور blame *n*	تومنه substantial *adj*
تور انگور grape *n*	تومنه کول curdle *v*
تور لگول scandalize *v*	تومور tumor *n*
تور لگونه scandal *n*	توند مزاجه grumpy *adj*
تور والی blackness *n*	توندخوې ferocious *adj*
تورتم dark *adj*	تونل mine, tunnel *n*
تورلگول accuse *v*	توری کېدل stutter *v*
تورن suspect *n*	توری‌ aunt *n*
توره sword *n*	تورل cast, carve *iv*
توره دره blackboard *n*	توبنه resource *n*
تورول denounce *v*	توبول pour, waste *v*
توربالی warrior *n*	تي خور ماشوم baby *n*
توسعه expansion *n*	تي لرونگي mammal *n*
توصېه prescribe *v*	تياره darkness *n*
توغندې rocket *n*	تياره murky *adj*
توقع کول live off *v*	تياره somber *adj*
توقيف detention *n*	تياره کول darken *v*
توک وهل stuff *v*	تياری arrangement *n*
توک، جلد volume *n*	تيت و پرک sporadic *adj*
توکيزې ځبرې cartoon *n*	تير beam *n*
تول amount to *v*	تيره کونکي sharpener *n*
تولول run up *v*	تيسس thesis *n*
تولېد produce *n*	تيکنالوژي technology *n*

oil *n* تيل	blister *n* تناكه
theory *n* تيورى	switch *n* تنى
stone *v* تيره ويشتل	unbutton *v* تنى خلاصول
inhale, gasp *v* تيگا وهل	alert *v* تبار سې
stuffy *adj* تر بوخته	dusk, gloom *n* تباره
bang *v* ترك	overshadow *v* تباره
tie, attach, bind *v* تړل	provide *v* تبارول
coagulation *n* تړل	preparation *n* تباري
closed *adj* تړل شوى	disintegrate *v* تبت و پرك كول
close *adj* تړلى	scrambled *adj* تبت والى
pertinent *adj* تړلب	disperse *v* تبت وپرك كول
tepid *adj* ترم	dispersal *n* تبت وپرك كونه
warm *adj* ترم	deceit *n* تبر ايستنه
warmth *n* ترموالى	trip *v* تبر وتل
warm up *v* ترمول	defraud *v* تبرايستل
trailer *n* تره	terms *n* تبرشوى
covenant, pact *n* ترون	past *adj* تبره
stipulate, ally *v* ترون كول	acidity *n* تبره والب
stammer *v* ترى ترى كبدل	last night *adv* تبره شپه
thirsty *adj* ترى	sharpen *v* تبره كول
abduct, kidnap *v* تبنتول	sharp *adj* تبره، نبغ
abduction *n* تبنتونه	deception *n* تبروتنه
escape, flee *v* تبنتبدل	swallow, ingest *v* تبرول
hike *n* تگ	offense, outrage *n* تبرى
trajectory *n* تگ كرښه	coerce, offend *v* تبرى كول
itinerary *n* تگلاره	offensive *adj* تبرى كوونكى

ت
ث
ج

ث

constant adj ثابت
prove v ثابتول
effusive adj ثابتونکې
secondary adj ثانوي
second n ثانيه
stability n ثبات
steady adj ثبات، ټينګ
record n ثبت
record v ثبتول
recorder n ثبتونکی
register v ثبتېدل
argument, proof n ثبوت

ج

pushy adj جابر
Japan n جاپان
Japanese adj جاپاني
herald n جاچي
charisma n جادو
sorcerer n جادو ګر
magician n جادوګر

oppress v تېرى ګول
aggression n تېرې
aggressive adj تېرې کونکې
disgusting adj تېرې کونکې
elapse, expire v تېربدل
fleeting adj تېربدنه
transition n تېربدنه
speedy adj تېز
loudly adv تېز والي
acid n تېزابي
spotlight n تېزه رڼا
brush up v تېزول
speedily adv تېزي
let out v تېزې سره وتل
sprout v تبغ وهل
phone n تېلېفون
phone v تېلېفون کول
escapade n تبنبته

جادوبي hermetic *adj*	جذبونکي absorbent *adj*
جادويي magical *adj*	جراح surgeon *n*
جار victim *n*	جرآت dare *n*
جارو broom *n*	جرآت کول dare *v*
جارو کول sweep *iv*	جرسي jersey *n*
جارول victimize *v*	جرګه convention *n*
جاري affluent *adj*	جرم crime, felony *n*
جاري ساتل keep on *v*	جرمن German *adj*
جاري incessant *adj*	جريان process *n*
جاري ساتل carry on *v*	جريبمه کول forfeit *v*
جاسوس spy *n*	جروبى cascade *n*
جاسوسي espionage *n*	جز component *n*
جال net *n*	جزا punishment *n*
جامه habit *n*	جزا ورکول punish *v*
جامي costume, robe *n*	جزا، جمله sentence *n*
جانګی underwear *n*	جزرورکول ebb *v*
جبه bog, swamp *n*	جزمي orthodox *adj*
جت gypsy *n*	جزیه نابا لغ minor *adj*
جدا کول cordon off *v*	جسارت daring *adj*
جدا کبدنه confiscation *n*	جست zinc *n*
جدي توب seriousness *n*	جسم body *n*
جدي، تينګ serious *adj*	جسما physically *adv*
جذام leprosy *n*	جسماني bodily *adj*
جذامي سړی leper *n*	جسمي sensual *adj*
جذب کول soak up *v*	جشن festivity *n*
جذب کبدل gravitate *v*	جعل کاري forgery *n*

جعل کاری کول fake v	جلبونکپ incorrigible adj
جعلي نوم pseudonym n	جم جگره thunderstorm n
جعلي counterfeit v	جمع additional adj
جعلي counterfeit adj	جمع digestion n
جغرافیه geography n	جمع شوی digestive adj
جغل کپدنه gravely adv	جمع کپدل turn out v
جگ چائینک urn n	جمعه Friday n
جگره battle, fight, war n	جمناستپک acrobat n
جگره کول battle, fight v	جمهوریت republic n
جگره مار quarrelsome adj	جنازه funeral n
جگره وهنه tactics n	جنت paradise n
جگوالپ altitude n	جنډه flag n
جگول elevate, lift v	جنس gender, sex n
جگونه elevation n	جنسپ generic adj
جگپدل go up v	جنسي sexuality n
جلا apart adv	جنسي تبادل truck n
جلا isolation n	جنگ bottle v
جلا off adv	جنگ ته راپلل defiance n
جلا شوی deductible adj	جنگپ fighter n
جلا کول deduct, detach v	جنگپ بپری warship n
جلا کپدنه schism n	جنگپالپ battleship n
جلاب laxative adj	جنگي سامان armaments n
جلاکپدنه estranged adj	جنگیالي militant adj
جلال majesty n	جنوب ختیځ southeast n
جلاوالی insulation n	جنوب لوبدیځ southwest n
جلبول fascinate v	جنوبي southern adj

southerner *n* جنوبي	جولاي *n* July
south *n* جنوبي قطب	sanctuary *n* جومات
January *n* جنوري	cottage *n* جونګره
embryo, fetus *n* جنين	essence *n* جوهر
catholic *adj* جهاني	substance *n* جوهر
Jew *n* جهود	pocket *n* جيب
dowry *n* جهيز	prison *n* جبل
meal *n* جواری	girl *n* جينې
gamble *v* جواري كول	lock up *n* جيل
apparent *adj* جوت	
adulterate *v* جوته كول	
adult *n* جوته كونكی	
rye *n* جودر	
sock *n* جورابه	
composition *n* جورښت	**چ**
bargain *n* جوړه	
bargain *v* جوړه راتلل	hand over *v* چا ته وركول
conjugate *v* جوړه كول	teapot *n* چائينک
couple *n* جوړه، تريا	print *n* چاپ
fabricate, make *v* جوړول	surround *v* چاپېرول
concoct *v* جوړول	ingratiate *v* چاپلوس
renovation *n* جوړونه	flatter *v* چاپلوسي
maker *n* جوړوونکی	print *v* چاپول
optician *n* جوړوونکي	printing *n* چاپونه
concur *v* جوربدل	enclosure *n* چاپېربال
teenager *n* جوريي	alternative *n* چاره
	chart *n* چارټ، نقشه
	shovel, spade *n* چارۍ

چاغ chubby, fat *adj*
چاقو knife *n*
چاک rift *n*
چاک. درز gap *n*
چاکلیت chocolate *n*
چال چلند treatment *n*
چالاک cute *adj*
چالان switch on *v*
چالباز tactical *adj*
چاود leak *n*
چاودل burst *iv*
چاودلی broke *adj*
چاودلی split *n*
چاودنه explosion *n*
چاودنه rupture *n*
چاودونکې مواد dynamite *n*
چاودبدل blow out, leak *iv*
چاودبدنه blowout *n*
چاودبدونکې explosive *adj*
چاونې garrison *n*
چای tea *n*
چای جوش kettle *n*
چاتلي dirty *adj*
چپ opponent *n*
چپ sedate *v*
چپاو invasion *n*

چیتپا quietness *n*
چپراس hinge *n*
چپراسول hinge *v*
چینه clock *n*
چپول gag *n*
چپول، دروغ gag *v*
چت ceiling *n*
چراغ دستي flashlight *n*
چرگ cock, rooster *n*
چرګه chicken, hen *n*
چرګوری chick *n*
چشمه glasses *n*
چشمې eyeglasses *n*
چغزی brittle *adj*
چغندک tumultuous *adj*
چغنده squeaky *adj*
چغه catchword *n*
چغې shout, shriek *n*
چغې کول exclaim *v*
چغې وهل screech, shriek *v*
چغبدل squeak *v*
چک چکې کول cheers *n*
چک کپ وهل applaud *v*
چک وهونکې rodent *n*
چکچکې کول acclaim *v*
چکر وهونکی wanderer *n*

tapestry *n* چکن شوب پرده	hook *n* چنگ، کړی
sauce *n* چکنب	Wednesday *n* چهارشنبه
dice *n* چکه پاو	silence *n* چوپتبا
grapefruit *n* چکوتره	satellite *n* چوپرپ
intrigue, ploy *n* چل	terrace *n* چوتره
construct *v* چل جورول	prick *v* چوخول
conspire *v* چل کول	mucus *n* چوخرپ
trick *n* چل، تبر ایستنه	top *n* چور لنډی
moral *adj* چلند	contemplate *v* چورت وهل
walk *n* چلند	swivel *v* چورلکه
drive *iv* چلول	whirl *v* چورلول
transaction *n* چلونه	beet *n* چوغندر
unfair *adj* چلي	whip *n* چوکه
cross *n* چلیپا	goad *v* چوکه کول
cross *v* چلیپا رابښکل	prod *v* چوکول
cross *adj* چلیپا شوی	furniture *n* چوکۍ
navigation *n* چلبدنه	detonate, rupture *v* چول
turf *n* چم	lime *n* چونه
block *v* چمبه وهل	frog *n* چونګبنبه
brisk *adj* چمتو	braid *n* چوتپ
mobilize *v* چمتو کول	tap *n* چوبنکه
expedition *n* چمتو والب	tap into *v* چوبنکول
anticipation *n* چمتوالی	tap into *n* چوبنکونه
exploit *v* چمتوکول	pleat *n* چوپ
lawn, meadow *n* چمن	pleated *adj* چوپ شوی
crab *n* چنکاښ	peep *v* چونهبدل

چيچل munch, sting v	ح
چيمپنزى chimpanzee n	
چينجى worm n	حارق العاده miraculous adj
چتک prompt, quick adj	حاشبه fringe n
چتکتبا haste n	حاصل product, yield n
چتکول hasten v	حاصل خبزه fertility n
چتلتوب grime n	حاصل ورکول yield v
چتلپ filth n	حاصلول get by v
چتى unprofitable adj	حاضر present adj
چتپ absurd adj	حاضر کول present v
چتپ گرزېدنه roam v	حافظه memory n
چرچپ کول revel v	حاکم bossy adj
چناسک moldy adj	حاکميت arbitration n
چناسپ mold n	حاکميت لرل dominate v
چڼل refine v	حال دا چپ whereas c
چڼول filter v	حال وبنه recount n
چنپاپپ violet n	حالت circumstance v
چبرته where adv	حامپ patron n
چبرپ whereabouts n	حبرول notify v
چبنپ لوبنپ porcelain n	حد ټاکل measure v
	حد، بريد limit n
	حذف omission n
	حربپ مهمات ammunition n
	حرص avarice, greed n
	حرصتوب greedy adj
	حرف جنګي charade n

حرکت movement n	حواله کونکی drawer n
حریص ambitious adj	حېثبت prestige n
حریم frontage n	حېرانوونکی astounding adj
حریص avaricious adj	حېرانوونکی amazing adj
حس کول sense v	حیا modesty n
حساب arithmetic n	حیاناک lowkey, modest adj
حساس sensitive adj	حیرانوونکي staggering adj
حساسیت backlash n	حیرانوونکی boil over v
حسد envy n	حیراني speculate v
حسدکول envy v	
حشره insect n	
حصار castle n	
حفاظت کول care for v	
حفه کول smother v	خ
حق غوښتل claim v	
حکم commandment n	خاټول tulip n
حکم کول decree v	خارج ته تلل come out v
حکمت wisdom n	خارج څانگه branch out v
حکومت government n	خارجول drop out v
حکومت کول govern v	خارجي exterior adj
حل کول work out, solve v	خارجي ،پردی foreign adj
حماقت folly n	خارجي سړی foreigner n
حمله assault, fit n	خارښت کول itch v
حمله کول assault v	خاشخاش poppy n
حواله ، مسوده draft n	خاص concrete n
حواله کول draft v	خاص رویش mannerism n
	خاصه غونډه get together v

خاصیت characteristic adj	خبری talk v
خاگینه omelette n	خبری اترپ dialogue n
خاکسار lowly adj	خبری کول speak iv
خاکه contour, sketch n	خبرپال reporter n
خاکه جوړول sketch v	خپ خپ تلل stalk v
خال ace n	خپرول advertise v
خال وهل vaccinate v	خپرونه televise v
خال، نښه spot n	خپروونکب broadcaster n
خالداره freckled adj	خپرپدل emanate v
خالق brute adj	خپر paw n
خالي Saturday n	خپسه nightmare n
خالي کول move out v	خپگان disapproval n
خالي devoid adj	خپل خوښب volunteer n
خاموش defuse, soothe v	خپل کاري automatic adj
خانه سامان butler n	خپل هډ akin adj
خاني lordship n	خپل وا که autonomous adj
خاوره clay, dirt, dust n	خپله کول displease v
خاورین لوښب crockery n	خپلواکي autonomy n
خاوند master n	خپلوان in-laws n
خاپن deserter n	خپلوب proximity n
خبر message, news n	خپلوي kinship n
خبرتیا notification n	خپه sad adj
خبرداره کیدل watch out v	خپه کول grieve, sadden v
خبرداري awareness n	خپه کیدل resent v
خبرنامه handout n	خپه کیدنه distressing adj
خبرول instruct, report v	خپور widespread adj

خپورول	broadcast v	خرابول	consume, strain v
خپوټی	wimp adj	خرابېدل	cut out v
ختل	ascend, climb v	خرابېدل، يخيدل	wear out v
ختمول	Finnish adj	خراپ غونډول	aggregate v
ختمول	log off v	خرافات	bigotry n
ختمبدل	die out v	خرافاتي	myopic adj
ختنه	climbing n	خرخ	expenditure n
خته کول	impact v	خرخلاو	sold-out adj
ختبخ	east n	خرخول	sell iv
ختيخه پوله	eastbound adj	خرخونکب	seller n
ختيث	orient n	خرپداري	shopping n
ختگر	mason n	خرپدل	snore n
ختکی	melon n	خرپبل	shave v
خته	mud n	خرپ	faded, gray, misty adj
ختين	muddy adj	خزانه دار	cashier n
خچنپ	gum n	خزلپ	rubbish n
خخلپ	garbage n	خزنده	reptile n
خداي پاماني	farewell n	خزه	moss n
خدای په امان	bye e	خس مار	gangrene n
خدمت کول	hospitalize v	خسر	father-in-law n
خر	donkey n	خسک	bug n
خراب	evil adj	خسوف	eclipse n
خراب	twist, strain n	خسيس	miser n
خراب شوی	strained adj	خصوصاً	especially adv
خرابتيا	demolition n	خطا	blunder n
خرابوالی	decay n	خطا ایستل	deceive v

خند اچول v obstruct, preempt	خطا کبدل v err
خند،ګڼ dense adj	خطا وتلی mistaken adj
خندول v compress	خطر n hazard, risk
خو c but	خطر کې اچول v risk
خوا بدوونکی odious adj	خطر ناک risky adj
خوا بدی شوی n iodine	خطرناکه terrible adj
خوا بدي کول n devaluation	خطیب n preacher
خوا ته ختل v soar	خفګان n sorrow
خوا خوري congenial adj	خفه unhappy adj
خوا خوري n compassion	خفه v traumatize
خوا ګرزي n nausea	خفه کول v asphyxiate
خواخوري benign adj	خلاصه n overview
خواخوري kindly adv	خلاصه v summarize
خواخوري n sympathy	خلاصول v extricate, unravel
خواخوري کول v sympathize	خلاصون n acquittal
خوار miserable adj	خلاصونه n redemption
خواري n misery	خلف n successor
خواري کښ diligent adj	خلق کول v create
خواږه n candy, sweets	خلک n folks, people
خواږه کچلان n yam	خلوت n privacy
خواږه n diet, food	خلیج n gulf, bay
خواښې n mother-in-law	خمیره n yeast, ferment
خواشینوونکی spineless adj	خنجر n dagger
خواشینی wretched adj	خندا n laugh
خواهش v implore	خندل v laugh
خوب لېدل iv dream	خنډ n obstacle

خوب لېده dream n	predilection n خونسه
خوبولي dizzy adj	like, select v خونسول
خوټپدل spirit, soul n	selection n خونسونه
خوځند vibrant adj	admirer n خونسوونکي
خوځنده motive n	treat v خونسي
خوځنډ shaky adj	fragrance n خوش بوی
خوځبدل wiggle v	humor n خوش طبعي
خور sister n	genial, happy adj خوشال
خورا ډبر innumerable adj	jolly, glad adj خوشاله
خورا ستر huge adj	rejoice v خوشاله کول
خوراک dish n	cheer, cheer up v خوشالول
خورورکونه tanned adj	gratify v خوشالول
خور noise n	delegation n خوشالوونکی
خور ژبب elegant adj	euphoria n خوشالي
خور ورمه redo v	pleasing adj خوشالبدل
خوره نغمه melody n	gratifying adj خوشالبدنه
خوروالی sweetness n	bliss n خوشالي
خورول sweeten v	dung n خوشاپب
خورل eat iv	aromatic adj خوشبویه کول
خورن خاب restaurant n	carefree adj خوشحاله
خوسا putrid adj	emission n خوشب
خوسا کبدل rot v	forsake iv خوشب کول
خوساکبدنه rot n	regret v خوشبنب
خوسالي joy n	pig, hog n خوگ
خوسکی calf n	mouth n خوله
خوسپ jubilant, merry adj	sweater n خوله کوونکی

perspire v خوله کبدل	belly n خبته
sweat n خولي	glutton n خبتو
sweat v خولي کول	alms n خبرات
hat n خولۍ	relative adj خبس
cap n خولی،سر پټونی	household n خبلخانه
relish, savor v خوند	sardine n خبنتي
enjoy v خوند اخپستل	imagination n خيال
flavor n خوند مزه	daydream v خيال پلو
taste v خوند ورکول	ideal adj خيالي
taste n خوند ورکول	betrayal n خيانت
delicious adj خوندور	betray v خيانت کول
zest n خوندور	benefactor n خير رسوونکی
safe adj خوندي	bounty n خيرات
savings n خوندي	squalid adj خيرن
secure v خوندي کول	soil v خيرنول
custody n خوندي توب	soggy adj خيشت
immunize v خوندي کول	soak v خيشتول
bleeding n خونريزي	tent n خيمه
bloody adj خونړی	daughter-in-law n خينه
compartment n خونه	
bloodthirsty adj خوني	
fantasy n خپال پلو	
fancy adj خپالي	
fiction n خپالي	
discrimination n خپانت	
double-cross v خپانت کول	

خ

د اوبو سپی beaver n	
د اوبو لکولو واله canal n	
د اوردې مودې long for v	
د اورۍ هډوکی collarbone n	
د اوسپنې اوزار hardware n	
د اوسېدو وړ habitable adj	
د بادام ونه almond n	
د بالښت پوښ pillowcase n	
د باندې out, outside adv	
د باندې لېرنه export v	
د بتانو رنګ shoepolish n	
د بحث لاندې fallhood n	
د بحث وړ debatable adj	
د بدلېدو وړ elastic adj	
د برښنا ماهر electrician n	
د برم خاوند sublime adj	
د برې نښان trophy n	
د بم چاودنه spark off v	
د بم ګولی bombshell n	
د بندو پارسوب arthritis n	
د بندیخان امر jailer n	
د بېرغ لکړه flagpole n	
د بېړی راشیل oar n	
د بېړی عرشه deck n	
د بېړی لکړه boom v	
د بېلجېمي Belgian adj	

د

د اورېدو وړ audible adj	
د اپریل میاشت April n	
د اتکا وړ dependable adj	
د اتلتوب heroic adj	
د اجازې وړ admissible adj	
د اجرا وړ applicable adj	
د اختر شپه vigil n	
د ادعا په توګه allegedly adv	
د ارې څنځیر chainsaw n	
د استوا کرښه equator n	
د اسمان لار galaxy n	
د اشپزانو مشر chef n	
د اشرا فو ډله aristocracy n	
د اطفایې غړی fireman n	
د افریقا پيشو lioness n	
د الانو کپسه romance n	
د امپراتور ښځه empress n	
د انتظار کوټه lobby v	
د اندازې وړ extenuating adj	
د انګورو باغ vineyard n	
د انګوروشراب wine n	
د اوبو پیشی۔ otter n	
د اوبو ذخیره reservoir n	

د بيسبال لوبه baseball n

د بيليارد لوبه billiards n

د پاپ مقام papacy n

د پاچا نایب regent n

د پام ور noticeable adj

د پای final adj

د پروړۍ کوټه haystack n

د پنبې ګوته toe n

د پهلواني athletic adj

د پوستې نښه postmark n

د پوهنتون rector n

د پوهنتون رئس chancellor n

د پوهېدو ور forgivable adj

د پیسو بکس piggy bank n

د پیغور sarcastic adj

د تابع کېدو ور docile adj

د تالونو کلي cleft n

د تباشیر تخته chalkboard n

د تجزیې له پاره settle for v

د تجویز ور advisable adj

د تسل ور satisfactory adj

د تصادف حالت accident n

د تعمیر فرش ground floor n

د تقاطع ځای crossing n

د تقسیم ور traumatic adj

د تل دپاره forever adv

د تلفاتو شمېر death toll n

د تمیز خاوند judicious adj

د تنخا رسېد payslip n

د تورن دفاعیه plea n

د تورو مچ nosy adj

د تي سر nipple n

د ټولو څخه لوړ crowning n

د ثنا ور praiseworthy adj

د جاذبې قوه magnetism n

د جراحي مبل probe v

د جراخي surgical adv

د جزا ور punishable adj

د جشن festive adj

د جلا کېدو ور detachable adj

+د جمع اعلام plus adj

د جنګ نقشه navy n

د چا نوم بدلول defame v

د چاپ ماشبېن printer n

د چکر ځای mall n

د چلولو لاره driveway n

د ځمکې جورول landfill n

د ځمکې لاندې underground adj

د څاروو خواړه mash v

د څاروو خواړه mask n

د څراغ پوښ lampshade n

د څېرۍ مېوه acorn n

د رى کرى noose *n*		د خبرونې ساعت alarm clock *n*
د زره له کومې heartfelt *adj*		د خطر زنګ siren *n*
د زره ورخ valve *n*		د خطري زنګ alarm *n*
د زغملو ور affordable *adj*		د خلکو ازمبنبت genocide *n*
د زنګ پرچ belfry *n*		د خندا ور laughable *adj*
د زنګون سترګه kneecap *n*		د خواشبنې ور regrettable *adj*
د زنغوزپ ونه pine *n*		د خواشينى ور deplorable *adj*
د زهرو ضد دارو antidote *n*		د خوب خونه bedroom *n*
د زبربدنې ورځ birthday *n*		د خوب سامان bedding *n*
د زينې پانکب staircase *n*		د خوب کالي nightgown *n*
د ژبې ټکونه spank *v*		د خوب کلپ pajamas *n*
د ژوند vital *adj*		د خوب کوټه chamber *n*
د ژوند رنګ lifestyle *n*		د خوځيدنې قوت springboard *n*
د ژوند معنا live up *v*		د خوراک edible *adj*
د ژوند وخت lifetime *adj*		د خوسي غوښنه veal *n*
د ژوندانه شيان livelihood *n*		د خوګ غوښنه pork *n*
د سبر ونه cypress *n*		د دابر اواز dial tone *n*
د سپينو لوښى silverplated *adj*		د ډاج ور pass around *v*
د سترګو لبدنه eyewitness *n*		د ډالر سلمه برخه cent *n*
د سر پوستکپ scalp *n*		د ډبرو سکاره coal *n*
د سرپخه dandruff *n*		د ډکولو مواد stuffing *n*
د سرپو څخه جوړ lead *n*		د رايپ کاغذ ballot *n*
د سرطان ناروغي cancer *n*		د ربط تورپ preposition *n*
د سکبټ لوبه کول skate *v*		د رسونپ ور approachable *adj*
د سندر غاړو ډله choir *n*		د رمز ترجمه decipher *v*
د سوکانو لوبه boxing *n*		د رنګولو برش paintbrush *n*

د سونګ لرګي firewood *n*	د غوښې لعاب gravy *n*
د سپنګار مېز dresser *n*	د غونډۍ سر hilltop *n*
د سياحت ډله tourism *n*	د غويو ګاډۍ cart *n*
د بنار شا و خوا suburb *n*	د غويو ګاډۍ cart *v*
د ښخولو ځای catacomb *n*	د فارم انګړ farmyard *n*
د شا لغته kickback *n*	د فلم کېسه scenario *n*
د شاباسۍ وړ admirable *adj*	د قبر شنانښته gravestone *n*
د شارحې نښه colon *n*	د قبر کنبستل grave *n*
د شپې nocturnal *adj*	د قربانۍ ګډورې scapegoat *n*
د شپيلۍ يو ډول clarinet *n*	د قربانۍ ځای altar *n*
د شجرې gene *n*	د قيامت ورځ resurrection *n*
د شطرنج ګوتک pawn *v*	د قيمت کوزېدل bring down *v*
د شګو بيديا desert *n*	د ګډوډۍ طرفدار anarchist *n*
د شمعې چوکه candlestick *n*	د ګرمي وخت heatwave *n*
د طبيعت بدلول dentures *n*	د ګوتې نښه fingerprint *n*
د عفونې ضدکول disinfect *v*	د ګوډ لکړه crutch *n*
د علم vandalism *n*	د کار ځی workshop *n*
د غاړي څخه aside from *adv*	د کاغذ کثوره wrapping *n*
د غاښ درد toothache *n*	د کاله مېرمن housewife *n*
د غاښونو منګ tartar *n*	د کب بچيان fried *adj*
د غرمې ډوډۍ lunch *n*	د کب وزر fin *n*
د غره غوايي bison *n*	د کباپ سيخ spit *iv*
د غلې ګودام elevator *n*	د کبانو ساتنځی aquarium *n*
د غڼې خاله cobweb *n*	د کتابونو بکس bookcase *n*
د غڼې خاله spiderweb *n*	د کرکې scornful *adj*
د غوږ درد earache *n*	د کرنې وړ ځمکه arable *adj*

د کسافت بیلر trash can n	د ماښام ډوډۍ dinner n
د کلورا ناروغۍ cholera n	د ماښام ډوډۍ supper n
د کلیسا جرګه synod n	د مترسیستم metric adj
د کمري لېنز lense n	د مثال exemplary adj
د کنج تیږه cornerstone n	د محکمي غړی bricklayer n
د کوټې فرش upholstery n	د مخلفت antagonize v
د کوڅې څراغ lamppost n	د مخه تیارول prepare v
د کور خاوند housekeeper n	د مخه خبرول foreshadow v
د کور کار housework n	د مخه سنجول premeditate v
د کورنۍ مشر patriarch n	د مخه سوچ premeditation n
د کورنۍ نوم surname n	د مخه نبونه preoccupation n
د کوره د باندې abroad adv	د مراتبو سلسله hierarchy n
د کونسل دفتر consulate n	د مرګ کټ deathbed n
د لارښودنه کتاب guidebook n	د مرګ لومه death trap n
د لاس بریدو ور attainable adj	د مړي سوزیدنه crematorium n
د لاس زولانه handcuffs n	د مړینې معائینه autopsy n
د لبنباتو فارم dairy farm n	د مشرانو جرګه senate n
د لرګو سکاره charcoal n	د مطلق واکدار almighty adj
د لږ وخت لپاره briefly adv	د معلوماتو زېرمه database n
د لمانځه اداب liturgy n	د مقایسه کېدو ور comparable adj
د لوښو خونه pantry n	د مقایسې ور comparative adj
د لیدنې visual adj	د ملاتبر guts n
د لیکلو څرمن parchment n	د ملګرتیا ور amicable adj
د لیکلو کار clerical adj	د منځ څخه through pre
د لیمو شربت lemonade n	د منځنیو پیړیو medieval adj
د مادي فلسفه materialism n	د مننې ور bearable adj

cider n د مېو شیره	ventilation n د هوا بدلون
harp n د موسقی اله	delegate n د هئيت غړي
admire v د مبنې په نظر کتل	league n د واټن واحد
hull n د مبوو او پوستکي	conjugal adj د واده
laundry n د مينځلو کالي	lard n د وازګې غوړي
lovable adj د مينې وړ	ice skate v د واورو لوبه
orchard n د ميوو باغ	destination n د وتلو ځای
clinic n د ناروغانو کتنځی	doorbell n د ور زنګ
ambulance n د ناروغانو موټر	doorstep n د وره زینه
seat n د ناستي ځاې	fraternal adj د ورورۍ
astrology n د نجوم علم	gun down v د وسلو تربیه
ball n د نڅا مجلس. توپ	divisible adj د وشبلو وړ
degeneration n د نسل کمېدنه	hairbrush n د وېښتو برش
consensus n د نظرونو موافقه	hairdo n د وېښتو ډول
asthmatic adj د نفس تنګی	washable adj د وینځلو وړ
upside-down adv د نقل تمري	noteworthy adj د یادونې وړ
scenic adj د نندارې	cool down v د یخ لاندې
unavoidable adj د نه پرېښودلو	iceberg n د یخ یوه ټوټه
illegible adj د نه لوستلو وړ	icebox n د یخي بکس
unbelievable adj د نه منلو وړ	Judaism n د یهودو دین
apocalypse n د نوي عهد انجیل	ice cube n د یخ ټوټه
profile n د نېم مخ تصویر	herself pro دا پخپله
honk v د هارن اواز	academic adj داپلاتون فلسفي
bone marrow n د هډوکو مغځ	hyphen n داتصال نښه
egg white n د هګی سپین	take in, turn in v داخل ته تلل
boyfriend n د هلک ملګر تیا	come in v داخل ته راتلل

داخلي inside adj	دايره circle n
داخلي intern v	دايره كول circle v
داخلي dogmatic adj	دايروي circular adj
داداري ور manageable adj	دايي midwife n
دار gallows n	دايي / نيا nanny n
دارايي asset, means n	دباره كتل crosswalk n
دارو drug n	دبلی can n
دارو وركول drug v	دبلياردلوبه pool n
داروغبي disease n	دبني aquatic adj
داره fang n	دبوتو علم botany n
داس ګانه trimmings n	دپاره for pre
داسب such adj	دپاسه upon pre
داش furnace n	دپاكول اله bleach n
داغ blot, scar n	دتره څوي cousin n
داغ ،نښه brand n	دتودوخی مقياس calorie n
داغ پلمونی soil n	دتيري په توګه outmoded adj
داغ ګر خبدل blot v	دجامو اخيستل clothe v
داغ كول stain v	دجراپوكاليس garter n.
داغ لګول spot v	دجنګ حمله bottleneck n
دالان gallery, porch n	دچاپولو حق copyright n
دانه pimple n	دچرګ اذان crow n
داهاكو ډبره limestone n	دحمام چينه bathrobe n
داوبو سبل deluge n	دخاروي ډله bestial adj
داودي ګل daisy n	دخطر نښه beacon n
داوسپنې خولپ helmet n	دخلكو حكومت democracy n
دابلبدو ور docility n	دخير دعا benediction n

ددرې پل viaduct n	درستوالې accuracy n
ددماغ ساحه minefield n	درستې precision n
ددنيا د تر کانو ډله convent n	درسي کتاب textbook n
ددۀ his adj	درشل threshold n
ددوو ښځو لرنه bigamy n	درغل traitor n
ددې په وجه because of pre	درغل treacherous adj
ددبن سپکاوې sacrilege n	درغلب fallacy n
ددپې hers pro	درغلي treachery, treason n
دربول batter v	درک grasp n
دربونه battery n	درلود ل include v
دربېدل throb n	درلودل contain v
دربېدل throb v	درمل healer n
درجن dozen n	درمل کول remedy v
درجه bulldoze v	درملتون pharmacy n
درجه species, grade n	درمن harvest n
درجه حرارت temperature n	درمندول harvest v
درجه دار classy adj	درناوې homage, regards n
درد pain, ache, sore n	درنښت decency, dignity n
دردمن painful adj	دره valley n
دردمند sore adj	درواغ lie n
دردناک excruciating adj	درواغجن liar adj
دردول afflict v	دروغ ويل lay iv
درز crevice n	درول cease, halt, stall v
درزپ seamstress n	دروند burdensome adj
درست inflict v	دروندوالې heaviness n
درست precise adj	درونه installation n

three *adj* دری	review *n* دسره کتنه
tripod *n* دری پنبیز	دسرو *adj* golden
triple *adj* دری گونی کول	handkerchief *n* دسمال
platform, pulpit *n* دربخ	December *n* دسمبر میاشت
desist, persist *v* دربدل	fuel *n* دسونگ مواد
stagnant *adj* دربدلی	discipline *n* دسپلبن سمون
stand *n* دربدنه	conspiracy *n* دسیسه
lingering *adj* دربدونکی	beach *n* دسیند غاړه
stage *v* دریخ	city hall *n* دبنار سالون
status *n* دریخ، موقف	bailiff *n* دبناروالی وکیل
chimney *n* دریخهٔ	wilderness *n* دبنت
third *adj* دریمه برخه	hostile *adj* دبنمن
ski *v* دردنگ	hostility *n* دبنمنب
tablet, board *n* دره	animosity *n* دبنمنی
cardiology *n* دزره ناروغي	diabetes *n* دشکرب ناروغي
tolerable *adj* دزغملو ور	litany *n* دعا
hometown *n* دزبردنه	invoke, pray *v* دعا کول
lifeguard *n* دژوند ساتل	dignitary *n* دعزت مقام
accordion *n* دساز بوه آله	curable *adj* دعلاج ور
dial *n* دساعت مبخ	lawsuit *n* دعوه
dawn *n* دسباوون رڼا	muffler *n* دغاړب دشمال
despicable *adj* دسپکتیا ور	dentist *n* دغاښنونو ډاکټر
enterprise *n* دستگاه	launch *n* دغرمب ړوړی
culture, customs *n* دستور	grievance *n* دغم علت
shortly *adv* دستي	this, these *adj* دغه
borderline *adj* دسرحد کرښه	chide *v* دغور تاوول

ridge n دغونډپو لر	دلگی مشر n sergeant
defense n دفاع	دلوري طبقي adj bourgeois
defend v دفاع کول	دلی کول n hustle
defender n دفاع کوونکی	دلی کېدل v pile
bureau, office n دفتر	دلیل v reason
bookkeeper n دفتر دار	دلیل n reason
bookkeeping n دفتر داري	دماغ n mind
considerable adj دقدر ور	دماغی حلل n psychopath
grill n دکباب سیخ	دماغي adj mental
heatstroke n دکرمی اسباب	دماغي پرده adj cerebral
pollen n دګل ګرده	دمخنیوي ور adj avoidable
cherry n دګلاس مبوه	دمړي سوځول v cremate
condone v دګنا بخښنبل	دمشکل انتخاب n dilemma
fingertip n دګوتې سر	دمعدې adj gastric
implement v دکار وسیله	دمفکورو علم n ideology
miner n دکان کار ګر	دملابند n vertebra
diaper n دکتان ټوکر	دمنلو ور adj believable
checkbook n دکتنې کتاب	دمنلو ور adj acceptable
tram n دکوڅې ګاډی	دمه نبونه n relaxation
wrist n دلاس بند	دموټر یوه پرزه n crank
console v دلاسه کول	دمینې څرګندول v court
denote v دلالت	دنامه غوټی n navel
implicate v دلالت کول	دنڅا سالون n ballroom
here adv دلته	دنده n dues, duty, job
dime n دلسو سنټو سکه	دنظر ټکې n viewpoint
platoon n دلګب	دنګبدونکب v plunge

دننه indoor, inland *adv*	دوزخ hell *n*
دننه inside, within *pre*	دوسیه dossier, folder *n*
دننوتلو حق admission *n*	دوسیه coverup *n*
دننوتو لار entree *n*	دوشنبه Monday *n*
دننی inland *adj*	دوطن homemade *adj*
دننی interior *adj*	دوکان shop *n*
دنه منلو inadmissible *adj*	دوکاندار salesman *n*
دنوح بېرکې ark *n*	دوکه باز swindler *n*
دنپا parsley *n*	دولت لګول turn over *v*
دهقان peasant *n*	دولت مند کول enrich *v*
دهلبز corridor *n*	دولسم twelfth *adj*
دوا medication *n*	دومره merely *adv*
دوا خانه drugstore *n*	دونو وهل log *v*
دواړه both *adj*	دونب پوستک bark *n*
دوام continuation *n*	دوه two *adj*
دوامداره lasting *adj*	دوه ټرکونه tow truck *n*
دواورپ توپان blizzard *n*	دوه ځله twice *adv*
دوباره حاصلول win back *v*	دوه ژوندی amphibious *adj*
دوباره کتنه reentry *n*	دوه ګون dual *adj*
دوجود یوه برخه bust *n*	دوه ګون duplicate *v*
دود custom, tradition *n*	دوه ګونب duplication *n*
دور era *n*	دوه مخي hypocrisy *n*
دوربینونه binoculars *n*	دوهم وار again *adv*
دوره circuit, epoch *n*	دوي they *pro*
دوروری brotherly *adj*	دبب giant *n*
دوریتول اله broiler *n*	دبرش thirty *adj*

particle n ذره

nuclear adj ذروي

mention n ذکر

mention v ذکر کول

sponsor n ذمه وار

insure v ذمه وهل

mentality n ذهنيت

gusto n ذوق

hobby n ذوقي کار

ر

captain n رئس

chairman n رئيس

recollect v را په زړه کېدل

upcoming adj را تلونکی

encompass v را چاپېرول

encircle v را چاپېربدل

stem v را ولاړېدل

composed adj را ټول شوی

prostate n را ټول کړ شوی

muster v را ټولول

unearth v رابرسېره کول

religion n دبن

piety n دبنداري

religious adj دبني

sacrament n دبني دود

wall n دبوال وزمه

hearth n دبوالي بخاري

bunk bed n دبوان

shrouded adj دبوی پلی

notable adj ديادونب ور

thirteen adj ديارلس

diploma n ديپلوم

diplomacy n ديپلوماسي

worldly adj دينوي

theology n دينيات

ذ

haircut n ذ وبينتو تباري

intrinsic adj ذاتی

attribute v ذاتي

personal adj ذاتي

store n ذخيره

fund v ذخبره کول

رابطه	link *n*	راټولوونکی	collector *n*
رابلل	beckon *v*	راټولبدنه	collection *n*
راپه دېخوا	since *pre*	راټولبدونکب	gregarious *adj*
راپور	report *n*	رانسکل	attract *v*
راتلل	come *iv*	رانسکنه	attraction *n*
راتلونکی	coming, next *adj*	راګرئبدل	return *v*
راتلونکی وخت	future *n*	راګرئبدنه	return *n*
راتګ	coming *n*	راکبرول	allure *n*
راخوټول	erupt *v*	راپه	vote *n*
راخوتپدنه	eruption *n*	راپه کول	vote *v*
راز	secret *n*	ربر	rubber *n*
راسته کول	coach *v*	ربرول	persecute *v*
راشه درشه کول	haunt *v*	ربروونکی	nuisance *n*
راشي	avalanche *n*	ربروونګی	trouble *v*
راشبن کبدل	germinate *v*	رپ	shelf *n*
راضي	content *adj*	رپبدل	flutter, waver *v*
راضي کول	appease, content *v*	رتبه	estate *n*
راضب کول	satisfy *v*	رحبم	graceful *adj*
راکره ورکره	trade *v*	رخت	cloth *n*
راکببل	trail *n*	رخصتي	vacation *n*
رانقلول	quote *v*	رخصتب	holiday *n*
رانبول	purchase *v*	رده	vein *n*
رانبول	purchase *n*	رده ول	refuse *v*
راهبه	nun *n*	رده ونه	refuse *n*
راهسب	since *c*	ردول	rebut *v*
راورل	bring *iv*	رژبدل	fade *v*

regime n رژیم	moisture n رطوبت
errand n رسالت	heal, mend v رغول
booklet n رساله	formation n رغونه
cafeteria n رستورانت	oasis n رغیانه
parade n رسم گذشت	competition n رقابت
invest v رسمآ مقررل	code n رمز
formal adj رسمي	sickness n رنځ
legalize v رسمي کول	color, dye n رنگ
controversy n رسوا	pale adj رنگ الوتی
infamous adj رسوا	tone n رنگ ورکول
convalescent adj رسوا شوی	colorful adj رنگداره
controversial adj رسوایي	painter n رنگمال
settle v رسول، اداکول	paint, color v رنگول
approach n رسونه	dying adj رنگونه
rope n رسی	index n رهنما
receipt n رسید	leading adj رهنمایي
leash n رسی	ascetic adj رهبز گاري
arrive, get up v رسبدل	get away v روانبدل
mature adj رسبدلی	departure n روانبدنه
arrival, influx n رسبدنه	conformist adj روایتي
ribbon n رشمه	ghost n روح
buy off v رشوت ورکول	monastic adj روحاني
convince v رضا کول	spiritual adj روحي
convincing adj رضاکونه	psychic adj روحي
consent n رضایت	suck v رودل
brethren n رضایي ورونه	bring up, educate v روزل

روزنه upbringing n	ريونده oriented adj
روزونکی trainer n	ريردونه shaken adj
روس Russia n	رټنه outcast adj
روسان Russian adj	رټه کول stain n
روضه shrine n	رډ plump adj
روغ رمټ intact, unhurt adj	رډه والي plain adj
روغتون infirmary n	ربنتنی committed adj
روغه peace n	ربنتنی truthful adj
روغه جوړه compromise n	ربنتونی wholehearted adj
روغه کول arbitrate v	ربنتيا truth n
روغبدل get over v	ربنتيا کرنه verification n
روک frank adj	ربنتياکول verify v
روماتېزم rheumatism n	ربنتبا fact n
رومي tomato n	ربنتبا honest adj
روړدی tame v	ربنتبنې factual adj
روړدي addicted adj	رڼا کېدل glimmer n
روړدبدنه addiction n	رياست presidency n
روبنان light n	رياست کول preside v
روبنانتيا lighting n	رېدپ anemia n
روبنانه light adj	رېدپ ګل anemic adj
روبنانه کور lighthouse n	ربشخند ridiculous adj
روبنانول brighten, light v	ربشخند وهل ridicule v
روڼ brilliant, clear adj	رپرد tremor n
رونول clear v	رپردول shake iv
ريا کاره hypocrite adj	رپردبدل tremble v
رياضي math n	رببنسکی shred n

shred v ربنیسکی کول	زربوز muzzle n
silk n ربنم	apricot, plum n زردالو
root n ربنه	rotten adj زرزست
sandpaper n ریگ مال	vegetation n زرغونوالی
	silversmith n زرگر
	millennium n زرکاله
	partridge n زرکه
ز	microwave n زره بین
	heart n زره
beseech iv زاري کول	cardiac arrest n زره نیوونکی
shabby adj زاړه	inwards adv زره او څیگر
molar n زامني غاښ	lonesome adj زره تنگوونکی
jaw n زامه	cardiac adj زره ته منسوب
cradle n زانگو	decorative adj زره راښکونکی
hammock n زانگو ډوله بستره	look at v زره راښکونکی
hermit, loner n زاهد	stunning adj زره راښکونکی
bruise, wound v زخمي کول	intriguing adj زره راښکوونی
jealousy n زخه	inspire v زره رکونه
learning n زده کړه	merciful adj زره سواند
learn iv زده کول	pitiful adj زره سواندې
learner n زده کوونکی	pity n زره سوب
thousand adj زر	clemency n زره سوی
once c زر تر زر	heartbeat n زره غورځېدنه
agriculture n زراعت	venture v زره کول
agricultural adj زراعتي	falter v زره کبدل
giraffe n زرافه	downtrodden adj زره ماتب

زړه ماتی broken *adj*	زما my *adj*
زړه نا زړه fickle *adj*	زمرود emerald *n*
زړه نا زړه کېدل hesitate *v*	زمری lion *n*
زړه نا زړه کېدل hesitant *adj*	زمزمه کول hum *v*
زړه ور courageous *adj*	زندان dungeon *n*
زړه ورتوب audacity *n*	زنگ rust *n*
زړه ورکول hearten *v*	زنگ کول rust *v*
زړه ورل enchant *v*	زنگ وهلې rusty *adj*
زړه ورونکې enchanting *adj*	زنگ،ترنگیار bell *n*
زړور bravery *n*	زنگون knee *n*
زړور، بې باک bold *adj*	زنگبدا، ټال swing *n*
زړوکې scarf *n*	زنگبدل swing *iv*
زرې seed *n*	زنگبدنه vibration *n*
زړی لرونکی nutty *adj*	زنه chin *n*
زبنت ډېر lavish *adj*	زنی۔ juvenile *n*
زـبنت ډېر utmost *adj*	زه I *pro*
زبنت زبات very *adv*	زه پخپله myself *pro*
زغم fortitude *n*	زهر poison, venom *n*
زغمل endure, undergo *v*	زهر جن poisonous *adj*
زغمونکې passive *adj*	زهر ناک virulent *adj*
زغمونکی broadminded *adj*	زهر ورکول poison *v*
زګبروی groan *n*	زهرناک toxin *n*
زګبروی moan *v*	زوال decadence *n*
زګبروی moan *n*	زور violence, stress *n*
زلزله earthquake *n*	زور اچول emphasize *v*
زما mine *pro*	زور ورکول push *v*

زورور stressful, violent *adj*	**زیات تلل** come over *v*
زورور گوزار dash *v*	**زیاتول** augment *v*
زور turmoil *n*	**زیار** attempt *n*
زور antiquated *adj*	**زیان** detriment *n*
زور اس hack *v*	**زیتون** olive *n*
زور سامان lumber *n*	**زیرزمیني** underpass *n*
زور سینگار old-fashioned *adj*	**زیري کول** startle *v*
زوزات descendant *n*	**زیري ورکونه** startled *adj*
زوم groom *n*	**زیر** boisterous *adj*
زوم son-in-law *n*	**زیر وبنبتان** bridle *n*
زوه pus *n*	**زیره** coastal *adj*
زباتوالب excel *v*	**زیره کرنبه** coastline *n*
زباتول propagate *v*	**زیربدنه** birth *n*
زبارت pilgrimage *n*	**زیلانس** womb *n*
زبر جامب lingerie *n*	**زینه** ladder, stairs *n*
زبر خانه basement, cellar *n*	
زبرب کول herald *v*	
زبر hoarse, rough *adj*	
زبرد brusque *adj*	
زبلانئی uterus *n*	**ژ**
زبم اچول exude *v*	
زبن saddle *n*	**ژاوله** bubble gum *n*
زیا تول Spain *n*	**ژبارل** translate *v*
زیات carnage *n*	**ژباره** interpretation *n*
زیات اخیستل overcharge *v*	**ژبارونکی** interpreter *n*
زیات تعداد major in *v*	**ژبه** language, tongue *n*
	ژر soon *adv*

owing to *adv* ژر ادا کول	biography *n* ژوند لیک
cram *v* ژر ژر خورل	quicken *v* ژوند ورکول
dupe *v* ژر غولبدونکی	exist *v* ژوندکول
scour *v* ژرژر ګرخبدل	vitality *n* ژوندون
yoke *n* ژغ	live *adj* ژوندی
rescue *v* ژغورل	creature *n* ژوندی مخلوق
rescue *n* ژغورنه	alive *adj* ژوندي
continental *adj* ژغورونکی	animation *n* ژوندیتوب
winter *n* ژمی	vivacious *adj* ژوندۍ
bachelor *n* ژنکی	human being *n* ژوندۍ موجودات
injury *n* ژوبله	chew, bite *v* ژوول
hurt *adj* ژوبلوالی	whiskers *n* ژویو بریتونه
blemish *v* ژوبلول	cry *n* ژرا
blemish *n* ژوبلونه	tearful *adj* ژراند
injurious *adj* ژوبلوونکی	cry, weep *v* ژرل
zoo *n* ژوبڼ	crying *n* ژربدونکی
zoology *n* ژوپوهنه	border *n* ژک
deep, abysmal *adj* ژور	marginal *adj* ژک
profound *adj* ژور پوه	hem, rim *n* ژۍ
cockpit *n* ژور خای	bile, yolk *n* ژیر
leech *n* ژوره	blond, yellow *adj* ژیړ
bumpy *adj* ژورب لروونکی	
deepen *v* ژوربدل	
life *n* ژوند	
biology *n* ژوند پوهنه	
animate, live *v* ژوند کول	

ژ

س

ساراني گازره parsnip n

سا اخیستل breathtaking adj
سا اخبستنه respiration n
سابندول belch v
سابندي belch n
سات تیري entertainment n
ساتل keep, protect iv
ساتلي secure adj
ساتندوپ policeman n
ساتنه safety n
ساتنئی storage n
ساتوندوپ warden n
ساتونکپ guard n
ساتوونکی custodian n
ساتپري fun n
ساحل seashore n
ساحه area, sphere n
ساختگپ phoney adj
ساده frenetic, mad adj
ساده توب simplicity n
ساده کول simplify v
ساده والی naive adj
ساده والپ childish adj
ساده چوله plain n
ساده چوله plainly adv

ساراپپ چرک pheasant n
ساري contagious adj
ساري epidemic n
ساز غرول strike up v
سازنده musician n
ساعت hour n
ساعت تبري pastime n
ساعت جورونکی watchmaker n
سالون hall n
سامان equipment n
سان linen n
سانتي متر centimeter n
ساه voyage n
ساړه cold adj
ساړه chill n
سابنس پوه scientist n
سبا tomorrow adv
سپارل bow out v
سپارښت commend v
سپاهي soldier n
سپتمبر September n
سپر fender n
سپرم sperm n
سپیزه زار Greenland n
سپک frivolous adj

سپک تماس graze n	سپرونکپ explorer n
سپک جسم buoy n	سپرن lousy adj
سپک خولی defiant adj	سپره louse n
سپک والې disgrace n	سپرې lice n
سپک ورک paltry adj	سپې dog n
سپک گذار touch n	سپین white adj
سپک گڼل disdain n	سپین زر silver n
سپکاوی libel n	سپینه وپنا frankness n
سپکتل look down v	سپینول whiten v
سپکه ول disgrace v	سپېڅلی immaculate adj
سپکوالې dishonor n	ستاسپ your adj
سپکول debase v	ستاسپ خپل yours pro
سپکونه reproach n	ستایل recommend v
سپما economy n	ستاپل praise n
سپما غرې sober adj	ستاپلول praise v
سپما کول downsize v	ستاپنه adulation n
سپمول amortize v	ستپلر stapler n
سپموونکی thrifty adj	ستر enormous, vast adj
سپنج sponge n	ستر پادري archbishop n
سپنگور blackberry n	ستر گک وهل blink v
سپورمیـ moon n	ستروالی immensity n
سپین outspoken adj	ستروالې Highness n
سپین سترگي impertinence n	سترگک wink n
سپین ویونکي outspoken adj	سترگک وهل wink v
سپڕل unfold n	سترگه eye n
سپڕنه description n	ستـرگی پرې پټول ignore v

س

سترکپ پټول v snooze	سترپا n fatigue
سترکپ تروونکی n blindfold	سترپاوالی adj relaxing
سترکپ ورترل v blindfold	ستبکر n sticker
ستل ،بوکه n pail	سخاوت n generosity
ستن n column, needle	سخت adj crispy
ستنه n bracket, mast	سخت توپان n tempest
ستنول v prohibit	سخت زړی adj inhuman
ستنبدل v revert	سخت ډارول v terrify
ستنبدنه n recurrence	سخته تجربه n ordeal
ستوری n star	سختي n intensity
ستوري پیژندنه n astronomy	سخي adj charitable
ستوغ adj steep	سر n head
ستومانتیا n exhaustion	سر پټونی n shelter
ستومانه کېدل v come up	سر پیچلی adj watertight
ستومانوونکی adj tedious	سر تنبه adj obstinate
ستومانوونکي adj boring	سر تنبگي n obstinacy
ستومانوونکپ adj tiresome	سر ته رسول v finish, fulfill
ستوماني n boredom	سر تبرپ n guerrilla
ستونزه n collapse	سر تبرپدنه adj gruelling
ستونی n throat	سر چینه n origin
ستونځه n hardship	سر دردپ n headache
ستړی adj weary	سر شمېرنه n census
ستړی ستومانه adj tired	سر غوخول v decapitate
ستړي والي n tiredness	سر لوری کول v canonize
ستړیا n tedium	سر لپک n preface
ستړیا کنبل n lounge	سر مشق n dummy

بو تیتول bow v	سره یو ځای together adv
سراب mirage n	سره کېدنه fusion n
سربرن زخم bruise n	سروی survey n
سربره extra adv	سریځه introduction n
سرپ chair v	سرتیتونه bow n
سرته رسول achieve v	سرگردان stray adj
سرته رسولنه achievement n	سرگردانه devious adj
سرحد boundary, frontier n	سربزه prologue n
سرسري لیکل scribble v	سربنده violin n
سرسرپ کتل glimpse v	سربښ glue, paste n
سرعت speed iv	سربښ کول paste v
سرعت speed n	سربښناک adhesive adj
سرکس circus n	سربښول glue v
سرکش break away v	سزا ورکول penalize v
سرکه vinegar n	سزا penalty n
سرلیک title n	سست impotent adj
سرمایه داري capitalism n	سستول give away v
سرمایه ورکول capitalize v	سطرنج chess n
سره gold n	سفارت embassy n
سره with pre	سفر journey n
سره اخښل mix v	سفر کول travel v
سره اوښتل tangle n	سفر کوونکی traveler n
سره سم according to pre	سفر لودیځ ته westbound adv
سره غاړه larynx n	سفرل بکس briefcase n
سره له دې despite c	سفبر ambassador n
سره ورکول manure n	سکاره کول char v

scholarship n سكالرشپ	pie n سمبوسه
reel n نخا سكاتپلبندي	tenor n سمت
coin n سكه	semester n سمستر
scooter n سكوټر	lush adj سمسور
hundred adj سل	ocean, sea n سمندر
centenary n سل كاله	marine adj سمندري
refer to v سلا مشوره كول	seafood n سمندري غذا
consult v سلا وركول	seasick adj سمندري ناروغ
salad n سلاته	walrus n سمندري نولی
greetings n سلام	piracy n سمندرپ غلا
greet v سلام اچول	gull n سمندرپ موغه
series n سلسله	strap n سمه
sovereign adj سلطنتي	rear adj سموالی
hundredth adj سلم	harmony, right n سموالپ
behave v سلوک کول	conform, rectify v سمول
sob n سلگی	atonement n سمون
hiccup n سلگپ	disposable adj سمونه
sob v سلگپ وهل	cave n سمځ
cylinder n سلبندر	calculation n سمبر
corresponding adj سم	senator n سناتور
reform n سم	circumcision n سنت کول
straight, valid adj سم	circumcise v سنت کول
immediately adv سم د لاسه	prudence n سنجش
hold up v سم ودربدل	deliberate v سنجول
censorship n سمبال	deliberate adj سنجول شوی
equip v سمبالول	document n سند

anvil n سندان	bore, stab v سوری کول
singer n سندر غاړی	hole n سوری
chant, song n سندره	pierce, drill v سوری کول
bulwark n سنگر	piercing n سوری کونکی
Tuesday n سه شنبه	perforate v سوری کېدل
morning n سهار	tardy adv سوست
awful adj سهم ناک	Marxist adj سوسیالست
ease n سهولت	gift n سوغات
fault n سهوه	sniff v سوغول
mistake, mistake iv سهوه کول	fist n سوک
sow iv سهیلي قطب	famine n سوکړه
socialism n سو شیالېزم	cease-fire n سوله
beg v سوال کول	rub v سولول
beggar n سوالگر	hoof n سوه
trim v سوتره	Switzerland n سویزرلاینډ
shop v سودا اخبستل	Sweden n سویس
merchant n سوداگر	Swiss adj سویسي
commerce n سوداگري	ardent adj سوځند
red adj سور	burn iv سوځول
fry v سور کول	burn n سوځېدنه
redden v سور کبدل	soda n سوډا
jackal n سور لنډیان	dismal adj سوړ
inflammation n سوربخن	hare n سوی
tune n سورول	diplomat n سیاستمدار
tune v سورول	lawmaker n سیاستوال
cavity, outlet n سوری	diplomatic adj سیاسي

س

competitor n سیال	man n سړی
compete v سیالي کول	cannibal n سړي خور
correct adj سیخ	guy n سړېچ
bar n سیخ، میله	chill v سړېدل
correction n سیخالی	nostril n سړمی
correct v سیخول	lung n سږی
straighten out v سیده کېدل	seal n سگ لاهو
swarm n سیل	sightseeing v سباحت کول
swamped adj سیلاب	cigar n سبار
cement n سیمنټ	planet n سباره
barrier, zone n سیمه	politics n سباست
barge n سیند	politician n سباست مدار
cinema n سینما	runner n سبال
breast n سینه	relax v سباله
chest n سینه، تټر	fluid n سباله ماده
décor n سینگار	rivalry n سبالي
corruption n سینگار شیان	rival v سبالي کول
spruce up v سینگار کول	refuge n سبب
decorate v سینگارول	rod n سبخ
spooky adj سیوري	serum m سبرم
cigarette n سیگرېټ	torrent n سبل
base n ستہ	flood v سبلاب
helm n ستپرنگ	flooding n سبلاب
road n سړک	gust n سبلی
cause n سړک پخول	gale n سبلي
cause v سړک پخول	district, region n سبمه

شاته کېدنه n retirement	سبمه اپز adj regional
شاته تپتدل v lean back	سبمه بز adj parochial
شاع n laser	سبنجاق n pin
شاعري n poetry	سبند n river
شاکوپی n hunchback	سبندوبچ n sandwich
شاملول v comprise	سبنه بغل n pneumonia
شامول v enroll	سبنگار v adorn, garnish
شاهانه adj regal, royal	سبنگارول v embellish
شاهد n witness	سبورن adj shady
شاهدي n testimony	سبوری n shade, shadow
شاهکار n masterpiece	سبوري n prowler
شاهي دولت n monastery	سبځل v ignite
شاو خوا adv about	
شاول کو ل v plummet	
شاړه n waste	**ش**
شاگرد n apprentice	
شابد adv perhaps, may-be	شا n back
شبکه n network	شا وخوا adj indirect
شپارلس adj sixteen	شاباس adj overdone
شپه n night	شابآسی ویل n applause
شپول n hurdle	شات n honey
شپون n shepherd	شاتر n precursor
شپږ adj six	شاته adj backward
شپږم adj sixth	شاته pre behind
شپیته adj sixty	شاته کېدل کېدل v retire
شپیدي n twilight	

pipe n شپلندوي	bet iv شرط ترل
reed n شپلی	legal adj شرعي
whistle n شپلې	oriental adj شرقي
whistle v شپلې کول	eastern adj شرقي
ostrich n شتر مرغ	firm n شرکت
rich adj شتمن	blush, shame n شرم
opulence n شتمني	disgraceful adj شرم ناک
wealth n شتمني	degrading adj شرمناک
affluence n شتمنب	timid adj شرمندوکی
availability n شته وال	rebuke n شرمول
ancestry n شجره	shame v شرمول
personality n شحصبت	bashful adj شرميندونکی
stiff adj شخ	blush v شرمبدل
off-the-record adj شخصي	ashamed adj شرمبدلی
own v شخصب	hang around v شرمبدونکی
private adj شخصب	log in v شروع کول
stiffen v شخول	measles n شری
brawl n شخړه	aristocrat n شريف
rigor n شدت	nobleman n شريف سړی
stifling adj شدید	chicken pox n شرپ
fierce adj شدبد	partner n شرپک بانپ
alcoholic adj شرابي	motto n شعار
rum n شراپ	poet n شعر
delinquency n شرارت	instinct n شعور
syrup n شربت	intuition n شعور
condition, bet n شرط	affair n شغل

شـفاهي orally *adv*	شـلخب dock *n*
شـفايي oval *adj*	شـلم twentieth *adj*
شـفتالو peach *n*	شمارل countdown *n*
شـفر password *n*	شمال north *n*
شـفر جورول codify *v*	شمالي northern *adj*
شـفقت کول condescend *v*	شمالي قطب arctic *adj*
شـقيقه temple *n*	شمزی backbone *n*
شـک distrustful *adj*	شمشتي turtle *n*
شـک suspicion, doubt *n*	شمشتی tortoise *n*
شـکايت complaint *n*	شمع candle *n*
شـکايت کول complain *v*	شمع دان chandelier *n*
شـکر کبنل thanks *n*	شمبر کوونکی calculator *n*
شـکري diabetic *adj*	شمبرل calculate, count *v*
شـکل feature, form *n*	شمبرنه number *n*
شـکل بدلونه disguise *n*	شمبرونکی counter *n*
شـکمن doubtful *adl*	شمبربدونکب accountable *adj*
شـکمن کبدل doubt *v*	شناخته tombstone *n*
شـکنجه torture *n*	شنه پلب green bean *n*
شـکنجه کول torture *v*	شنه مانب greenhouse *n*
شـکور basket *n*	شنیلی sod *n*
شـکول extort, pluck, rip *v*	شند barren, sterile *adj*
شـکونه severance *n*	شهادت ardor, passion *n*
شـکونب porcupine *n*	شهادت ورکول attest *v*
شـکب dubious *adj*	شهرت fame, honor *n*
شـل paralysis *n*	شهرت ورکول popularize *v*
شـل کول paralyze *v*	شهزادگی princess *n*

ش

شیره juice n	شهو ت لرل lust v
شیریخ ice cream n	شهواني lustful adj
شیطان demon, devil n	شهواني prurient adj
شیندل sprinkle, splash v	شهوت reputation n
شدل gross, rude, vulgar adj	شهوت پرسته lewd adj
شدلتبا vulgarity n	شو پشو کبدل diver n
شدلوالي rudeness n	شوإر sprawl v
شر کول whip v	شوإره awkward adj
شرل banish, deport v	شوخ naughty adj
شرنه exile, expulsion n	شودیاره کول till v
شگه pebble, sand n	شور کول sound v
شگون omen n	شور ما شور overcrowded adj
شببه minute n	شور ما شور row n
شبردان faucet n	شور، غالمغال sound n
شبره pulp n	شورناک noisy adj
شبره ترپ زببنبل sap v	شوق dedication n
شببشه glass n	شوق او ذوق enthusiasm n
شبطان evil n	شوقي amateur adj
شبظاني satanic adj	شوکمار swindle n
شبن green adj	شوکه extortion n
	شوم sinister adj
	شومه bait n
	شونډه lip n
	شونډپ ginger n
	شی thing n
	شیدپ milk n

ش

ص

صاف pure, serene adj

صافي کول puree n

صبر ناک stoic adj

صحت health n

صحت مند healthy adj

صحرايي پيشو lynx n

صحنه stage n

صحيح okay adv

صدر اعظم premier adj

صراحي jug n

صرف او نحوه grammar n

صفت adjective n

صفت اسم participle n

صفر zero n

صلاحيت authorization n

صلاحيت ورکول authorize v

صليبي جګره crusade n

صميمي candor n

صميمي hearty adj

صندوق case n

صنف يا ډول sort n

صوتي acoustic adj

صوفي recluse n

صومعه cloister n

ض

ضامن bail n

ضايع کول devour, mess up v

ضايع کول throw away v

ضايع کول put away v

ضايع کونکی wasteful adj

ضد contradiction n

ضرب multiplication n

ضربول multiply v

ضررناک delete v

ضررناک detrimental adj

ضرورت binding adj

ضروري necessary adj

ضم کېدل merge v

ضمانت guarantee n

ضمانت کول guarantee v

ضمير conscience n

ضميمه attached adj

ضميمه attachment n

ضمبر pronoun n

ص
ض

ظ

ظالم monstrous *adj*

ظالم شهواتي *n* sadist

ظالمانه despotic *adj*

ظاهر كېدل emerge *v*

ظآهرآ apparently *adv*

ظرفيت capacity *n*

ظلم oppression *n*

ع

عاجزي meekness *n*

عادانه just *adj*

عادت practice *n*

عادي customary *adj*

عادي habitual *adj*

عادي كول acclimatize *v*

عاق كول disinherit *v*

عالم learned *adj*

عالي August *n*

عام public *adj*

عامول publish *v*

عبادت prayer *n*

ط

طاعون plague *n*

طب طبابت medicine *n*

طبابت therapy *n*

طبراق backpack *n*

طبعي منظره landscape *n*

طبقه بندي assortment *n*

طبيعت nature *n*

طبيعي natural *adj*

طبيب doctor *n*

طبيب physician *n*

طرز method *n*

طرفدار incomplete *adj*

طريقه formula *n*

طعنه irony *n*

طفيلي parasite *n*

طلاق divorce, divorcee *n*

طلاقول divorce *v*

طلسمي charismatic *adj*

طمعدار كول alluring *adj*

طوفاني gusty *adj*

طياره airliner *n*

ط
ظ
ع

عصب nerve n	عبادت adorable adj
عصبي nervous adj	عبادت کول adore v
عصبی edgy adj	عبث futile adj
عصبی ناروغي epilepsy n	عبثوالی futility n
عصبی ڈاکتر psychiatrist n	عجب prodigy n
عصر reign n	عجلب والی oddity n
عصري کول modernize v	عجیبه bitterly adv
عصري کبدل update v	عجیبه marvelous adj
عضله muscle n	عجبب queer, weird adj
عطر perfume n	عدالت justice n
عقاب eagle n	عذاب torment n
عقیده belief, creed n	عذاب ورکول torment v
عقبده doctrine n	عربی ژبه Arabic adj
عکاسب photography n	عرض appeal n
عکس photo, picture n	عرض کول apply for v
عکس اخبستل photograph v	عریضه application n
عکس المل itchiness n	عریضه کول sue v
عکس جورول canvas v	عزت respect n
عکس کبنل portray v	عزت کول care about v
علاج cure n	عزم constancy n
علاج کول cure v	عسکر combatant n
علاقه spice n	عسکر سیمه terrain n
علامه earmark v	عسکري تربیت infertile adj
علامه symptom n	عشارب decimal adj
علاوه پر دې furthermore adv	عشقي سندرب serenade n
علمی scientific adj	عصابانی neurotic adj

ع

غ

غار n cavern, den

غاررہ اینبودنه v surrender

غالبوزه n bum

غالمغال n shouting

غالی n carpet

غارہ اینبودل v succumb

غارہ غرونکب v disobey

غاریزه n tonic

غارک ته adv ashore

غاښ n dent, tooth

غاښ پاکی n toothpick

غاښ جورول v dent

غابنور کونه adj harrowing

غابنیز adj dental

غابب n disappearance

غابه n scope

غبار n haze

غبر ګون n twin

غبرک adj double

غبرګول v double

غبرګونی n cloning

غپا v bark

غچ n revenge

غچ اخبستل v revenge

عمر n age

عمل n deed, feat

عمل کول v abide by

عملي کوونکی n conductor

عملیات n operation

عمومي adj common

عمومي اسناد n archive

عمومي بخښنه n amnesty

عمومي کول v generalize

عمومب ګنه n edition

عنصر n element

عیاش adj luxurious

عیب v defect

عیسوي سمبول n crucifix

عیسوي ملا n minister

عیني n objective

عبب n flaw

عببي adj faulty

غچپدل creak v	غلامي bondage n
غچپدنه creak n	غلبيل strainer n
غذاپي مواد groceries n	غلبل riddle n
غر mount, mountain n	غلبلول sift v
غربي western adj	غلط inaccurate adj
غركبدل go under v	غلط پوهبدل misconstrue v
غرمه noon n	غلط تعبيرول misunderstand v
غرنى mountainous adj	غلط تعبيرول misinterpret v
غرځه antelope n	غلط ثابتول disprove v
غررنه growl v	غلط ثابتول refute v
غركى cobblestone n	غلط ختل falsify v
غريب poor, indigent n	غلط شمبرل miscalculate v
غزل lay n	غلط قضاوت misjudge v
غزول extend, stretch v	غلطه erroneous adj
غزبدنه stretch n	غلطه مانا كول pervert v
غزبدونكي resilient adj	غلطي error, goof n
غسل bath n	غلطي كول goof v
غشى bolt n	غلطب oversight n
غصبول levy, usurp v	غله cereal, grain n
غصبي jumpy adj	غلول swindle v
غصه bitterness n	غلوونكي elusive adj
غل robber, thief n	غلى composure n
غلا burglary, theft n	غلى hush up v
غلا كول embezzle, steal v	غلي quiet, silent adj
غلامول enthrall v	غلبم enemy, foe n
غلامونكى enthralling adj	غم mourning, grief n

غ

غم شریکېدنه condo n	غورکېدل pulsate v
غم کول deplore v	غوربدل grumble, rumble v
غمجن derail v	غوربدنه roar n
غمجن downcast adj	غوربدونکې grouchy adj
غمجنتیا derailment n	غوز walnut n
غمجنه پېښه catastrophe n	غوسه anger n
غمول exasperate v	غوسه کېدل anger v
غمی gem, jewel n	غوغا uproar n
غمګېن کېدل distress v	غولول beguile, trick v
غنچه cluster n	غولونکی seduction n
غنم wheat n	غولونکې evasive adj
غنم رنګه سرې brunette adj	غولونه enticement n
غوا cow, oxen n	غولوونکي misleading adj
غوبه cowboy n	غولی courtyard n
غوجل stable adj	غولی پاکوونکی mop v
غوجن carnal adj	غوماشي mosquito n
غوره elect v	غومبسه wasp n
غوره excellent adj	غونجېدل shrink iv
غوره seldom adv	غونجېدنه traction n
غوره توب expediency n	غوندې like pre
غوره شوی designate adj	غوند brigade n
غوره والې excellence n	غوند پلورنه wholesale n
غوره ګنل prefer v	غونډاري کول agglomerate v
غورهار rumble n	غونډارې round adj
غورکنګ wave n	غونډه briefing, session n
غورکول omit, oust v	غونډوالې hunched adj

غ

غوربن fatty adj	غوندول hunch n
غور ear n	غوندی hill n
غور خیری earwax n	غوندی لمن hillside n
غور نبول eavesdrop v	غوندیدل cluster v
غوروالی earring n	غووته immersion n
غوروالب pendant n	غویی bull n
غوښتل covet, desire v	غوته buckle, button n
غوښتل شوی demanding adj	غوته کول enhance v
غوښتنه demand, petition n	غوته کونه shoelace n
غوښتنه کول request v	غوته ورکول downturn n
غوښتوونکی applicant n	غوتی blow n
غوښن رنگ carnation n	غوخ incision n
غوښه flesh, meat n	غوخول clip, amputate v
غوبب ox n	غوخونه interruption n
غیب وینه oracle n	غوخوونکی cutter n
غیر رسمي informal adj	غوخوونکب اله cutlery n
غیر عادي unusual adj	غور greasy adj
غیر قانوني illegal adj	غور یاشه buttonhole n
غیر متحمل unrealistic adj	غورپ gulp n
غیر معمولي way out n	غورپول gulp v
غیر واقعي unreal adj	غوره مالي flattery n
غیرخاِضرب absence n	غوره مالي کول coax v
غټ والب greatness n	غورول anoint, grease v
غته بلا monster n	غورونه lubrication n
غته چنگاښ toad n	غورپ grease n
غته گوته thumb n	غوربدل blossom v

غ

غبر موافق discordant adj	غتول glorify v
غبر بقبني ambivalent adj	غرپ sip n
غبزه تاک pathetic adj	غرپ کول sip v
غبر bosom n	غرغره کول gargle v
غبر کبدل embrace v	غرل، پیچل twist v
غبر نیول wrestle v	غرمببدل roar v
	غرندول loosen v
	غرنه، پیچنه twist n
ف	غروسکه constellation n
	غروشکه wreath n
فابرپکه factory n	غروندی apostrophe n
فاتح conqueror n	غری brick, ingot n
فاحشه خانه brothel n	غریتوب membership n
فارغ التحصبل graduate v	غرې personnel n
فارم farm n	غږ call n
فاسد corrupt v	غږ کول call v
فاسد corrupt adj	غږیز vowel n
فاسدول bribe v	غبنتلی strong adj
فاسفورس phosphorus n	غبنتلی struggle v
فاصله distance n	غبنتلپ drastic adj
فاصله span v	غنه spider n
فاصله ساتل space out v	غنیدنه growth n
فاکولته faculty n	غبر اخلاقي amoral adj
فابده revenue n	غبر خاضر absent adj
فبروري February n	غبر رسمي fishy adj
	غبر مستقبم sideways adv

فعالول acute *adj*	فرار banishment *n*
فعاليت behavior *v*	فرارپ fugitive *n*
فعل verb *n*	فراغت graduation *n*
فقره clause *n*	فرانسه France *n*
فكر ponder *v*	فرانسوي French *adj*
فكر reflection *n*	فرش floor *n*
فكر كول consider *v*	فرصت opportunity *n*
فلز metal *n*	فرضآ supposing *c*
فلزي metallic *adj*	فرضي so-called *adj*
فلزي wire *n*	فرضيه hypothesis *n*
فلزي مزى cable *n*	فرعي دفتر branch office *n*
فلسفه philosophy *n*	فرق difference *n*
فلم movie *n*	فرقه sect *n*
فلم film *n*	فرقه مشر corporal *n*
فلتر filter *n*	فريكونسى frequency *n*
فنجپ fungus *n*	فزيك physics *n*
فنلند Finland *n*	فساد contamination *n*
فني technical *adj*	فسخه كول cancel *v*
فواره fountain *n*	فسخه كونه annulment *n*
فوج troop *n*	فشار pressure *n*
فوري عكس snapshot *n*	فشارول pressure *v*
فوق العاده remarkable *adj*	فصاحت eloquence *n*
فوټ بال football *n*	فضليت morality *n*
فيشني trendy *adj*	فضوله شيان junk *n*
فيصله decision *n*	فعال agile, active *adj*
فيصله شوى interested *adj*	فعالول activate *v*

ف

deciding *adj* فیصله کن	law, precept *n* قانون
decide, untie *v* فیصله کول	lawyer *n* قانون پوه
patch *v* فیصله کول	legislate *v* قانون جوړول
patch *n* فیصله کول	law-abiding *adj* قانون منونکی
philosopher *n* فیلسوف	statute *n* قانون
fuse *n* فیوز	lawful *adj* قانوني
	legality *n* قانونیت
	franchise *n* قانوني حق
	hold out *v* قایم ساتل
ق	constipation *n* قبضیت
	acceptance *n* قبول شوب
down-to-earth *adj* قابل عمل	tribe *n* قبیله
assassin *n* قاتل	dim *adj* قت
smuggler *n* قاچاق ورونکی	dim *v* قت کول
furious *adj* قار	height *n* قد
angry *adj* قارجن	esteem *v* قدر کول
embitter *v* قارول	step-by-step *adv* قدم په قدم
geese, swan *n* قاز	stroll, walk *v* قدم وهل
courier *n* قاصد	step *n* قدم، پل
judge *n* قاضي	contract *n* قرار داد
crucial *adj* قاطع	sacrifice *n* قرباني
guidelines *n* قاعده	loan *n* قرض
rhyme *n* قافیه	loan *v* قرض کول
last *v* قالب کول	debrief *v* قرض ورکول
dictionary *n* قاموس	debit *n* قرضداري
insatiable *adj* قانع کبدونکی	stationery *n* قرطاسیه

ف
ق

قوم n clan
قوماندان n commander
قوماندہ n mandate
قوہ n force
قوي n buildup
قوي adj burly, obese
قوي کول v fortify
قویتر n stranger
قویتوب adj compelling
قوپ adj potent, robust
قى کول v throw up
قید n adverb
قیر n asphalt, tar
قیراط n carat
قیمتي adj costly
قیمه n meatball
قیمومیت adj mandatory
قې n vomit
قې کول v vomit
قبدول v qualify
قبمت ټپتول v mark down
قبمتب adj pricey
کربدل n aberration

قرعه lot adv
قرینه context n
قسم قسم various adj
قسمت destiny, fate n
قشر، پوټکی crust n
قصاب butcher n
قصابي butchery n
قصدا willfully adv
قصدآ knowingly adv
قضاوت award n
قضبه premise n
قطاع sector n
قطب نما compass n
قطبي polar adj
قطعه ارتباط unplug v
قطعي definite adj
قفل latch n
قلف ساز locksmith n
قلم pen n
قلمرو dominion n
قناعت satisfaction n
قهر fury, wrath n
قهوه coffee n
قوت power, energy n
قوسونه parenthesis n
قولنج colic n

ک

کاپي کوونکی copier n	کاشقه spoon n
کاپي ویستل clone v	کاشوقه tablespoon n
کات کول crease n	کاغذ paper n
کات کول crease v	کافر heathen n
کاتولیزم Catholicism n	کافي copy n
کاچوغپ silverware n	کافي اخیستل copy v
کار work, task n	کافي ذخیره deposit n
کار بټر carburetor n	کافین caffeine n
کار پیل کول go in v	کافپ adequate adj
کار فرما employer n	کاکا uncle n
کار کول service, toil v	کال year n
کار کوونکي laborer n	کالي clothes, garment n
کار کپدل collaborate v	کالیزه anniversary n
کار ور workable adj	کالب dress n
کار ګر worker n	کالب اغوستل dress v
کار ګران labor n	کالبو الماري wardrobe n
کارتوس cartridge n	کاملا fully adv
کارجن squeamish adj	کامه comma n
کارک cork n	کان کیندل mine v
کاروان caravan n	کاندید candidate n
کارول employ v	کانتین canteen n
کارګر employee n	کانګرو kangaroo n
کارپګر grassroots adj	کاهو lettuce n
کاسه bowl, shell n	کانپی ore, stone n
	کب fish n
	کب نبوونکی fisherman n

ک

pride n کبر	lizard n کربوری
haughty, cocky adj کبر جن	jacket, coat n کرتۍ
groove n کبله	globule n کردۍ ذره
leap year n کبیثه کال	crystal n کرستل
cuff n کپ، ولچک	obscene adj کرغېرن
cage n کپس	antipathy, hate n کرکه
capsule n کپسول	abhor, loathe v کرکه کول
book n کتاب	cultivate v کرل
bookstore n کتاب پلورنځی	cultural adj کرل شوی
library n کتابتون	cabbage n کرم
librarian n کتابدار	cultivation n کرنه
pedantic adj کتابي ملا	authenticate v کره کول
glance, observe v کتل	granite n کرونده
woven adj کتل شوی	crap n کریپ
visit v کتل کول	crappy adj کریپي
mass n کتله، ډله	crane n کرین
glance, inspection n کتنه	perennial adj کرۍ کال
fold v کتول	gravel n کرپر
visitor n کتونکي	vengeance n کسات
palm n کجوری ونه	avenge v کسات اخیستل
mule n کچر	profession n کسب
pumpkin n کدو	artisan n کسب ګر
placate, silence v کرارول	mechanic n کسبګر
hush n کراربدنه	envious, jealous adj کستمن
karate n کراټي	deficit n کسر
freight n کرابه	beloved adj کسران

ک

کش draw n	کلک، شدید severe adj
کشاله hangup, problem n	کلکه حمله onslaught n
کشر junior adj	کلکوالی firmness n
کشفول detector n	کلکول fasten, tighten v
کشکول pull v	کلکولب hardness n
کشول drag v	کلمه gut n
کشبش pastor n	کلمب lyrics n
کشبشب pastoral adj	کلنی annual, yearly adj
کف facing pre	کله when adv
کفر blasphemy n	کله کله uncommon adj
کفر وبل profane adj	کلوله bun n
کفرب heretic adj	کلونیا cologne n
کفن shroud n	کلي key n
ککر infested adj	کلي بند key ring n
کلا fort n	کلیدره keyboard n
کلابندب siege n	کلیزه calendar n
کلالي ceramic n	کلیسا church n
کلام speech n	کلیسا مشر dean n
کلپ padlock n	کلیوالي countryside n
کلتور civilize v	کلب village n
کلچ clutch n	کلبزه almanac n
کلچه cookie n	کلبوال villager n
کلسترول cholesterol n	کلبوالي rural adj
کلک durable, solid adj	کم petty adj
کلک زخمي کول maim v	کم ارزښته little by little adv
کلک لرګب hardwood n	کم اصل degenerate adj

ک

کم اصل کبدل degenerate v	کمبدنه spasm n
کمبود deficient adj	کمبدونکي flexible adj
کمپله blanket n	کمبس shirt n
کمپولاژ camouflage n	کمبنه humble adj
کمپولاژ کول camouflage v	کنترول control n
کمپوډر pharmacist n	کنترولول control v
کمپیوتر computer n	کنجکي coronary adj
کمر precipice n	کنجوس stingy adj
کمر بند wafer n	کنده depth n
کمرزوري sissy adj	کندو bin n
کمزورتبا weakness n	کنسرت concert n
کمزوری cowardly adv	کنفرانس خونه auditorium n
کمزوری defenseless adj	کنډک regiment n
کمزوری کول weaken v	کنګالول rinse v
کمزوري weak adj	کنګل کول freeze iv
کمزوری feeble, frailty adj	کنبدل excavate v
کمزوری کول disabled adj	کنبدنه grave adj
کمزورپتوب disability n	که چبري if c
کموالی brevity n	که څه هم though c
کمول cut back, reduce v	کهکشان gal n
کمونست socialist adj	کوبه knob n
کمونه decrease n	کوپراتیف cooperative adj
کمونبزم communism n	کوپره coconut n
کمی shortage n	کوپون coupon n
کمیسار commission n	کوتره dove n
کمین unassuming adj	کوتره pigeon n

ک

کوتک baton, bat n	کورنی نوم n ash
کوچ butter n	کورنی family n
کوچنی child, infant n	کورنی کار homework n
کوچنی ببرل keg n	کورنی مرغان poultry n
کوچنی جهیل lagoon n	کورنی څناور pet n
کوچنی کور lodge v	کورودانی thank v
کوچنی ټوټه chip n	کوز underneath pre
کوچنیان children n	کوزده engagement n
کوچنیتوب childhood n	کوزه برخه downtown n
کوچنیوالی juvenile adj	کوزول overhaul v
کوچنی خونه kiosk n	کوزړی jar n
کوچنی کوټهٔ booth n	کوزېدل get down, get off v
کوچنی ټوټه crumb n	کوشش endeavor n
کوچنب بوټې herb n	کوشش کول essay n
کوچنب سپې puppy n	کوشېر کول weld v
کوچنب کلب hamlet n	کوشېر کوونکی welder n
کوچی migrant n	کوفته hamburger n
کور home n ,	کوکاین cocaine n
کور ته تلل repatriate v	کول waiter n
کور جوړونه quarters n	کولبه کول plow v
کوربنه hostess n	کولمه intestine n
کوربه host n	کولول roll v
کورس course n	کوم which adj
کورس ډله chorus n	کوم ته چې whom pro
کورنی ښوونکی tutor n	کومکي subsidiary adj
کورنی domestic adj	کومکي پاڼه leaflet n

کومکی helpful *adj*	کور وور winding *adj*
کوناټپ hip *n*	کور وور ځای labyrinth *n*
کونست communist *adj*	، کور crooked *adj*
کونستر گی pad *n*	کوروالی curve *n*
کونسل consul *n*	کوروالی curve *v*
کونډ widower *n*	کوروالی warped *adj*
کونډه widow *n*	کوښنیښ worthwhile *adj*
کونب کبر shellfish *n*	کوښنیښ کول try *v*
کوټ gout *n*	کوڼ deaf *adj*
کوټلپ غوښبهٔ mincemeat *n*	کوڼ کول deafen *v*
کوټه heap, lump *n*	کوڼ والی deafening *adj*
کوټه کول heap, amass *v*	کوڼوالی deafness *n*
کوټه، چانس room *n*	کیسه story, tale *n*
کوټی colt *n*	کیسه ویل narrate *v*
کوڅه street *n*	کیفیت character *n*
کوڅی۔ lock *n*	کیله banana *n*
کوڅی کول lock *v*	کیلو متر kilometer *n*
کوڅپ queue *n*	کیلو واټ kilowatt *n*
کوډ گر wizard *n*	کیلو گرام kilogram *n*
کوډله hut, kennel *n*	کیمیا chemistry *n*
کوډله shack *n*	کیمیا پوه chemist *n*
کوډگر exorcist *n*	کیمیاوي chemical *adj*
کوډگره witch *n*	کیندل dig *iv*
کوډپ witchcraft *n*	کینه spite *n*
کوډپ کول bewitch *v*	کینه ور spiteful *adj*
کور oblique, prone *adj*	کینو tangerine *n*

ک

bed n کټ

identical adj کټ مټ

replicate v کټ مټ کول

fence n کټاره

muzzle v کټپوز ور اچول

stool n کټکی

bag, envelope n کثوړه

agony, anguish n کراو

pan n کراۍ

garrulous adj کرتن

crunchy adj کرسن

window n کرکۍ

wind up v کرکۍ خلاصول

aggravation n کرکبچنوالې

procedure n کرنلار

action n کرنه

activity n کرنې

attitude n کره وره

crook n کروپ

factor n کرونې

crack v کریکه کول

connection n کرۍ

ring iv کرۍ کول

convoluted adj کرۍ والې

hanger n کرۍ

agonize v کړبدل

agonizing adj کړبدنه

clinch, tilt v کړول

flex, recline v کړبدل

diversion n کړبدنه

installment n کنبت

demean v کنبته کول

derogatory adj کنبته کېدل

denigrate v کنبته کنل

squeeze v کنبپکنبل

become iv کېدل

vulnerable adj کېدونکی

possible adj کېدونکې

rein n کبزه کول

parable n کبسه

cake n کبک

press v کبمنډل

engrave v کبندل

engraving n کبندونکی

sit iv کبنبناستل

intercede v ګواښ کول

ل

لاس رپر	trolley n
لاس ګاډۍ	wheelbarrow n
لاس کې نېول	handle v
لاس لنډول	evict v
لاس لېک	endorsement n
لاس لیک	autograph n
لاس لیک کول	subscribe v
لاس ماغو	glove n
لاس موندل	master v
لاسته راورل	obtain v
لاسته راورنه	input n
لاستې	handle, hilt n
لاسلیک کول	check in v
لاسب بکسه	handbag n
لاسب بم	grenade n
لاسب کتاب	handbook n
لاسب لېک	script n
لاسي	manual adj
لاسي کتاب	manual n
لالهنده	wander v
لالهندب	predicament n
لامبل	bathtub n
لامبو وهل	swim iv
لامبوزن	swimmer n
لانجه	knot n
لاندب	below adv

لاپې وهل	bluff, boast v
لاپي	carcass n
لار	path, route n
لار بندول	blockage n
لار، سرک	way n
لارښود	guide n
لارښودل	guide v
لارښودنه کول	advise v
لارښونه	direction n
لارښوول	conduct v
لارښوونکی	leader n
،لارښوونه کول	direct v
لارښوونې	coaching n
لاره	coarse adj
لاره نيول	take away v
لاره وركول	stray v
لاړې	saliva n
لازم	prerequisite n
لاس	hand n
لاس اچول	scuffle, trespass v
لاس اخیستل	relinquish v
لاس اخیستنه	abstinence n
لاس ته راورل	acquire v
لاس رسېدنه	access n

under *pre* لاندې	moment *n* لږ وخت
beneath, below *pre* لاندې تر	scarcity *n* لږوالپ
down *adv* لاندې خوا	minority *n* لږوالی
precipitate *v* لاندې غورځول	diminish, lessen *v* لږول
let down *v* لاندې کول	subtract *v* لږول
overcome *v* لاندېـ کول	contraction *n* لږونه
lighter *n* لایټر	discount *v* لږوول
flashy, sporty *adj* لباسي	discount *n* لږونه
handful *n* لپه	sequence *n* لړ
monotonous *adj* لټ	shock *v* لړزه
explore, seek *v* لټول	shudder *n* لړزه
search *n* لټونه	convulse *v* لړزول
curious *adj* لټوونکی	devastating *adj* لړزوونکی
stagnation *n* لټي	quake, quiver *v* لړزېدل
undress *v* لڅول	shiver *n* لړزېدنه
archaeology *n* لرغون پېژندنه	haggle, stir *v* لړل
ancient *adj* لرغونی	scorpion *n* لړم
wood *n* لرګی	mist *n* لړه
wooden *adj* لرګين	set up *v* لړکی
have, possess *iv* لرل	ten *adj* لس
remote *adj* لرې	decade *n* لس کاله
revoke, shun *v* لرې کول	loudspeaker *n* لسپکر
get out *v* لرې کېدل	list *n* لست
brief, scarce, less *v* لږ	list *v* لست کې نيول
sizable *adj* لږ زيات	tenth *n* لسم
nuance *n* لږ فرق	tempting *adj* لسوونکی شی

agitator *n* لسوونکي	weed *v* للونل
offset, switch *v* لبنته	celebrate *v* لمانځل
ditch, gutter *n* لبنتي	worship, cult *n* لمانځنه
trench *n* لبنتی ویستل	toilet *n* لمباځی
army *n* لبنکر	bathe *v* لمبل
ruby *n* لعل	flame *n* لمبه
damnation *n* لعنت	blaze *v* لمبه کبدل
damn, curse *v* لعنت ویل	spa *n* لمببدنه
dismantle *v* لغړول	quicksand *n* لمدي شګي
cove *n* لغم	sun *n* لمر
abrogate *v* لغوه کول	sundown *n* لمر پربواته
accent *n* لفظ	sunrise *n* لمر خاته
nickname *n* لقب	sunset *n* لمر لوبده
eardrum *n* لقب پا جابداد	sunburn *n* لمر وهلی
stork *n* لګ لګ	solar *adj* لمریز
inefficient *adj* لکاوو	sunglasses *n* لمریزي ښینبي
expense *n* لکنبت	touch *v* لمس کول
engaged *adj* لکپا	incite, provoke *v* لمسول
engage, amuse *v* لکپا کول	commotion *n* لمسون
embark *v* لکپا کپدل	enticing *adj* لمسونکي (شپ)
strike, verge *iv* لکپدل	affection *n* لمسونه
busy *adj* لکیا	grandchild *n* لمسی
inhabit *v* لکیا کول	footnote *n* لمن لپک
lecture *n* لکچر	officiate *v* لمونځ ور کول
tail *n* لکی	humidity *n* لندبل
tail *v* لکی	water *v* لندول

dampen v لندبدل	له غمه ډک sorrowful adj
brief, concise adj لند	له کاره شړل chase away v
shortsighted adj لند پاری	له کاره وبستونکب dismissal n
collect v لند لمونځ	له لاسه وتلی missing adj
shorthand n لند لیک	له معنا ډک meaningful adj
temporary adj لند مهال	له منځه تلل vanish v
glimpse n لند نظر	له منځه ورل abolish v
short adj لند، پاتي	له وراېه afar adv
anecdote n لنده کبسه	له وربخو پرته cloudless adj
terse adj لنده مجزه خیره	له وبرې تښتیدل chicken out v
abridge, shorten v لندول	له وېنو ډک gory adj
scoff v لنډې وهل	لهجه dialect n
abstract adj لندېز	لوازمر furnishings n
abbey n لنگر	لوبتکه toy n
abbot n لنگر خانه	لوبغاړي player n
from pre له	لوبغالي playground n
unthinkable adj له اټکله لرې	لوبه farce, game n
uproot v له بېخه ویستل	لوبې play n
unleash v له پرې خلاصول	لوبې کول play v
mutilate v له پښو غورځول	لوبیا kidney bean n
impunity n له جوا خلاصون	لوت مار vulture n
writhe v له درده تاوېدل	لوټ booty, loot n
mutually adv له دواړو خواوو	لوټ ماري burglar n
inasmuch as c له دې کبله	لوټا rob v
resumption n له سره نبونه	لوټل burglarize v
mysterious adj له سرو ډک	لوټول loot, overrun v

ل

hoodlum, scam *n* لوچک	preliminary *adj* لومړنې
bare, naked *adj* لوڅ	main, original *adj* لومړنی
uncover *v* لوڅول	basics *n* لومړني
west *n* لودیځ	priority *n* لومړي توب
daughter *n* لور	settler *n* لومړي کېدل
towards *pre* لوري ته	primacy *n* لومړي والی
hunger *n* لوږه	first *adj* لومړی
starve *v* لوږه کالل	debut *n* لومړی کوشـش
glorious, lofty *adj* لوړ	creativity *n* لومړی والی
increasing *adj* لوړ شوی	initials *n* لومړي
major in *n* لوړ نمره	snare *n* لومه
superiority *n* لوړ والی	snare *v* لومه نیول
upheaval *n* لوړه	humid, wet *adj* لوند
aspire *v* لوړه ارزو لرل	damp *adj* لوند والی
climax *n* لوړه درجه	celibacy *n* لوندي
plateau *n* لوړه سطحه	principle *n* لوۍ مشـر
swear *iv* لوړه کول	gate *n* لوۍ ور
advantage *n* لوړوالب	spill *iv* لوېدل
sovereignty *n* لوړوالي	fall *iv* لوېدل،غورځېدل
exalt *v* لوړول	downfall, spill *n* لوېدنه
increase, inflation *v* لوړېدل	tumble *v* لوېدنه
increase *n* لوړېدنه	disintegration *n* لوېدنه (سـقوط)
lesson *n* لوست	fall *n* لوېده
pot *n* لوښپ	saloon *n* لوپه خوفه
container *n* لوښی	highway *n* لوپه لار
fume *n* لوگپ	bulk *n* لوپوالی

ل

exaggerate v لوبول	sale n لبلام
massive, major adj لوي	dormitory n لبلبه
supermarket n لوي پلورنځی	battalion n لبوا
tycoon n لوي تجار	eager, zealous adj لبوال
cataract n لوي جروبی	furor n لبوالتبا
floodlight n لوي څراغ	eagerness n لبوالتيا
metropolis n لوي ښار	madly adv لبونتوب
superpower n لوي طاقت	madness n لبونتوب
medallion n لوي نښان	distraught adj لبونږ
descent n لويدنه	frenzied, maniac adj لبونی
midget n لويشتکی	madman n لبونی سړی
cathedral n لويه کليسا	madden v لبونی کول
aspiration n لويه هيله	wolf n لبوه
magnify v لويول	look v ليدل
liter n لبتر	invisible adj ليدل کېدونکی
perspective n لبد	observation n ليدنه
discern v لبدل	spectator n ليدونکي
view n لبدنه	writing, letter n ليک
away, far adv لبرې	write iv ليکل
eliminate v لبرې کول	written adj ليکل شوی
migrate v لبرد بدل	trail v ليکه
dispatch, send v لبرل	intravenous adj ليکه توب
consignment n لبرنه	writer n ليکوال
sender n لبرونکب	composer n ليکونکی
epistle n لبک	notary, clerk n ليکوونکی
file n لبکه	striped adj ليکب

ل

auction v ليلام ر	break iv ماتيدل
auctioneer n ليلامكوونكى	defeat n ماتى
auction n ليلامول	defeat v ماتى ور كول
solder v ليم كول	crash, malfunction v ماتبدل
lemon n ليمو	breakable adj ماتبدونكى
arc n ليندى	item n ماده
leg n لينگى	corporal adj مادي
avid adj ليوال	serpent, snake n مار
berserk adv ليونتوب	march v مارش كول
insanity n ليونتوب	marshal n مارشل
crazy, insane adj ليونى	marker n ماركر
	type v ماركه كول
	market n ماركيټ
	Marxist adj ماركبست
	porous adj ماسادام
م	afternoon n ماسپښينبن
	masochism n ماسكوژم
prehistoric adj ما قبل التاريخ	trigger v ماشه
malfunction n مات	trigger n ماشه
bankrupt adj مات شوى	brat, kid n ماشوم
frustration n ماته	machine n ماشين
shipwreck n ماته ببرى	machine gun n ماشين دار
foil v ماته وركول	mechanism n ماشين دستگا
fracture n ماتوالب	mechanize v ماشيني كول
rip apart, violate v ماتول	motor n ماشيني موټر
breach, break n ماتونه	brain n ماغزه

cargo n مال	mansion n مانۍ
landlord n مالک	edifice n مانۍ
landlady n مالکه	disappointing adj ماېوس کډېنه
cotton n مالوچ	disappoint v ماېوس کول
subsidy n مالي مرسته	disappointment n ماېوستوب
molecule n ماليکول	discuss v مباحثه کول
salt n مالګه	swap n مبادله
salty adj مالګېن	interchange v مبادله کول
financial adj مالي	warfare n مبارزه
finance v مالیه	combat v مبارزه کول
mammoth n ماموت پیل	congratulations n مبارکي
official adj مامور	congratulate v مبارکي ویل
let iv مانع	overstate v مبالغه کول
maneuver n مانو وره	monitor v مبصر
manners n ماهده	dazzle v مبهوت
deft, expert adj ماهر	armistice n متارکه
pelican n ماهي خورک	aggressor n متجاوز
caliber n ماهېت	circulation n متحدالمال
liquid n مایع	synonym n مترادف
thwart v مایل	progressive adj مترقي
captivate v مایل کول	lash n متروکه
countess n ماینه	fanatic adj متعصب
desperate adj مایوسه	reciprocal adj متقابل
despair n مایوسي	depend v متکي کېدل
eve, evening n ماښام	maxim, proverb n متل
sailor n ماڼو	concentrate v متمرکز کول

متمرکز کېدل focus on v	مجرم criminal adj
متن text n	مجرم culprit, felon n
متناسب compatible adj	مجسم کول embody v
متناسبوالی compatibility n	مجسمه idol, statue n
متناوب alternate adj	مجسمه جورونه sculpture n
متهم defendant n	مجلس conference n
متوجه attentive adj	مجموعه digest v
متوسط ordinary adj	مجهز کول furnish v
متيازې urine n	مجموع totality n
متيازې کول urinate v	مچه kiss n
مثال example n	مچول kiss v
مثال ورکول exemplify v	مچی bee n
مثانه bladder, cyst n	مچی خاله beehive n
مثبت positive adj	محاسب accountant n
مثبت (هو) affirmative adj	محافظه guardian n
مثلث triangle n	محافظه کار conservative adj
مجادله کول contend v	محتاط careful adj
مجادله کوونکی contender n	محتاط cautious adj
مجازي کبسه allegory n	محترم respectful adj
مجبوره کول force v	محتکر bear iv
مجبورول compel v	محدود cramped adj
مجبورول terrorism n	محدودول limit v
مجبوریت being n	محدودیت limitation n
مجرا expiation n	محرک stimulus n
مجراکول expiate v	محروموالی bereaved adj
مجرد buzzer n	محرومول deprivation n

محرومول deprive v	مخالفت کول conflict, confront v
محسوس palpable adj	مخالفت کونه dissident adj
محصول output n	مخالفه ډله opposition n
محکمه courthouse n	مخامخ affront n
محکمه بدلول extradite v	مخامخ head-on adv
محکمه ته سپارل extradition n	مخامخ opposite adj
محکي کېدنې antecedents n	مخامخ شوی opposite adv
محلل solvent adj	مخامخ کېدل meet iv
محلول lotion n	مخامخ کېدنه front adj
محلي situated adj	مختاړی prefix n
محلي ځای local adj	مختلف otherwise adv
محنیوی impediment n	مخدره مواد narcotic n
محور axis n	مخرب destructive adj
مخ face, surface n	مخروط cone n
مخ اړول avert v	مخصوصا particularly adv
مخ په لمر خاته eastward adv	مخکنۍ فرض presupposition n
مخ په وراندې onwards adv	مخکې تلل go ahead v
مخ ته forward adv	مخکې کېدنه antecedent n
مخ نیول curb v	مخکې څکل foretaste n
مخ نیونه rebuff v	مخکېدل precede v
مخ نبوپ drawback n	مخکېنۍ precaution n
مخ ور کرځول face up to v	مخلوط فلزات alloy n
مخابره کول communicate v	مخلوط concoction n
مخالف averse adj	مخنیونه barrage n
مخالف کول contradict v	مخنیوی avoidance n
مخالفت conflict n	مخنیوی کول bypass v

مخنبوب prohibition n	مراجعه كوونكى client n
مخه trend n	مراسم ceremony n
مخه نيول avoid v	مراكشي سړى moor v
مخه اړول veer v	مربا marmalade, jam n
مخه لبدل preview n	مربع square n
مخه نبول prevent, clog v	مربوط شيان belongings n
مخه ور count n	مرتكب كبدل perpetrate v
مخي ته تلل come about v	مرجع reference n
مداخله interference n	مرچ pepper n
مداخله كول interfere v	مرچ او مصاله condiment n
مدار orbit n	مرحله instance, phase n
مدافع وكبل advocate v	مرخبزى mushroom n
مدافعه fencing n	مردار filthy adj
مدخل doorway n	مردك bullet n
مدرسه seminary n	مردكب pill n
مدعي plaintiff n	مرستندوي aide n
مدلل demonstrative adj	مرستندويه conducive adj
مدني civil adj	مرسته help, relief v
مدني پوهنه civic adj	مرسته كول aid, assist v
مدبر principal adj	مرسته كونكب helper n
مدبر director n	مرستون asylum n
مدبون owe v	مرسل addressee n
مذهبي solemn adj	مرغي sparrow n
مذهبي سندرب hymn n	مركب complex adj
مذهبي مبلغات missionary n	مركب setup n
مذهب feast n	مركز center, focus n

centralize v مركزي كول	pore n مسام
conversation n مركه	parity n مساوات
converse v مركه كول	equality n مساوي
marble n مرمر	equate v مساوي كول
currency n مروجي پيسي	concern n مسآله
Mars n مريخ	dictator, tyrant n مستبد
mortality n مرگ	eligible adj مستحق
dead end n مرگوني پاي	cozy adj مستريح
esophagus n مري	rectangle n مستطيل
frame n مزاج	rectangular adj مستطيل شكله
comedy n مزاحيه ډرامه	efficiency n مستعد
henchman n مزدور	colony n مستعمره
splint n مزرى	colonize v مستعمره كول
lash out v مزمت كول	documentary n مستند
chronic adj مزمن	consumer n مستهلك
sturdy adj مزى	prank n مستي
enjoyment n مزي	mosque n مسجد
culpability n مسئووليت	deform v مسخ كول
tournament n مسابقه	laughing stock n مسخرچي
bird n مسارغه	clown n مسخره
massage n مساژ	mime v مسخره كول
massage v مساژ كول	bishop n مسخي ملا
masseur n مساژ كوونکی	chuckle v مسكا كول
passenger n مسافر	shambles n مسلح
voyager n (مسافر (سمندري	career n مسلك
seasoning n مساله	professional adj مسلكي

مسلمان Muslim adj	مشوره admonition n
مسول responsible adj	مشوره كول counsel v
مسولبت responsibility n	مصئون immune adj
مسي copper n	مصئونيت immunity n
مسيحا Messiah n	مصارف consumption n
مسيحي christian adj	مصرع verse n
مسيحيت Christianity n	مصرفول spend iv
مشاور counselor, adviser n	مصرفبدنه spending n
مشتريان clientele n	مصروف bustling adj
مشتق derivative adj	مصنوعي artificial adj
مشخص concrete adj	مصيبت bale n
مشر boss n	مضاعف multiple adj
مشر توب leadership n	مضر displeasing adj
مشرتوب guidance n	مضر malignancy n
مشرك pagan adj	مطالعه study v
مشروب drink, liquor n	مظاهره كول call out v
مشروط conditional adj	معادل equivalent adj
مشروع legitimate adj	معاصر contemporary adj
مشري كونكى domineering adj	معاف exempt adj
مشعل torch n	معافي forgiveness n
مشغولا amusement n	معامله كول dealings n
مشغولوالي mixed-up adj	معاون auxiliary adj
مشغوليت business n	معاينه كول go over v
مشكل arduous adj	معتدل mild adj
مشكوك problematic adj	معجزه marvel n
مشهور famous adj	معدني مواد mineral n

معذرت excuse n	مفلس penniless adj
معزولول depose v	مفبد fruitful adj
معشوقه sweetheart n	مقابل against pre
معطر fragrant adj	مقابله encounter n
معقول sane adj	مقابله كول encounter v
معقولبت sanity n	مقابله كوونكى contestant n
معلومات data, information n	مقاله article n
معلومات لرل acknowledge v	مقام position, seniority n
معمار architect n	مقامي irreversible adj
معماري architecture n	مقاومت consistency n
معمولي ذكر كول touch on v	مقايسه comparison n
معنا كول mean iv	مقايسه كول compare v
معنى spell n	مقبوضه engrossed adj
معنى كول spell iv	مقدار quantity n
معنى كونه spelling n	مقدس divine adj
معيار criterion n	مقدسات relic n
معياري standardize v	مقررول constitute v
مغازه magazine n	مقصد meaning n
مغذي nutritious adj	مقناطيس magnet n
مغرور proud adj	مقناطيسي magnetic adj
مغشوش confusion n	مقننه قوه legislature n
مغشوشول confuse v	مقوا cardboard n
مفاهمه communication n	مكاتبه كول correspond v
مفرد singular adj	مكار foxy adj
مفكر thoughtful adj	مكعب cube n
مفكوره concept, idea n	مكعب غوندي cubic adj

مكمكلبدنه coercion n	ملي كول nationalize v
مكمل avowed adj	ملي متر millimeter n
مكمل كول wrap up v	مليت nationality n
مل comrade n	ملگرتوب companionship n
ملا clergy, priest n	ملگرتيا association n
ملا ساتوونكي supporter n	ملگرتيا accomplishment n
ملاتفه scroll n	ملگرتيا كول accompany v
ملاتړ backing n	ملگرو ډله fellowship n
ملاتړ vouch for v	ملگرى friend, colleague n
ملاتړ كول confirm v	ملگرې accomplice n
ملاتړل back v	ملب practical adj
ملاريا malaria n	ملب گرام milligram n
ملامتول condemn, rebuke v	مماس tangent n
ملاوستنى belt n	ممانعت hindrance n
ملاگب priestess n	ممكن feasible adj
ملابي priesthood n	ممنون thankful adj
ملخ locust n	ممين lover n
ملغلرب pearl n	مناسب agreeable adj
ملكه queen n	مناظره debate v
ملكبت ownership n	منافق dishonest adj
ملنډب mockery, satire n	منافقت dishonesty n
ملنډب وهل deride, mock v	مناقشه debate n
ملهم ointment n	منتحب كبدل get in v
ملوث كول desecrate v	منتقل كبدل relocate v
ملونه rein v	منتقل كبدنه relocation n
ملي national adj	منجم astronomer n

منسوخول call off *v*	منوونکی submissive *adj*
منشور prism *n*	منوونکی obedient *adj*
منشب secretary *n*	منوونکي believer *n*
منصبدار detective, officer *n*	منی autumn *n*
منصف referee *n*	منځنی central *adj*
منطق logic *n*	منځنی intermediary *n*
منطقي logical *adj*	منځنی حالت mediocrity *n*
منظره panorama *n*	منځګر middleman *n*
منظم systematic *adj*	منځګری arbiter, umpire *n*
منظم کول coordinate *v*	منځګري mediator *n*
منظمول spearhead *v*	منځګريتوب mediate *v*
منظورول sanction *v*	مند ه اخيستل track *v*
منظوري commendation *n*	مندکی spray *v*
منع ban *n*	مندل shove *n*
منع کول ban, forbid *v*	منډه وهل run *iv*
منغور hateful *adj*	مهاجر emigrant *n*
منفي negative *adj*	مهاجرت exodus *n*
منفب pessimistic *adj*	مهاجرت کول emigrate *v*
منقل heater *n*	مهارت know-how *n*
منل concede, confess *v*	مهال وبش timetable *n*
منل شوی inevitable *adj*	مهربان benevolent *adj*
منلی indisputable *adj*	مهربانه gracious *adj*
منلی حقيقت axiom *n*	مهرباني mercy *n*
منلب favorable *adj*	مهلک deadly, fatal *adj*
مننه gratitude *n*	مهم significant *adj*
مننه کول appreciate *v*	مهم توکی indispensable *adj*

someday adv مهم شخص	motherhood n موروالی
peanut n مو پلپ	hemisphere n مورګه
material, matter n مواد	vent n مورک
equation n موازنه	mosaic n موزک
balance v موازنه کول	melodic adj موزيکي
parallel n موازي	museum n موزيم
trunk n مواصلاتي	founder n موسس
consonant n موافق	season n موسم
comply, agree v موافق کېدل	seasonal adj موسمي
approval n موافقه	music n موسيقي
accord, approve n موافقه کول	relative n موصول
cellphone n موبايل	issue, topic n موضوع
tune up v موتر جورول	camp v موقتي اوسېدل
efficient adj موثر	truce n موقتي روغه
humanities n موجودات	detour n موقتي لار
presence n موجودېت	provisional adj موقتي
courteous adj مودب	state v موقف
apologize v مودبانه	dismiss v موقفول
polite adj مودپ	wax n موم ژاوله
duration, period n موده	mummy n موميا شوی
mother n مور	embalm v موممبابپ کول
parents n مور او پلار	detect, find v موندل
loophole n مورچل	diagnosis n موندنه
ambush v مورچه	receptive adj موندونکی
maternity n مورنی خوي	underlying adj موندپز
maternal adj مورنی۔	we pro مونږ

موټر automobile n	ميلون million n
موټر سايكل bike n	ميلونر millionaire n
موټر وان trucker n	مينتوب courtship n
موټروان chauffeur n	مينه craving, love n
مور replete adj	مينه کول love v
مور us pro	مت arm n
مورک mouse n	مت ترونکی badge n
موړکان mice n	مځکنی terrestrial adj
موړی، ستن stake n	مځکه earth, ground n
موبنل nip v	مډال medal n
موبننه nip n	مړ dead adj
مياشت month n	مړ lifeless adj
مياشتنی monthly adv	مړ کول lynch v
ميدان arena n	مړ کېدل depart, die v
ميده شوی crushing adj	مړ مړ تلل sham n
ميده کول crush, mince v	مراوې کول wither v
ميراث inheritance n	مراوې کېدل dwindle v
ميرمن madam n	مرتوالي pervert adj
ميره stepmother n	مرز quail n
ميري زی stepbrother n	مرستون tomb n
ميرکن bonfire n	مړول feed iv
ميکروب microbe n	مړی corpse n
ميل liking n	مړينه death n
ميلمستيا banquet n	مړينه deceased adj
ميلمه پال stewardess n	مړبدل glut n
ميلمه کول invite v	مښنام brunch n

scrub v منبل	billionaire n ملبنر
connect v منبلول	favor n مبنه
friction n منبود	fondness n مبنه
beak, bill n منبوکه	affectionate adj مبنه ناک
apple n منه	purity n مبنځل
extent n مبچ	fruit n مبوه
tack n مبخ	fruity adj مبوه داره
rivet v مبخ کول	courage n مبرانه
riveting adj مبخ کونه	manly adj مبرنی
field n مبدان	husband n مبره
pulverize v مبده کول	spouse n مبره
hashish n مبدول	married adj مبروښه
heritage n مبراث	ant n مبرک
heir n مبراث خور	buffalo n مببنه
hereditary adj مبراثي	
patrimony n مبراثي ښتمني	
lady, mistress n مبرمن	
table, desk n مبز	
tablecloth n مبز پوښ	**ن**
dwell iv مبښته کبدل	
hotel n مبلمستون	inept adj نا امبده
guest n مبلمه	restless, uneasy adj نا ارام
hospitality n مبلمه پالنه	uncomfortable adj نا ارامه
receptionist n مبلمه پالونکی	uneasiness n نا ارامي
entertain v مبلمه کول	unfamiliar adj نا اشنا
entertaining adj مبلمه کونکی	hopeless adj نا امبد
	pessimism n نا امبدي

ن

premature _adj_ نا بالغه	unsteady _adj_ نا منظم
misfit _adj_ نا ببر	unfriendly _adj_ نا مهربان
unequal _adj_ نا برابر	vacant _adj_ نا نیول شوی
unsuccessful _adj_ نا بریالی	uneven _adj_ نا هوار
meanness _n_ نا تر سي	undeserved _adj_ نا ور
loose _adj_ نا تړلی	inappropriate _adj_ نا وړه
fictitious _adj_ نا چله	malpractice _v_ نا وړه اداره
perjury _n_ نا حقه لوړه	pent-up _adj_ نا وبلي
unaware _adj_ نا خبره	surprise _v_ نا خا په یخای
unsafe _adj_ نا خوندي	unexpected _adj_ نا خاپه
conflicting _adj_ نا خوښنه	stop by _v_ نا خاپي دربدنه
discontent _adj_ نا راضه	unnoticed, vague _adj_ نا خرګند
illicit _adj_ نا روا	exotic _adj_ نااشنا
unhealthy _adj_ نا روغ	genius _n_ نابغه
untrue _adj_ نا رښتیا	novice _n_ نابلده
unprotected _adj_ نا ساتلی	annihilation _n_ نابود
ungrateful _adj_ نا شکره	annihilate, annul _v_ نابودول
undesirable _adj_ نا غوښتی	seedy _adj_ ناپاکي
disobedience _n_ نا فرمانب	pollution _n_ ناپاکب
flop _n_ نا کامبدل	shortlived _adj_ ناپوره
incoherent _adj_ نا لایقه	ignorant, unwise _adj_ ناپوه
uneducated _adj_ نا لوستی	ignorance _n_ ناپوهي
unreasonable _adj_ نا معقول	pending _adj_ ناتمامه
mystic, uncertain _adj_ نا معلوم	languish _v_ ناتوانه کېدل
defective _adj_ نا مکمل	borough _n_ ناحیه
unsuitable _adj_ نا مناسب	insecurity _n_ ناخوندیتوب

outdated *adj* نادوده	impractical *adj* ناشونى
dissatisfied *adj* ناراض	unlikely *adj* ناشونى
invalid *n* ناروغه	impossibility *n* ناشونى کار
orange *n* نارنج	fine *n* ناغه
heinous *adj* ناروا	pear *n* ناک
sick *adj* ناروغ	hassle *n* ناکاره
dissonant *adj* ناروغتبا	miscarriage *n* ناکاره ورونکي
sicken *v* ناروغول	fall through *v* ناکام کبدل
ailment. Illness *n* ناروغي	flunk *v* ناکامه کبدل
ill *adj* ناروغي	defection *n* ناکامي
elm *n* نارون	failure *n* ناکامب
Norway *n* ناروى	fail *v* ناکامبدل
breakfast *n* نارى	instability *n* ناکراري
manliness *n* نارينتوب	inability *n* نالايقي
outcry *n* نارپ سورپ	saucer *n* نالبکپ
virility *n* نارپنتوب	illiterate *adj* نالوستى
grace *n* ناز	renowned *adj* نامتو
flirt *v* ناز کول	celebrity *n* نامتو سرى
fondle *v* ناز ورکول	illegitimate *adj* نامشروع
delicate, tender *adj* نازک	immature *adj* نامکمل
gauze *n* نازکه جالى	blameless *adj* ناملامته
caress *v* نازول	disobedient *adj* نامنونکپ
stepsister *n* ناسکه خور	disagree *v* ناموافق
imprecise *adj* ناسم	infrequent *adj* ناموندونکى
ulcer *n* ناسور	doll *n* نانزکه
publisher *n* ناشر	baker *n* نانوايي

puppet *n* نانځکه	abuse *v* ناره گټه کول
dissimilar *adj* ناوته	vice *n* ناپب
lake *n* ناور	hairdresser *n* ناپي
novel *n* ناول	plant *n* نبات
novelist *n* ناول لیکونکی	compost *n* نباتي سره
obscenity *n* ناولتوب	pulse *n* نپض
tainted *adj* ناولي شوي	deduce, infer *v* نتیجه کښنل
sewage *n* ناولي اوبه	by-product, result *n* نتېجه
pollute *v* ناولي کول	liberation *n* نجات
aqueduct *n* ناوه	rid of *iv* نجات حاصلول
nasty *adj* ناوی	astrologer *n* نجوم پوه
foul, shocking *adj* ناوره	plot *v* نحشه کول
misuse *n* ناوره استفاده	flaunt *v* نخري کول
mitigate *v* ناوره استفاده کول	draftsman *n* نخشه کښ
malnutrition *n* ناوره تغذیه	Netherlands *n* ندر لیند
misbehave *v* ناوره چلند کول	vow *v* نذر کول
incapacitate *v* ناوره کول	male *n* نر
bride *n* ناوې	virile *adj* نر
lieutenant *n* نایب وکیل	boldness *n* نر توب
nitrogen *n* نایتروجن	boar *n* نر خوگ
barber *n* نایي	balmy, placid *adj* نرم
abruptly *adv* ناخاپه	soft *adj* نرم پوست
sudden *adj* ناخاپي	gentleness *n* نرموالي
tantrum *n* ناخاپي غصه	soften *v* نرمول
revulsion, fright *n* ناخاپي	leniency *n* نرمي
bunker *n* ناره وزمه ببرک	relent *v* نرمبدل

نری meager, tenuous *adj*	نشرېه publication *n*
نری رنخ tuberculosis *n*	نشه ecstasy *n*
نری شوی attenuating *adj*	نشه drunk *adj*
نری غاړی کډو squash *v*	نشه توب drunkenness *n*
نری لار lane *n*	نصېحت feedback, advice *n*
نري کېدل attenuate *v*	نظام system *n*
نری اوِرده دره splinter *n*	نظامي کلا fortress *n*
نرب emaciated *adj*	نظر ingenuity *n*
نرب باران drizzle *n*	نظریه believe *v*
نرب زړی sentimental *adj*	نظریه opinion *n*
نرب ملا waist *n*	نظم poem *n*
نزاکت delicacy *n*	نغاړل muffle *v*
نزدې adjoining *adj*	نغررل guzzle *v*
نزدې کول border on *v*	نغرل gobble *v*
نژدې around *pre*	نغری fireplace *n*
نژدې handy *adj*	نفر person *n*
نژدېوالې vicinity *n*	نفرت loathing, dislike *n*
نس abdomen, bowels *n*	نفرت کول detest, dislike *v*
نسج tissue *n*	نفس تنگي asthma *n*
نسحه prescription *n*	نفوس population *n*
نسکور upset *v*	نقاشب drawing *n*
نسکوروالی reversible *adj*	نقدي پېسې cash *n*
نسل generation *n*	نقشه lay-out, map *n*
نسواري brown *adj*	نقصانول abort *v*
نشانه mark *n*	نقل photocopy *n*
نشر prose *n*	نقلول transcribe *v*

deportation n نقلیه وسایل	incalculable adj نه اټل کبدونکی
dummy adj نقلی	indivisible adj نه ببلبدونکی
legend n نکل	implacable adj نه پخلا کبدونکی
necktie n نکتایی	miss v نه پوهبدل
chute, duct n نل	disrepair n نه تر میمیدونکی
plumber n نل دوان	inseparable adj نه جلا کبدنکی
plumbing n نل دوانی	irreparable adj نه جوړبدنکی
nozzle n نلی	insoluble adj نه حل کبدونکی
appreciation n نمانځنه	unending adj نه ختمبدونکی
display n نمایش	irrevocable adj نه رګرزبدنکی
agent n نماینده	unbearable adj نه زغمبدونکی
agency n نمایندګي	immortal adj نه فنا کبدونکی
moisten v نمجنول	unfailing adj نه کمبدونکی
pattern, model n نمونه	impossible adj نه کبدونکی
today adv نن	adamant adj نه ماتبدونکي
tonight adv نن شپې	supple adj نه ماتبدووکی
exhibition n نندارتون	reject, veto v نه منل
bystander n نندارچي	rejection n نه منه
prospect n ننداره	immoral adj نه مړ کبدنه
enter, sink in v ننوتل	unforgettable adj نه هبربدوکی
next door adj ننوتځی	disentangle v نه ګډول
pull out v ننوبستل	ninth adj نهم
nor c نه	dolphin, whale n نهنګ
not adv نه	normal adj نورمال
unpredictable adj نه اټکل کبدونکی	tongs n نوسی
	pincers n نوسب

claw, nail *n* نوک	nickel *n* نیکل
dart *n* نوکداره گولۍ	auspicious *adj* نیکمرغه
servant *n* نوکر	nicotine *n* نیکوټین
serve *v* نوکري کول	kindness *n* نیکي
spur *n* نوکه	migraine *n* نیم سری
noun, name *n* نوم	cinder *n* نیم سوی سکاره
registration *n* نوم لېکنه	midnight *n* نیمه شپه
November *n* نومبر	badly *adv* نیمګړتوب
brand-new, latest *adj* نوی	defect *n* نیمګړتیا
originate *v* نوی را ایستل	insufficient *adj* نیمګړی
newcomer *n* نوی راغلی	objection *n* نیوکه
newborn *n* نوی زېږد	catch, take *iv* نیول
recovery *n* نوی کول	catching *adj* نیول شوی
newscast *n* نوی لنډیز	occupation *n* نیونه
newsletter *n* نوی لیک	bearer, occupant *n* نیوونکی
novelty *n* نوی والی	dance, dancing *n* نڅا
recruit *n* نوي عسکر	dance *v* نڅېدل
newlywed *adj* نوي واده کړي	cosmic *adj* نړیوال
renewal *n* نوې توب	universe, world *n* نړی
regeneration *n* نوې زېږېدنه	worldwide *adj* نړېوال
renew *v* نوې کول	near *pre* نږدی
granny *n* نیا	by, close to *pre* نږدې
transplant *v* نیالول	approach *v* نږدې کول
mattress *n* نیالۍ	come apart *v* نږدې ورتلل
direct *adj* نیغ	almost *adv* نږدې
caring, kind *adj* نیک	cordon, target *n* نښان

ن
ۍ

نبنـتل adhere, collide v	نبمول halve v
نبنته allocate v	نبمگرې جمله phrase n
نبنتوونکی coherent adj	نبنې popcorn n
نبنلول bar v	نبول grab, seize, hold v
نبنه clue, sign, token n	نبول شوی adoptive adj
نبنه ایز symbolic adj	نبول، درک کول grasp v
نبنه کول aim, sign, mark v	نبونکې hijacker n
نبنه کول trace v	نبونه hijack n
نبنه ویشتونکی marksman n	نبټه date n
نبا grandmother n	نبټه ټاکل date v
نبا او نبکه grandparents n	نبښ وهل sting n
نبالول plant v	
نبستې poverty n	
نبغ erect adj	
نبغ standing n	
نبغ، ور right adj	۵
نبغه pointed adj	
نبغول erect, put up v	
نبکتایي tie n	هئیت committee n
نبکمرغه fortunate adj	هئیت delegate v
نبکه ancestor n	هارمون hormone n
نبم half n	هالبند Holland n
نبم half adj	هاند کول strive iv
نبم کنبه ajar adj	هاوان توپ mortar n
نبم مخی silhouette n	هایدروجن hydrogen n
نبم وبده drowsy adj	هپستال hospital n
	هجا syllable n

هغوي په خپله themselves pro	هجرت colonization n
هک پک aghast adj	هدایات ورکونه bound for adj
هک پک کول amaze v	هدف ته رسبدل drive at v
هلته there adv	هدیره cemetery n
هلک boy n	هدبره graveyard n
هلکتوب boyhood n	هر every, each adj
هلۍ duck n	هر ساعت hourly adv
هلي کوپتر helicopter n	هر شی anything pro
هم and c	هر شب everything pro
همدا ډول likewise adv	هر کلی ovation n
همداسې also, too adv	هر کلب کول welcome v
همفکري unanimity n	هر یو anyone pro
همکار coordinator n	هر یوه ته apiece adv
همکاري contribution n	هر څه چب whatever adj
همکاري کول back up v	هر څوک anybody pro
هنداره mirror n	هرم pyramid n
هندسه geometry n	هره ورځ everyday adj
هندوانه watermelon n	هسپانوي Spanish adj
هنر art n	هسپانوب Hispanic adj
هنر craft n	هستوګني ځای inhabitable adj
هنر مند craftsman n	هسک heaven n
هنري artistic adj	هسکول bug v
هو yes adv	هغه چب what adj
هوا weather, air n	هغه دا (بنځه) she pro
هوا ايستل debunk v	هغه وخت کې while c
هوا بدلول ventilate v	هغوي those adj

هوا خوري كول v park	هيله كول v wish, urge
هوا نورد n aviator	هيله لرل pre barring
هوا نوردي n aviation	هيله من v yearn
هوا وركول v air	هيڅ adj neither
هوار n pavement	هيڅ يو هم نه pro no one
هوايي خط n airmail	هيڅكله pre none
هوايي فضا n airspace	هيڅكله نه adv never
هوايي كرښه n airline	هيڅوك pro nobody
هوايي ډگر n airport	هڅه n exertion, effort
هواپي لغته n kickoff	هڅه كول v attempt
هوس n whim	هڅونه n incentive
هوسا adj convenient	هګۍ n egg
هوسا كول n comfort	هيبتناكه adj sickening
هوسا كول v relieve	هيجان n excitement
هوسا كوونكى n comforter	هبرجن adj oblivious
هوسۍ n deer	هبرجنتوب n amnesia
هوسۍ غوښه n venison	هبرول n debris
هويت n identity	هبرول v forget
هوټل n inn	هبرول n oblivion
هوټل ساتونكى n bartender	هيله n expectation
هوټلۍ n barmaid	هيله لرل v look forward
هوښيار adj prudent, sensible	هيله مند adj hopeful
هيبتناك adj awesome	هبواد n homeland
هيجا n diphthong	هبواد، سيمه n country
هيچرې adv nowhere	هبوادوال n compatriot
هيله n urge, wish	

و

obligatory *adj*	واجب
incorporate *v*	واحد د بو بدن
bridal, marital *adj*	واده
marriage *n*	واده
wed *iv*	واده شوب
marry *v*	واده کول
beat *n*	وار
mystify *v*	وار خطاکول
bewilder *v*	وارخطايي
confusing *adj*	وارخطايي
clumsiness *n*	وارخطاېب
import *v*	واردول
importation *n*	واردونه
break open *v*	واز
fat *n*	وازګه
vest *n*	واسکټ
happening *n*	واقع کېدل
incident *n*	واقع کېدنه
collision *n*	واقعه
authentic *adj*	واقعي
genuine *adj*	واقعب
happen *v*	واقعب کېدل
authority *n*	واک

warrant *v*	واک ورکول
vaccine *n*	واکسین
dignify *v*	واکمن
prince, ruler *n*	واکمن
waltz *n*	والس نڅا
volleyball *n*	والي بال
governor *n*	والي
snow *v*	واوره وربدل
snow *n*	واوره وربدل
snowfall *n*	واورب وریا
watt *n*	واټ
bunch *n*	وابنکی
grass, weed *n*	وابنه
streetcar, wagon *n*	واګون
fiddle *n*	وابلون
pest *n*	وبا
outer *adj*	وتلی
prominent *adj*	وتلب
exit, intrusion *n*	وتنه
outgoing *adj*	وتونکی
fund *n*	وجه
inventory *n*	وجودي
dried, dry *adj*	وچ
proven *adj*	وچ وابنه
drought *n*	وچکالب
arid *adj*	وچه

و

drain, dry v	وچول	perceive v	ور کول
drainage n	وچونه	insert v	وراچول
dryer n	وچوونک	nephew n	وراره
brutal adj	وحشت	overthrow n	وران
savage adj	وحشي	damaging adj	وران شوی
wild boar n	وحشي پیشو	sabotage v	ورانکاري کول
orangutan n	وحشي سری	overthrow v	ورانول
bestiality v	وحشب کول	havoc n	ورانونه
bestiality n	وحشب والی	builder n	ورانوونکی
times, time n	وخت	ruin v	ورانپ کول
tact n	وخت پیژندنه	ruin n	ورانپ کول
occasion n	وخت وار	remittance n	وربنبنه
time v	وخت ټاکل	ask v	ورپسپ ګرخبدل
early adv	وختي	inject v	ورپیژندل
build iv	ودانول	resort v	ورتلل
building n	ودانی	replica n	ورته
premises n	ودانپ	alike, similar adj	ورته
stand up v	ودرېدل	likeness n	ورته والی
grow iv	وده کول	resemblance n	ورته والپ
match v	وده ول	resemble v	ورته والپ
sucker adj	ودونکی	sportman n	ورزش کار
door n	ور	restitution n	ورستوونه
remind v	ور په یادول	decay, fester v	ورستبدل
introduce v	ور پیژندل	perishable adj	ورستبدونکپ
janitor n	ور ساتونکی	anonymous adj	ورک نومی
entrust v	ور سپارل	give, grant iv	ورکول

intrude v ورننه ایستل	cloud n وریځ
infiltrate v ورننوتل	blur v وریځ
brother n ورور	day n ورځ
pass away v ورور ورکېدل	newspaper n ورځپاڼه
subsequent adj ورورستنی	daily adv ورځنی
brotherhood n ورورلي	paperwork n ورځنادارۍ کار
fraternity n ورورګلوي	routine n ورځنب کار
ultimate adj وروستنی	diary n ورځب یادانبتونه
later adj وروسته	flea n ورده
afterwards adv وروسته	fleece n ورګ
after pre وروسته	roast n وربته
fall behind v وروسته پاتب	roast, parch v وربتول
fall back v وروسته تګ	rice n وربجب
incur v وروسته کول	ministry n وزارت
hereafter adv وروسته له دب	wing n وزر
latter adj وروستی	hover v وزروهل
last name n وروستی نوم	rhythm n وزن
ultimatum n وروستی ټکی	murder, kill n وژل
incurable adj وروستی	zap v وژل
flicker v وروستی رپ	assassination n وژنه
thigh n ورون	killer, murderer n وژونکی
eyebrow n وروځب	weapon n وسله
lamb n ورک	arsenal n وسله تون
barbecue n وریت	gunman n وسله وال
broil v وریتول	armor n وسله ګرځونکي
cheerful adj ورین تندک	melancholy n وسواس

9

9

وسواسي meticulous adj	ول کونه curl n
وسواسي fussy adj	ول ول کول curl v
وسبله gimmick n	ولایت county n
وشتل shoot iv	ولاړ immobilize v
وصیت testament n	ولاړ still adj
وضع mood n	ولابت province n
وضع کوونکی conditioner n	ولتبج voltage n
وطن پالونکوی patriot n	ولچک کول handcuff v
وطن پالونکوی patriotic adj	ولس مشر president n
وطن پسی خفه homesick adj	ولسی شورا parliament n
وظیفه بدلول take over v	وله willow n
وعده commitment n	ولي curator n
وعده خلافی کول go back v	ولي کبدل melt v
وعظ sermon n	ولی shock n
وعظ کول preach v	ولب why adv
وفا fidelity n	ولب ابستل eradicate v
وفا دار پاتي کیدل stick to v	وندنی، کړی band n
وفادار faithful adj	ونه لوری inward adj
وفاداري allegiance n	ونه tree n
وفاداري loyal adj	ونډه وال shareholder n
وفادري loyalty n	وهل hit, beat, chastise iv
وقف devotion n	وهل knock, hit n
وقف کول dedicate v	وهل شوی beaten adj
وقفول devote v	وهم / خیال illusion n
وکالت proxy n	وهنه beating n
ول شوی curly adj	وور لید microscope n

garlic n وورہ	awake iv ویښ
creek, stream n ویاله	awakening n ویښنتوب
articulate v ویاند	awake adj ویښنبدل
desolate adj ویجاړ	able, parch, due adj وړ
detergent n ویجاړ	deserve v وړ کېدل
dilapidated adj ویجاړ شوی	merit n وړ والی
destruction n ویجاړتوب	predecessor n وړادینب
desolation n ویجاړتیا	candidacy n وړاندیز
damage, destroy v ویجاړول	farther adv وړاندې
destroyer n ویجاړوونکی	advance v وړاندې کول
numb adj ویدول	precedent n وړاندې والب
lament, woes n ویر	competence n وړتوب
lament v ویر کول	enable v وړکول
mourn v ویرکول	convey, carry v وړل
scare away v ویرہ ول	traffic n وړل راوړل
mistrust v ویسا نه کول	transport v وړل راوړل
balm n ویلنی	transit n وړنه
dissolve v ویلي کول	traffic v وړنه راوړنه
thaw v ویلي کېدل	boat n وړہ بېری
thaw n ویلي کېدل	cabin n وړہ خونه
soluble adj ویلي کېدونکی	chore n وړہ دنده
statement n وینا	chapel n وړہ کلیسا
blood n وینه	bulletin n وړہ ورځپاڼه
transfusion n وینه ورکونه	ability, fitness n وړوالی
bleed iv وینې کول	nurse v ووروکپالل
speaker n ویوونکی	nurse n ووروکپاله

9

nursery n وروکتون	exterminate v وپجارول
inferior adj وروکی	wail n وبر
subtitle n اعنوان وروکی	wail, groan v کول وبر
belittle v کول وروکی	fateful, tragic adj وبرجن
wane v کېدل وروکی	tragedy n کسه وبرجنه
trivialize v وروکنکول	panic, menace n وبره
petite adj وروکپ	terrifying adj وبره
lock up v دوکان وروکپ	terrorize v اچوونکی وبره
turret n مناره وروکپ	appall, dismay v وبرول
confidence n وریا	frightening adj وبرونه
woolen adj ورین	appalling adj وبروونکی
nap n اسټر ورین	hideous adj وبروونکپ
wool n ورۍ	constipate v وبربدل
self-esteem n ورپا	constipated adj وبربدلی
stink n ورم	dispensation n وبستنه
stink iv کول ورم	division n وبش
breath n ورمه	dispense v وبشل
hurt iv ورول	stew n وبشنه
hungry adj ورپ	say iv وبل
watchful adj وښ	voice n وبل
bracelet n وښی	related adj شوب وبل
pasture, prairie n وښبانه	mint n وبلنی
men n وګړي	homily n وبنا
exult v وبارل	wash v وبنڅل
web n پانه وبب	hemorrhage n کبدنه وبنپ
vitamin n وبتامبن	overlap v وبرول

hairy *adj* وبنتن	chilly, cloudy *adj* يخ
diagonal *adj* وبنته	coldness, ice *n* يخ
wake up *iv* وبنبدل	cool *adj* يخني
	frostbitten *adj* يخوالى
	cool *v* يخول
	frostbite *n* يخبدنه
	indecency *n* يرغل
	assail, invade *v* يرغل كول

يا

	assailant *n* يرغل گر
either *adj* يا	invader *n* يركوونكى
or, whether *c* يا	certain, sure *adj* يقيني
monument *n* ياد گار	ascertain *v* يقيني كول
memoirs *n* يادابنت	Sunday *n* يكشنبه
memo *n* يادابنتونه	unit *n* يكر
noteworthy *n* يادداشت	liver *n* ينه
mind *v* يادول	one *adj* يو
notation *n* يادونه	assemble *v* يو كبدل
memorable *adj* يادونب ور	unilateral *adj* يو ارخيز
memento *n* يادگار	another *adj* يو بل
note *v* يادگبرنه	each other *adj* يو د بل سره
yard *n* يارد	cod *n* يو دول كب
jasmine *n* ياسمين	uniform *n* يو شان
bandit *n* ياغي	uniformity *n* يو شان توب
insurgency *n* ياغي توب	assimilate *v* يو شانته كبدل
break away *v* ياغي كربدل	monotony *n* يو شى والى
orphan *n* يتيم	legion *n* يو غند عسكر
lose *iv* يجارول	

combine, unify v یو کول

integrate v یو لاس کول

neither adv یو هم نه

union n یو والی

jointly adv یو ځای

coexist v یو ځای اوسېدل

consolidate v یو ځای کول

associate v یو ځای کېدل

congregate v یو ځای کېدل

liaison n یو ځای کېدنه

once adv یو ځلي

something pro یو څه

somebody pro یو څوک

syringe n یو ډول پیچکاري

alligator n یو ډول تمساح

custard n یو ډول خواړه

cantaloupe n یو ډول ختکی

asparagus n یو ډول سابه

cocktail n یو ډول شراب

miniskirt n یو ډول کمیس

cricket n یو ډول لوبه

tennis n یو ډول لوبه ده

swordfish n یو ډول ماهي

solitary adj یواز ی

loneliness n یوازی

only adv یوازي

solitude n یوازېتوب

Greece n یونان

conscious adj یوه

spoonful n یوه کاشقه

bankrupt v یووالی

compound n یوځای

compound v یوځای کول

digress v یوې خوا ته کېدل

تا

type n تاپه

island n تاپو

peninsula n تاپو وزمه

appoint v تاکل

entrenched adj تاکل شوي

appointment n تاکلنه

norm n تاکلي اندازه

peculiar adj تاکلی

assessment n تاکنه

interval, stop n تال

postpone v تالول

respite n تالونه

loiter v تالبدل

تانک tank n	توپ وهنه bounce n
تانته cane n	توخی cough n
تات canvas n	توخبدل cough v
تپ wound n	توک توک کېدل cave in v
تغر rug n	توکه joke n
تک stitch, clash n	توکیزي څبري caricature n
تک تک غږ کول click v	توکب hoax n
تک تک وهل knock v	توکب humorous adj
تکان convulsion, jolt n	توکب کول joke v
تکان خورل jolt v	تول all, total adj
تکان ورکول jerk v	تول واکمني imperial adj
تکر clash, concussion n	تولنه assembly n
تکسي موټر cab n	توله entire adj
تکند torrid adj	تولول compact, gather v
تکول pound, thresh v	تولونه backlog n
تکی، خال mole n	تولیزه وژنه massacre n
تکي په تکي literal adj	تولگی class n
تکټ tag n	تولگیوال classmate n
تکب dot, point n	تولب gang n
تلی وهل toll n	تولبدل crowded adj
تن ton n	تومبدل stick iv
تنډه brow n	تومبونب paperclip n
تو پ وهل jump v	تونا tuna n
تو لنه congregation n	توټه scrap, piece n
توپ hop, leap, jump v	توټه کول scrap v
توپ وهل bounce, spring v	توټه توټه piecemeal adv

crumble v ټوټه ټوټه کول	persevere v ټينګار
tape recorder n ټيپ ريکارډر	persistence n ټينګار
boost v ټيل وهل	resist v ټينګار کول
telepathy n ټيلي پټي	establish v ټينګول
stable adj ټينګ	persistent adj ټينګپدونکي
clench v ټينګ نيول	humility n ټيت والي
tenacity n ټينګار	dwarf n ټيتکپ
withstand v ټينګار کول	degradation n ټيتول
strengthen v ټينګوالی	humiliate v ټيتول
condense v ټينګول	rebate n ټيټونه
mean adj ټيت	
depression n ټيټوالی	
base v ټيټول	
crouch v ټيټيدل	
cob n ټيټو	# ځا
shark, viper n ټک	
shrewd, wily adj ټک	hive, nest n ځاله
cheater n ټکمار	informer n ځان ايستل
fraud n ټکي	sneak v ځان ايستل
insincere adj ټکي	continent n ځان ژغورنه
cheat v ټکي کول	restrain v ځان ساتل
ruse, guile n ټکپ	vindicate v ځان سپينول
inflate v ټبل وهل	arrogance n ځان ستابنه
boost n ټپله کونه	martyr n ځان شهيدول
gripe n ټپنګ	towel n ځان وچونی
rigid adj ټپنګ	suicide n ځان وژنه
	respective adj ځان ځاني

pose v خان بودل	brightness, spark n خلا
pose n خان بونه	glow, twinkle v خلا
alone adj خانته	polish, varnish v خلا ورکول
monopolize v خانته کول	bright, shiny adj خلاند
egoism n خانمني	splendor n خلاند
native adj خاني	lightly adv خلانده
own adj خانگرتوب	lad n خلمی
specialty n خانگرتیا	youthful adj خلمی
special, typical adj خانگری	flamboyant adj خلند
specialize v خانگری کول	gleam n خلول
single adj خانگری، یو	varnish n خلوونکی
trait n خانگري ننـه	flare-up, shine v خلبدل
location, site n خای	glare n خلبدل
stationary adj خای په خای	strawberry n خمکنی توت
localize v خای کول	land n خمکه
souvenir n خاي	geology n خمکه پژندنه
supersede v خاي نیونه	our adj خمونږ
insertion n خايونه	ours pro خمونږه
place v خاب	ourselves pro خمونږه خپله
accommodate v خاب ور	wildlife n خناور
awning n خپری	cruelty n خناورتوب
suppress v خپل	delay n خندیدنه
foam n خک	chain, zipper n خنځیر
because c خکه	deadlock adj خنډ
hence adv خکه چه	interlude n خنډ
therefore adv خکه نو	defer, delay v خندول

postponement *n* خنډونه	monk *n* کپ خیله
overdue *adj* خنډپدل	any *adj* خینپ
belated *adj* خنډپدلی	caterpillar *n* خینپ حشرات
forest, jungle *n* خنګل	sometimes *adv* خینپ وختونه
sway *v* خنګپدل	hang *iv* خپرول
answer, reply *n* خواب	dangle *v* خپریدل
answer, reply *v* خواب ورکول	lather *n* ډگ
respond *v* خوابول	harsh *adj* خپر
adolescent *n* خوان	gaze *v* خپر کپدل
young *adj* خوان	gifted *adj* خپرک
youth *n* خوانی	harshness *n* خپروالپ
intercession *n* خواښ	
mischief *n* خور	
annoy, harass *v* خورول	**خ**
nagging *adj* خورول شوی	
harassment *n* خورونکپ	well *n* خا
pinch *n* خورونه	sheets *n* خادر
intruder *n* خوروونکی	oversee, spy *v* خارل
worrisome *adj* خوروونکی	scout *n* خارندوپ
bothersome *adj* خوروونکپ	maintenance *n* خارنه
bother *v* خورپدل	attorney *n* خارنوال
summit *n* خوکه	caretaker *n* خارونکی
shackle *n* خولنپ	beast *n* خاروی
son *n* خوي	cattle *n* خاروي
pendulum *n* خورند	animal *n* خاروپ
astute, clever *adj* خیرک	

خان بچول elude v	display, divulge v خرگندول
خانګه bough, branch n	خرگندول، وبل express v
خاخكی drop n	خرگندونه exhilarating adj
خانبت midday n	خرگندبدنه appearance n
خپاند wavy adj	خربدونكی browser n
خپركی chapter n	خکل drink iv
خپره shed iv	خکبدل creep v
خپلیـ footwear n	خلور four adj
خپلپ sandal n	خلور ګوټيز square adj
خپه shower, tide n	خلورم fourth adj
خراغ lamp n	خلورمه برخه quarter n
خربول fatten v	خلوبښت forty adj
خرخ rotation, spool n	خلی milestone, tower n
خرخه pulley n	خلی monumental adj
خرخول rotate, spin v	خمخب وهل row v
خرخپ تمانچه revolver v	خنده bank, brim, edge n
خرخبدل revolve v	خنګ په خنګ collateral adj
خرکندتبا visibility n	خنګ لګول lean iv
خرل graze v	خنګل elbow n
خرمن leather n	خنګلاره sidewalk n
خرګدوالی leaning n	خه اندازه some adj
خرګند conspicuous adj	خه څول how adv
خرګند والی clarity n	خو diverse, few adj
خرګندوالی openness n	خو ورځنی transient adj
خرګندوالپ distinction n	خوارلس fourteen adj
خرګندوالپ patent adj	خوک who pro

څوک څب whoever pro	**څ**
څوکه apex, crest n	
څوکه peak n	څا اچوونکی terrorist n
څوکۍ chair n	څار fear, horror n
څیرل tease v	څار شوی afraid adj
څیربدل browse v	څار شوب eerie adj
څټ rear, reverse n	څار ونکب paranoid adj
څټک hammer n	څار وونکب petrified adj
څټل lick v	څارول awe n
څخوبی leakage n	څارول daunt v
څخول drip, drop v	څارونکی formidable adj
څخبدل distill, trickle v	څارونکب dreadful, scary adj
څخبدنه tricky adj	څارونه dreaded adj
څربکه pang n	څاروونکی terrific adj
څنساک beverage n	څاروونکب disastrous adj
څنستن owner n	څاربدنه daunting adj
څنستن تعالب God n	څال سپر shield n
څنسونکی drinker n	څالر dollar n
څبره portrait, effigy n	څاړ certainty n
څبرل inspect v	څاړ conclusive adj
څبرنه inquest n	څاړ ساتل solace n
څبرنه کول research v	څاړ ور کول assure v
څبرۍ oak n	څاړمنتوب credibility n
	څاړه کول ensure v
	څاړینه assurance n
	څاکي mailman n

epitaph *n* ډبر لېک	fashionable *adj* ډولۍ
rocky *adj* ډبرين	bread *n* ډوډۍ
thicken *v* ډبلول	diner *n* ډوډۍ خورونکی
motorcycle *n* ډپ ډبۍ	nourish *v* ډوډۍ ورکول
dramatic *adj* دراماتېک	nourishment *n* ډوډۍ ورکونه
shot *n* ډز، ستن	depot *n* ډيپو، تحويلخانه
gunfire *n* ډزب	moron *adj* ډير احمق سړي
full *adj* ډک	outlive *v* ډير پاينست کول
bumper *n* ډک ګلاس	starchy *adj* ډير تشريفاتي
pier, wharf *n* ډکه	atrocious *adj* ډير ظالم
flip *v* ډکه کول	outshine *v* ډير ځليلبدل
fill, saturate *v* ډکول	late *adv* ډيل
crowd, flock, team *n* ډله	stem, stock *n* ډډ
ringleader *n* ډله مشر	restraint *n* ډډه
procession *n* ډلبيز تګ	stench *n* ډډوزمه
Denmak *n* ډنمارک	bloat *v* ډډبدل
pond, pool *n* ډنډ	colonel *n* ډګروال
lean *adj* ډنګر	abound *v* ډېر
atrophy *v* ډنګربدل	lots, many *adj* ډېر
sunken *adj* ډوب	much *adv* ډېر
engulf *v* ډوبول	worse *adj* ډېر بد
soak in *v* ډوبيدل	outlast *v* ډېر پاينست کول
drown, sink *v* ډوببدل	worsen *v* ډېر خرابول
plunge *n* ډوببدنه	excessive *adj* ډېر زبات
breed, style *n* ډول	icy *adj* ډېر سوړ
breed *iv* ډوله جوړول	needy *adj* ډېر ضروري

روند blind adj
روند blindness n

ﻍ

دغ echo n
دغ کول hello e
دغ لور وونکی microphone n
رلب hail n
رلب اوربدل hail v
رمنځ comb n
رمنځول comb v
ريره beard n

---

destitute adj دپر غريب
red-hot adj دپر قوي
tiny adj دپر کوچنی
tremendous adj دپر لوي
towering adj دپر لور
prodigious adj دپر لوي
dire adj دپر وبروونکی
often adv دپر ځلي
least adj دپر کوچنی
terror n دپره وبره
intensify v دپرول
intensive adj دپروونکی
abundance n دپربښت
lantern n دپوه

ﺭ

propose v راندپ کول
hitch n رچول
blind v رندول
wreckage n رنگ
stagger v رنگ بنگ کېدل
wreck v رنگول
before pre رومبی

شن

شنکاروالب revealing adj

شنکاري ټوپک shotgun n

شنکارب hunter n

شنکاربدل loom n

شنآره apparel n

شنکته تر downstairs adv

شنکته خوا downhill adv

شنکته راتلل come down v

شنکته غورځبدل fall down v

شنکته کبدل descend v

شنکر antenna, horn n

شنکلا beauty n

شنکلا پبژندنه aesthetic adj

شنکلی beautiful adj

شنکلب handsome adj

شنکنځا insult, abuse n

شنکنځل insult v

شنکنځل کول scold v

شنکنځل کبدل scolding n

شننگری ankle n

شنه fine, good adj

شنه پرنټ کول fine print n

شنه تر better adj

شنه خوي decorum n

شنه ذوق elegance n

شنه راغلی welcome n

شناپېری fairy n

شناخی fork n

شناخب pitchfork n

شنادي delight, laughter n

شنادي کول delight v

شنار city n

شناروال mayor n

شناري citizen n

شنارگی town n

شناغلی mister n

شناغلی gentleman n

شناغلب sir n

شنامار dragon n

شنانک tub n

شنایسته compulsive adj

شنایسته کول beautify v

شنخول bury v

شنخونه burial n

شنکار hunting, quest n

شنکار کول chase v

شنکارندوب standard n

شنکاره explicit adj

شنکاره کول assert, reveal v

شنکاره کبدل visualize v

civilization *n* بنه سلوک

discourage *v* بنه نه کېل

goodwill *n* بنه نبت

embrace *n* بنه هرکلي

goodness, virtue *n* بنه والي

good-looking *adj* بنه ښکاربدنه

stumble *v* بنوئبدل

exhibit, show *v* بنودل

implicit *adj* بنودل شوی

rust-proof *adj* بنودونکی

broth, soup *n* بنوروا

galvanize *v* بنورول

move *n* بنورونه

budge *v* بنوربدل

glide *v* بنوهبدل

teach *iv* بنوودل

simulate *v* بنوول

coach, teacher *n* بنوونکی

implication *n* بنوونه

academy *n* بنوونځي

smoothness *n* بنویوالی

lapse *v* بنوببدل

lapse *n* بنوببدنه

ladylike *adj* بنځنی

wife, woman *n* بنځه

wives *n* بنځي

female *n* بنځبنه

feminine *adj* بنځبني

cuss *v* بنبرا کول

juicy *adj* بنبراز

fertilize *v* بنبرازه کول

signify *v* بنبل

sister-in-law *n* بنبنه

welfare *n* بنبگنه

ک

garage *n* کاراج

reef *n* کاره

bribe, carrot *n* کازره

patience *n* کالل

put up with *v* کالل

patient *adj* کالونکي

footstep, pace *n* کام

pace *v* کام کول

reindeer *n* کاوزه

neighbor *n* کاونډي

neighborhood *n* کاونډیتوب

adjacent *adj* کاونډي

vehicle *n* کاډی

ornament *n* ګاڼه	pledge *v* ګروول
chat *v* ګپ شپ	mortgage *n* ګروی
talkative *adj* ګپاو	pledge *n* ګروپ
stroke *n* ګذار	pawnbroker *n* ګروپ وال
gram *n* ګرام	cordless *adj* ګرځندنه با تار
reflexive *adj* ګرامر لازمی	mobile *adj* ګرځنده
expensive *adj* ګران	tourist *n* ګرځندوي
difficulty *n* ګراني	tour *n* ګرځنت
intimacy *n* ګرانښت	circulate, turn *v* ګرځېدل
Dutch *adj* ګرد	turn *n* ګرځېدل
altogether *adj* ګرد سره	patrol *n* ګزمه
whirlpool *n* ګرداو	tow *v* ګشول
dusty *adj* ګردجن	flower *n* ګلُ
drift *v* ګردله	thumbtack *n* ګل تبخی
corpulent *adj* ګردی	flowerpot *n* ګل دانی
dissuade *v* ګرزول	embroidery *n* ګل دوزي
arrest *v* ګرفتارول	embroider *v* ګل دوزي کول
arrest *n* ګرفتارونه	bloom *v* ګل غوړېدنه
defrost *v* ګرم	rose *n* ګلاب
hot, spicy *adj* ګرم	pink, rosy *adj* ګلابي
conviction *n* ګرمتیا	nice *adj* ګلالی
heat *v* ګرمول	petal *n* ګلپاڼي
bit *n* ګرمټ	vase *n* ګلدانی
heat *n* ګرمي	glucose *n* ګلوکوز
staff *n* ګروپ	conjecture, guess *n* ګمان
collaboration *n* ګروپي کار	guess *v* ګمان کول

delude v گمراه	gown n گون
tariff n گمرکي تعرفه	wrinkle n گونجه
guilt, sin n گناه	wrinkle v گونجه کبدل
sin v گناه کول	crisp adj گونجي گونجي
sinful, sinner adj گناه گار	party n گوند، حزب
guilty adj گناهگار	genuflect, kneel v گونډه کبدل
pickpocket n کنډکپ	mute adj کونګ
sew, affix v کنډل	owl n کونګ
sewing n کنډنه	angle n کوټ
sewer n کنډونکی	corner n کوټ، کنج
tailor n کنډونکی	cripple v کوډ ول
daze v کنګسول	limp v کوډ کوډ تلل
dome n کنبزه	limp n کوډ کوډ تلل
cauliflower n کوپي	wobble v کوډ وړ تلل
ring n گوتمۍ	abdication n کوبنه
finger n ګوته	seclusion n کوبنه توب
warehouse n ګودام	secluded adj کوبنه کبدنه
haven n کودر	eccentric adj کوبنه کبر
zebra n کوره خر	hollow, shallow adj کوګ
earphones n کوشکي	sulphur n کوګړ
headphones n کوشکپ	sofa n کتکمۍ
goalkeeper n کول ساتونکپ	beneficiary n کتکوونکی
goal n کول، مقصد	earn, win v کتل
morsel n کوله	avail v کته
missile n کولۍ	gain, profit n کته
pellet n کولپ	gain, profit v کته کول

beneficial, useful *adj* کټور	negotiation *n* کربدنه
usefulness *n* کټورتوب	downpour *n* کڼ باران
winner *n* کټوونکی	numerous *adj* کڼ سمبر
interest *n* کتهٔ	brake *n* کڼ څنګل
blend *n* کډ	presume, suppose *v* کڼل
cohabit *v* کډ ژوند کول	guitar *n* کبتار
dazed, messy *adj* کډ وډ	fox *n* کبدره
blend *v* کډول	involve *v* کبرول
mixture *n* کډوله	gas *n* کبس
communion *n* کډون	quarrel *n* کبله
participate *v* کډون کول	quarrel, grouch *v* کبله کول
entry *n* کډون کونه	gallon *n* کبلبن
blender *n* کډوونکی	stomach *n* کبډه
chaotic, impure *adj* کډوډ	mug *n* کبډوی
promiscuous *adj* کډوډ	pack *v* کبډي کول
disturb *v* کډوډ کول	
shuffle *v* کډوډول	
chaos *n* کډوډي	
disorder *n* کډوډۍ	**با**
disorganized *adj* کډوډپدېنه	
mingle *v* کډبدل	remembrance *n* باد
cockroach *n* کرندی	remember *v* بادول
mileage *n* کرندیتوب	reminder *n* بادونه
accelerate *v* کرندي کول	friendship *n* باري
brink, cliff *n* کرنګ	hooligan *n* باغي
negotiate *v* کربدل	stupid *adj* ببرا

بو ځای simultaneous adj	بتبم fatherly adj
بو ځاي کول affiliate v	بخ frigid adj
بو ځاي کبدل adjoin v	بخ شوپ frosty adj
بو څو several adj	بخ لرونگی freezing adj
بواځب single n	بخچال freezer n
بواځبوالی singlehanded adj	بخول refrigerate v
بولس eleven adj	برغل handrail n
بولسم eleventh adj	برغل کول mug v
بونان Greek adj	برغل کونه mugging n
بوه انه penny n	برغمل hostage n
بوځاي توب congestion n	بو an a
بوځاي والب congested adj	بو کول desegregate v
بب ارزښته null adj	بو والی alliance n

Word to Word™ Bilingual Dictionary Series

Bengali ISBN 0-933146-30-2	**Haitian-Creole** ISBN 0-933146-23-X	**Russian** ISBN 0-933146-92-2
Chinese ISBN 0-933146-22-1	**Hindi** ISBN 0-933146-31-0	**Spanish** ISBN 0-933146-99-X
Farsi ISBN 0-933146-33-7	**Korean** ISBN 0-933146-97-3	**Tagalog** ISBN 0-933146-37-X
French ISBN 0-933146-36-1	**Portuguese** ISBN 0-933146-94-9	**Thai** ISBN 0-933146-35-3
German ISBN 0-933146-93-0	**Punjabi** ISBN 0-933146-32-9	**Turkish** ISBN 0-933146-95-7
Gujarati ISBN 0-933146-98-1	**Romanian** ISBN 0-933146-91-4	**Vietnamese** ISBN 0-933146-96-5

Please visit www.BilingualDictionaries.com to find release dates for future languages and current pricing.

Order Information

To order any of our Word to Word™ Bilingual Dictionaries or any other products from Bilingual Dictionaries, Inc., please contact us at (951) 461-6893 or visit us at www.BilingualDictionaries.com. Visit our website to download our current Catalog/Order Form, view our products, and find information regarding Bilingual Dictionaries, Inc.

 **Bilingual Dictionaries, Inc.**

PO Box 1154 • Murrieta, CA 92562 • Tel: (951) 461-6893 • Fax: (951) 461-3092
www.BilingualDictionaries.com